GUSTAVE FLAUBERT'S
MADAME BOVARY

Maman! maman! ce Monsieur du Luxembourg, que tu as dit (tu sais bien) que c'était un grand ami de papa!... il n'a pas salué!... Ah! par exemple, en voilà un malhonnête!

Gavarni, *Les Enfants terribles* [Brats]. "Mama, mama! That gentleman from the Luxembourg garden, the one that you said (you remember) was a good friend of papa! He didn't even say hello! He doesn't have any manners!" (*Source:* Gavarni [pseud. of Sulpice-Guillaume Chevalier], *Œuvres choisies*. Paris: Hetzel, 1846.)

GUSTAVE FLAUBERT'S
MADAME BOVARY

A REFERENCE GUIDE

Laurence M. Porter and Eugene F. Gray

Greenwood Guides to Fiction

GREENWOOD PRESS
Westport, Connecticut • London

Library of Congress Cataloging-in-Publication Data

Porter, Laurence M. 1936–
   Gustave Flaubert's Madame Bovary: a reference guide / Laurence M. Porter and
Eugene F. Gray.
     p. cm.   (Greenwood guides to fiction, ISSN 1535–8577)
   Includes bibliographical references and index.
   ISBN 0–313–31916–2 (alk. paper)
   1. Flaubert, Gustave, 1821–1880. Madame Bovary—Handbooks, manuals, etc. I. Gray,
Eugene F., 1936– II. Title. III. Series.
PQ2246.M3 P67, 2002
843'8—dc21   2002075320

British Library Cataloguing in Publication Data is available.

Library of Congress Catalog Card Number: 2002075320
ISBN: 0–313–31916–2
ISSN: 1535–8577

First published in 2002

Greenwood Press, 88 Post Road West, Westport, CT 06881
An imprint of Greenwood Publishing Group, Inc.
www.greenwood.com

Printed in the United States of America

The paper used in this book complies with the
Permanent Paper Standard issued by the National
Information Standards Organization (Z39.48–1984).

10 9 8 7 6 5 4 3 2 1

Contents

Preface

All his life, Gustave Flaubert's consuming passion was his art. He wrote and directed plays when he was a child. A sympathetic teacher encouraged him to write fiction when he was in secondary school. Friends helped him publish when he was quite young. After two unhappy years of law study, epilepsy and the comfortable family fortune freed him from the need to earn a living. His skeptical father died not long after, leaving him alone with his mother in an idyllic country setting on the River Seine, two and a half miles outside Rouen. He traveled, and later he acquired a small apartment in Paris, spending part of each year with fellow writers. But when he was writing, he did little else except to read voraciously, as most writers do. During a year and a half in the thick of composing *Madame Bovary,* he got together with his mistress, Louise Colet, only six times. He was working on his last novel, the postmodernist satire *Bouvard et Pécuchet,* when he died.

Flaubert's determination to achieve stylistic and structural perfection made *Madame Bovary* his masterpiece. Throughout the first half of the twentieth century, he was the novelist's novelist—and *Madame Bovary* the exemplary novel—in Western literature. "It remains perpetually the novel of all novels which the criticism of fiction cannot overlook; as soon as ever we speak of the principles of the art, we must be prepared to engage with Flaubert.... I shall have nothing more to say," declared Percy Lubbock in his famous study of the art of fiction, "that is not in some sense an extension and an amplification of hints to be found in *Madame Bovary.*"[1] Since the 1950s, William Faulkner has taken up Flaubert's mantle and inspired writers throughout the world. He owes much to Flaubert, a master of showing rather than telling who allows readers to draw their own conclusions. It is fair to say Flaubert has greater range. *Madame*

Bovary, the story of a spoiled, narcissistic, overeducated Norman farm girl who marries and then has two affairs out of boredom and who poisons herself when bankrupt and rejected in love, seems narrow. But Flaubert's oeuvre—which includes a grandiose panorama of all the theologies and heresies of the early Christian era (in *La Tentation de saint Antoine*); his mythic-historical novel of the Punic Wars (*Salammbô*); his saints' lives set in antiquity, the early middle ages, and the present (*Trois Contes*); his cynical depiction of the vanity of love and success in contemporary Paris under the constitutional monarch Louis-Philippe; and his satiric questioning of human knowledge in the mock-encyclopedic *Bouvard et Pécuchet*—this corpus far surpasses the scope of Faulkner's fictional world.

Flaubert's masterpiece, *Madame Bovary*, was published a century and a half ago. To appreciate the novel, we should ask how everyday life was different then, how those differences shaped the literature that mirrored them, and why *Madame Bovary* nevertheless remains so deeply appreciated and so influential. By realizing what Flaubert's contemporaries took for granted, we can better understand both the force of Emma Bovary's rebellion against society and the inevitability of her failure.

THE CATHOLIC HERITAGE

Before our era of mass immigration and ethnic diversity, France was a Catholic country. The Revolution had outlawed Catholicism for a time, but Napoleon I quickly reestablished that religion to give his empire an international basis of legitimacy. Not until the repeal of the Falloux Law in 1905 did France completely separate church from state. Although Flaubert and his family were not believers, their regular exposure to religion was inevitable. Imagine yourself, today, in one of the many Islamic countries of the world. Whether or not you attended services at the mosque, five times a day you would hear the muezzins' calls to prayer from the balconies of the minarets that dominate the skyline of major cities and towns. You would encounter persons in religious garb every day in the streets, and major life transitions would be marked by religious ceremonies. Similarly, in Rouen of the 1830s and early 1840s (the period in which *Madame Bovary* is set) the magnificent cathedral towered above the town; its bells pealed over the city regularly to call the faithful to mass. The chiming of bells "rising to heaven" was itself a long-established symbol for prayer and a reminder that those who heard it should pause to pray. Priests officiated at baptisms, christenings, marriages, and burials. Through the sacrament of confession, they directed the spiritual life of most families, often advising penitential restitution, indemnity, and community service, which today would be determined by secular courts of law.

The religious influence of servants on small children of the well-to-do classes should not be underestimated. In a middle-class household such as Flaubert's, children were usually sent to live with wet nurses during their first year or two of life, and even moderately prosperous households had servants, who might work for only room and board and who spent much time with the children. These servants were likely to be observing Catholics; directly or indirectly, they informed the children in their charge about the basic points of Catholic belief and shared with them, in addition, many innocent superstitions and pious legends, as we see in Flaubert's sympathetic portrayal of the illiterate maid-of-all-work Félicité lovingly raising Paul and Virginie in "Un cœur simple."

So the Catholic religion left a strong imprint even on the literary productions of nonbelievers in nineteenth-century France. Priests and monks were prominent characters in much realist-naturalist fiction: Balzac's *Le Curé de campagne*, Stendhal's *Le Rouge et le Noir* and *La Chartreuse de Parme*, Zola's *La Faute de l'abbé Mouret*, Flaubert's *La Tentation de saint Antoine* and "La Légende de saint Julien l'hospitalier." Several of the sacraments are described in detail as plot elements in Flaubert's fictions: extreme unction in *Madame Bovary;* baptism, confirmation, and communion in "Un cœur simple." Discussions of religion appear frequently in Flaubert's correspondence, itself an unintended literary masterpiece. In his youth, he had a transient but intense religious experience as he entered Jerusalem. That commercialized modern city, with its warring sects, bitterly disappointed his idealistic expectations. During his adolescence, he claims, he went through a two-year period of chastity, hating the flesh; during the latter years of his life, he styled himself as Saint Polycarp, a vehement critic of the corruption of his age. Friends playfully honored this self-identification with a yearly banquet. However misguided and narcissistic she may have been in her spiritual quest, Emma Bovary derived her religious aspirations from Flaubert's own. But her "tempérament plus sentimentale [sic] qu'artiste" (*Madame Bovary*, 1, 6, 96) sought physical and emotional titillation in all experience, whereas Flaubert himself diverted his desires for religious transcendence into the religion of Art. Each of his *Trois Contes*, the masterpiece of his late maturity, was a saint's life—and his disappointment with the religious counselors in *Madame Bovary*, the priest Bournisien (whose name suggests *borné*, "limited") and the bishop's bookseller, who selects devotional readings for Emma as heedlessly as if he were packing up glass beads (literally, "iron ware") for savages, derives not from their holding false beliefs, but from their lack of spirituality, intelligence, and commitment.

Convents often provided finishing schools for moderately well-off young women, including the spoiled farm girl Emma Bovary. As today, the Jesuits, a teaching order founded in 1540 to counter the intellectual influence of the Protestant Reformation, ran many fine secondary schools and universities. Although Flaubert's own teachers were secularists, he often encountered Jesuit-trained persons in everyday life.

ECONOMIC REALITIES

Finally, the religious life provided an occupation for many of the younger siblings of the wealthier families, while controlling the population growth that otherwise risked fragmenting hereditary fortunes. Primogeniture (the practice of deeding all one's land to the eldest son rather than dividing it among all the children of a family) and the difficulty of raising a dowry for many daughters (the original Santa Claus—Saint Nicholas—first made his name by providing dowries for each of three sisters) left younger siblings without suitable employment. Even the professions often were, in effect, hereditary. Flaubert's older brother, Achille, assumed their father's place as chief of surgery, with living quarters in the hospital; Gustave, the second child, was fortunate in being able to remain in their country residence, Croisset, with an inheritance sufficient to provide for his expenses starting shortly after he began his full-time career as a writer.

Men without an inheritance often had few alternatives but the church or military service, as the title of Stendhal's masterpiece *Le Rouge et le Noir* (the officer's red uniform or the priest's black cassock) suggests. The law, the profession into which his father tried to push the reluctant Flaubert so that he might earn a living, was a traditional dumping ground for moderately intelligent young middle-class men without a vocation. Léon in *Madame Bovary* and Frédéric Moreau in Flaubert's *L'Education sentimentale* are examples. Such economic factors often contributed to motivating adventures abroad: crusades, colonialism, or colonization of sparsely settled lands such as large areas of North America or, under the July Monarchy (1830–48), Algeria.

MARRIAGE AS A SOCIAL PROBLEM

Young women who did not wish to become virtual servants in their older brothers' households or to eke out a living at menial labor ordinarily had to choose between the religious life, marriage, or prostitution. Marriage for love was rarely permitted; the parents usually arranged unions in order to create political alliances, to consolidate land holdings, or to trade the prestige of a family name for access to a larger fortune. Because Emma's father, Old Rouault, feels no attachment to farming, he does not try to find a farmer husband for his only child, a man who could keep the farm in the family when Rouault became old; however, he is pleased to find an infatuated suitor who will not therefore ask for a large dowry. He may have felt flattered to become the father-in-law of a "doctor." That he sent his daughter to a convent school (comparable to finishing schools) attests to his social pretensions. Moreover, Emma is of little use for the farm work, and Rouault looks forward to having one less mouth to feed.

The sexual double standard, even more entrenched in France than in the United States, meant that Flaubert's male contemporaries often could freely seek physical and emotional satisfaction outside marriage. Today, Americans' furor over the love affairs of men of state, generals, and prominent businessmen in the United States often amuses the French.

Much of French literature, then—even misogynistic literature—adopts the woman's point of view as it explores imaginary compensations for loveless marriages. In medieval times, *l'amour courtois* elaborated a code of conduct for amorous but chaste relationships.[2] Novels from Madame de Lafayette's *La Princesse de Clèves* (1678) to Honoré de Balzac's *Eugénie Grandet* (1833) and Hervé Bazin's *Vipère au poing* (1948) all discuss how arranged marriages frustrate true love. Emma Bovary, in contrast, had thought that she loved Charles— who proves to be a faithful, loving husband and father and a good provider— because she had no basis of comparison, but her frustration in marriage relates her story to many others. In Catholic France, no divorce was allowed between 1816 and 1884. Even after 1884, for a time a woman could not divorce in order to marry a lover. Desperate women sometimes arranged to be caught in bed with a neutral third party.

THE CLASSICAL TRADITION IN SECULAR EDUCATION

Flaubert's secular education determined the quality of his imagination in ways that, today, are hard to realize. Until World War I, and in the United States as well as Europe, a standard secondary school academic program for the privileged males who went beyond the rudiments of literacy typically included one's first language, seven years of Latin, two years of Greek, rhetoric (a rigorous equivalent of today's freshman-level composition), mathematics, history, and philosophy. As a result, every educated person in the Western world had intensively translated his first language into Latin and back again; instruction focused on a core curriculum of Vergil's *Aeneid*, Horace's odes, Ovid's *Metamorphoses* (a compendium of tales from Greek and Roman mythology, including a creation myth), and Homer's *Iliad*, together with writings from the historians such as Xenophon, Tacitus, or Suetonius. Outside of school, the fame of the English novelist Sir Walter Scott in France between 1815 and 1830 predisposed many writers (Dumas *père*, Hugo, Vigny, etc.) to compose historical novels. Flaubert's *La Tentation de saint Antoine* (1849, 1856, 1874), *Salammbô* (1862), and "Hérodias" (1876) reflect these converging influences.

Which French works did professors and critics advise Flaubert and his contemporaries to read? The literary canon available to Flaubert was surprisingly limited by today's standards. Francophone literatures (those written in French abroad) did not yet exist; Flaubert read modern literatures mainly in translation; and his school curriculum focused on one hundred fifty years, roughly from 1630 to 1780. During Flaubert's youth, medieval French literature was still being discovered; sixteenth-century literature—with the exceptions of Rabelais and Montaigne—was just beginning to be appreciated; nineteenth-century literature, associated with romantic social defiance and revolution, was still suspect in the schools, although enthusiastic young instructors often introduced it to their pupils. The canonical Roman classics, together with the seventeenth- and eighteenth-century French masterpieces that were widely taught and were associated with the golden age of the monarchy when France had culturally dominated Europe all valued craftsmanship over innovation. As Pascal had put it, in order to emphasize the primary importance of form, "when two people are playing tennis, they both use the same ball—but one of them places it better." For a writer before the romantics to emphasize daring innovations of content and literary genre, without coherent structure, would have seemed like driving a golf ball into the woods or a tennis ball over the fence: no matter how hard and straight you hit it, you would be out of bounds. During his years of law study in Paris, Flaubert took an hour out every morning to read Homer's *Iliad* in the original Greek. Even during his thirties, when Flaubert was composing *Madame Bovary*, the authors he mentions admiringly more than once in his correspondence are Montaigne, Boileau, Cervantes, Goethe (most of all), Hugo, La Fontaine, Plutarch, Rabelais, and Sophocles. Note the virtual absence of contemporaries and the strong representation of sixteenth- through eighteenth-century French authors, plus the Ancients.

FLAUBERT'S INNER CONFLICTS

Flaubert's imagination boiled over with fantastic, sadistic visions; given his educational experience, it was natural for him to turn to history to find guiding principles of classical restraint. So his first major project eventually to be published, *La Tentation de saint Antoine*, depicts almost exclusively altered states of consciousness—dreams and hallucinations—brought about by prolonged isolation, fasting, and obsessive prayer. But Flaubert tries to discipline these by attributing them to a prominent historical figure, a Church Father, exotically situated in the Egyptian desert beside the Nile, and chosen from one of the most tumultuous periods of the history of the Christian church as it struggled to define itself in competition with many heresies. When he read the result of two years' passionate work to his friends, they rejected it in horror; they felt that "the cancer of lyricism" had infected Flaubert. They proposed a contemporary, local subject, treating ordinary people, as a corrective: that is, write about what you know. *Madame Bovary*, then, was an enforced cure, reluctantly undertaken, like a rigorous diet and exercise regime. Like the author of the 1849 version of *La Tentation de saint Antoine*, Emma is an intelligent, morbidly sensitive person with low impulse control—but totally obscure in history.

So as he writes *Madame Bovary*, Flaubert continually wars with himself. Authors often lingeringly imagine crimes that they fear to commit. In l'abbé Prévost's *L'Histoire du chevalier Des Grieux et de Manon Lescaut* (Manon Lescaut), Choderlos de Laclos's *Les Liaisons dangereuses* (Dangerous Acquaintances), Balzac's *La Cousine Bette,* or Emile Zola's *Nana,* for example, a wanton woman lies, cheats, and seduces men at will, ruining their lives. But then, suddenly, at the very end, the marvelous, brilliant Marquise de Merteuil is exposed and socially disgraced, disfigured by smallpox, financially ruined, and forced to take refuge in the provinces; Manon is arrested and deported in chains; Valérie Marneffe dies horribly from disease; Nana also contracts smallpox and literally rots to death, abandoned by all the men who lusted for her. The four male authors in question create a female protagonist in order to distance themselves from the temptation of her disorderly behavior, but their vicarious pleasure obviously remains strong. Such works have two endings, one for the main character and one for the implied author (the personality that can be inferred from the text as a whole, without recourse to biographical speculation). Together, these two endings say, "That looks like fun ... but I probably couldn't get away with it."

Flaubert writes such an ending—Emma Bovary ruins herself financially and then dies horribly from the arsenic that she thought would give her a peaceful release from her frustrations—but throughout the novel, his impersonal narrator frequently yields to a dreamy, sensual, ecstatic identification with his heroine, only to pull back sharply and denounce her self-deception and her mediocrity. Her pathetic, devoted husband, Charles, who finally succumbs to the appeal of Emma's deluded romanticism after her death and becomes so corrupted by it that he languishes and dies, represents an antiself for the author, a vehemently rejected possibility. But the ending of *Madame Bovary,* like those of Chateaubriand's incest fantasy *René* or of *Manon Lescaut,* remains shrouded by a lingering pall of morbid delectation.

It is our own weaknesses we most hate in others. During the time that Flaubert was composing *Madame Bovary* as an antidote to his own hysterical tendencies, he also tried to correct the hysterical personality of his new lover, Louise Colet.[3] She was a noted writer, perhaps underrated today. Flaubert delighted in her intelligence and, throughout 1852 and 1853 especially, wrote her brilliant, thoughtful letters detailing his struggles in writing *Madame Bovary.* He also carefully read everything she wrote then and tried to help her improve, making rigorous, astringent comments about her style and content. The major theme of his comments—often crudely and vividly sexist—is that of Professor Henry Higgins in *Pygmalion* or *My Fair Lady:* "Why can't a woman be more like a man?" He wanted to transform Louise Colet into an ideal male companion with a "virile" imagination (for explanations of this expression, see Flaubert's letters, which define it beyond satiety), still sexually available to him at his convenience, but undemanding, willing to tolerate long periods of neglect. Louise Colet was passionate and persistent. Once when, in desperation, she traveled from Paris to Croisset to confront him, Flaubert refused to let her in. Even his mother criticized him for how he treated her then. He must have been the great love of her life. She later devoted two bitter romans à clef to him. Emma Bovary's possessive, demanding relationships with Rodolphe Boulanger and Léon Dupuis may in part have been unfair parodies of Louise Colet's attitudes. Flaubert's marked androgyny, his religious devotion to his art, and his being in love with love and art more than with any individual ensured that he would stay with his mother until she died. He preserved lifelong friendships with women such as Elisa Schlésinger, Gertrude Tennant, and Juliet Herbert because they were undemanding. But it was George Sand, brilliant, independent, creative, forceful, who became most nearly his kindred spirit and who among his friends (with the possible exception of Zola) was most nearly his literary equal. Her depiction of the antihero in her novel *Horace* helped shape the male protagonists of the 1869 *L'Education sentimentale*, and her example decisively redirected Flaubert's imagination in the *Trois Contes* (1877), inspired by her idealistic vision.

With the final six lines of *Madame Bovary*, Flaubert extricates himself from the seductive power of Emma's sensibility as it survives in Charles and returns to pure satire. He sharply sketches the eventual financial and social triumphs of the unscrupulous, officious busybody Homais, the pharmacist. But, just as the proximate cause of Charles's ruin was his unwise agreement, on two occasions, to give Emma power of attorney and control over their finances, so Flaubert himself was foredoomed to ruin himself by trusting the direction of his own fortune to the callous, dishonest husband of his beloved niece. His keen intelligence, hard work, and perspicacity could not protect him from his blind devotion to his niece, whom he had helped to raise from infancy and who was, in effect, his only child. At length, having made a better marriage (it was she who proposed) when her first husband, Commanville, died, and having retired to the Villa Tanit in the South of France, named after the moon-goddess in Flaubert's *Salammbô*, she would become the guardian of his papers and his memory, making sure that most of his notes and plans remained together and, in time, writing some Flaubert scholarship herself.

THE IMPORTANCE OF *MADAME BOVARY*

Widely taught in required courses throughout the secondary school and college curriculum, *Madame Bovary* addresses major problems in human relations and ethics, the relationship of fiction to reality, the use and misuse of language, and the art of the novel.[4] Flaubert's sharp criticisms of the excesses of capitalist societies—greed, exploitation, and consumerism—apply to our own day. His keen analysis of people's difficulties in communicating with each other in dysfunctional relationships illuminates much of our own experience, regardless of our gender, ethnicity, or background. Despite the humble, obscure social setting in which it plays out, Emma's narcissistic personality disorder typifies the tragic hero throughout literature.[5] The fate of this charming, intelligent, but impulsive and deeply selfish person raises many feminist issues in the context of a society where women were not allowed to vote, move, open a bank account, hold a passport, or start a business without their husbands' permission until after World War II.

Flaubert was a master of irony and satire. In depicting the Restoration period (1815–48) and, by implication, the beginning of the Second Empire (1851–70), he exposed the hollowness of traditional social myths such as the moral superiority of the romantic idealist, the probity of the small tradesman, the sanctity of the family, and the transforming power of religious faith. So acute were his observations that he and his publisher were placed on trial for subverting public morals. As Roland Barthes observed, any text must be an oppositional text if it is to emerge as a separate entity. But in its time, *Madame Bovary* seemed particularly subversive, stirring up a storm of protest from reviewers who deplored the absence of any morally inspiring characters.

The towering example of Flaubert's craftsmanship continues to inspire authors throughout the Western world today. Perhaps only William Faulkner, in the twentieth century, will prove as influential. Flaubert's meticulous plotting and intricate, innovative use of point of view, with its deliberate ambiguities; his precise descriptions and tableaux; his harrowing depictions of financial difficulties, illnesses, and despair; his ironic citation of conversational commonplaces and solecisms; and his rich depictions of characters' velleities of resistance to temptation (a major motif throughout his works)—all these strengths have led later writers and teachers of creative writing often to look to his art for guidance. In the United States and the United Kingdom, more nineteenth-century French scholars devote themselves to Flaubert than to any other author. For the last century and a half, realists, naturalists, modernists, and postmodernists in turn have found ever-renewed inspiration in his works.[6]

THE INTENDED AUDIENCES FOR THIS REFERENCE BOOK

This reference book addresses two audiences: the introduction and chapter 1, designed for the general reader and the undergraduate, respectively set the novel in the personal context of Flaubert's life and retell and clarify the plot. For graduate students, teachers, and scholars specializing in Flaubert, nineteenth-century France, the novel, or comparative literature, chapters 2, 5, and 6 offer substantial essays on the sources and genesis of Flaubert's text, his art of narration, and his influence on world literature. All readers should find valuable suggestions in chapters 3 and 4, on the social, cultural, and philosophical background of the times, and in the bibliographic essay (chapter 7) and bibliography, which conclude the volume.

A NOTE ON THE AUTHORS

Eugene F. Gray wrote chapters 3 and 4; Laurence M. Porter wrote the preface, the introduction, and chapters 1, 2, 5, and 6; we collaborated on the bibliographical essay, chapter 7. Our previous work on the Flaubert chapter in the definitive "Cabeen" critical bibliography edited by David Baguley (see the second item listed under "Bibliographies") and on three other Flaubert books (*Critical Essays, Approaches to Teaching* Madame Bovary, *A Gustave Flaubert Encyclopedia*), as well as a doctoral thesis on Flaubert's treatment of point of view by Eugene F. Gray and the essays we each have devoted to *Madame Bovary,* have gradually prepared us to write this reference book throughout our careers.

Eugene F. Gray writes:

Growing up in a small town in Michigan, I did not have access to the cultural and literary resources of a large city. My father, who had a keen and logical mind, stimulated my interest in science and math in high school. I also studied music with a talented local teacher. At the University of Michigan I majored in physics and engineering. For the language requirement in physics I chose French, because there was a French family in my hometown with whom I could converse, and I soon became fluent. In 1958 I was chosen to work at the World's Fair in Brussels, Belgium, and it was during that year that I became interested in French culture. Upon my return to Michigan, I finished my degree in physics but also took the beginning courses in French literature for relaxation. Encouraged by Professor Robert Niess, I took literature courses for a semester to test the water, so to speak, and then entered the graduate program in Romance Languages. Professor Niess inspired me to concentrate on the nineteenth century and directed my dissertation on Gustave Flaubert. My research interests have been the somewhat antithetical areas of novelistic style and the relationships between writers and the sciences. When the desktop computer became popular, I saw that it could be valuable for the study of language and literature, and I designed two computerized multimedia language laboratories at Michigan State University. More recently I have been occupied in preparing a Web site devoted to nineteenth-century French caricaturists.

Laurence M. Porter writes:

This book brings me full circle to recall my initial commitment to French studies. Because I first came to Harvard from a small public high school, with one and a half years of French, and placed into fourth-year college French (in those days one did what one was told), the undergraduate years were an uncertain struggle. After college, I enlisted in the army to sort things out, reading the literary classics that one could purchase there cheaply and taking a correspondence course in German. When I decided to make a career in college French instead, I returned to Harvard in the winter of 1958. Working in Widener Library as a title searcher in Western European languages, passing time until I could begin graduate study in the fall, I audited a Flaubert seminar by the late René Jasinski, whose year-long nineteenth-century French literature course had been my favorite during undergraduate years. Professor Jasinski's encouragement, devotion to his calling, benevolence, erudition, and keen sensitivity to all forms of French literature were inspiring. He and Paul Bénichou had come to Harvard to escape the stuffiness of the Sorbonne. Their warmth and lack of affectation were memorable. Thanks to them, I am writing this now.

In 1963 my wife's job brought me to Michigan State University, where I settled down to teaching twelve courses a year. There were few Harvard graduates in nineteenth-century French studies at the time, but the late Benjamin F. Bart (Ph.D. 1947) and I eventually met when he visited East Lansing. He opened many doors for me—above all, securing me a contract to edit the *Critical Essays on Gustave Flaubert*. One Flaubert book led to another, and here we are, blessed with the most attractive Flaubert subject of all, the masterpiece *Madame Bovary*. We hope you may enjoy, or re-enjoy (as Flaubert might say), this wonderful, ironic, rich novel as much as we do.

ACKNOWLEDGMENTS

Some sentences and paragraphs, in modified form, come from various entries in Laurence M. Porter's edition of Greenwood Press's *A Gustave Flaubert Encyclopedia* (2001). From the fifty-some contributors to that volume and to Eugene F. Gray and Laurence M. Porter's edited volume *Approaches to Teaching Flaubert's Madame Bovary* (New York: The Modern Language Association of America, 1995), we have learned much, and we are grateful for their help.

In particular, we would like to thank these colleagues for their detailed suggestions concerning the impact of Flaubert's *Madame Bovary* on other writers: Anita Alkhas (University of Wisconsin at Milwaukee), David Bellos (Princeton University), Isabelle Cassagne (Lewis and Clark College), William Cloonan (Florida State University), Patricia Greene (Michigan State University), Cheryl Krueger (University of Virginia), Larry Kuiper (University of Wisconsin at Milwaukee), E. Nicole Meyer (University of Wisconsin at Green Bay), Stéphane Michaud (Université de Paris III: Sorbonne Nouvelle), Shawn Morrison (College of Charleston), Armine Kotin Mortimer (University of Illinois), William Paulson (University of Michigan), Luciano Campos Picanço (Davidson College), Carol Rifelj (Middlebury College), Sheila Teahan (Michigan State University), and Agnès Peysson Zeiss (Penn Charter School). We are also gratefully indebted to Fabrice J. Venezia, creator of the Flaubert info.com Web site, for his help in recommending electronic resources.

NOTES

1. Percy Lubbock, *The Craft of Fiction* (1921; reprint New York: Viking, 1957): 60, 92.

2. From the male viewpoint, Chrétien de Troyes opposed *l'amour courtois*, complaisantly explored the dangers of adultery in *Le Chevalier à la charette* (Lancelot, King Arthur, and Guinevere), and denounced the uxoriousness of an all-too-happy marriage that would keep a man from his combat duty (*Yvain*).

3. Flaubert knew that he himself was hysterical, and said so; he also depicted male hysteria in the barbarian chieftain Mâtho of *Salammbô*.

4. This final section of the preface is a modified, condensed version of Laurence M. Porter and Eugene F. Gray, eds., *Approaches to Teaching Flaubert's Madame Bovary* (New York: MLA, 1995), "Preface to the Volume," xi–xv.

5. See Laurence M. Porter, "Emma Bovary's Narcissism Revisited," in Graham Falconer and Mary Donaldson-Evans, eds., *Kaleidoscope: Essays on Nineteenth Century*

French Literature in Honor of Thomas H. Goetz. Toronto: Centre d'Etudes Romantiques Joseph Sablé, St. Michael's College, The University of Toronto, 1996: 85–97.

6. See Laurence M. Porter, ed., *A Gustave Flaubert Encyclopedia* (Westport, CT: Greenwood, 2001), "Influence on Other Writers," 363, and the forty-two other articles to which this entry in the Index refers, as well as those listed under *Madame Bovary,* 366.

Introduction

Gustave Flaubert's parents met in L'Hôtel-Dieu, the main hospital of Rouen. Set on the Seine in a flat expanse of dairy farms and orchards in Northwestern France, eighty miles northwest of Paris, this port was the largest town in Normandy. Flaubert's mother, Caroline-Augustine-Elisa Foucault, had become an orphan early in 1803.[1] In 1806, she went to live with her godmother, the wife of Jean-Baptiste Laumonier, the chief surgeon of the Hôtel-Dieu at Rouen. Flaubert's father (1784 – 1846) was serving under Laumonier as a surgical intern. The marriage, in 1812, was undoubtedly arranged because Achille-Cléophas had demonstrated exceptional ability in his profession and promised to become a worthy successor to his father-in-law when the latter retired. Achille-Cléophas's drive and intelligence made him upwardly mobile: his own father had been a veterinarian. Like many self-made men, when he had arrived professionally he proved conservative—continuing, for example, to believe in the virtues of bloodletting as a medical treatment.[2] Throughout his life, however, he remained a dedicated practitioner, spending many hours improving his surgical technique by practicing on cadavers and traveling far to perform operations for almost no money if they seemed of interest for the advancement of medical science.

FLAUBERT'S CHILDHOOD

The Flauberts' first-born child, Achille (1813–82), eight years older than Gustave, was dutiful and studious. Achille followed in his father's footsteps, becoming chief surgeon in his turn when his father died. From 1818 on, the family lived in the chief surgeon's official residence, an apartment within the hospital. Flaubert was born there. Work and family were closely interwoven for three generations, providing a stable, secure environment. That both the eldest son, the eldest daughter, and the granddaughter were named after the parents further reflected the family's sense of continuity. Moreover, the Flaubert family's devoted servant, Julie, was to remain with them until Gustave's death. She told him stories that helped to spark his love for fiction. Meanwhile, despite the frequent changes of regime, history reinforced the family's sense of security: France was at peace after a quarter-century of war (1791–1815), and no more wars would be fought on French soil until 1870.

Three siblings died in infancy before Gustave Flaubert (1821–80) was born on December 12.[3] Because he was eight years younger than his older brother, who had been away from home to study medicine, Flaubert felt closest to his younger sister, Caroline (1824 – 46). The two children played together often and wrote each other with great affection in adulthood. Caroline's daughter, also named Caroline, was to live with the Flauberts until her marriage, and Flaubert loved his niece deeply throughout his life.

Flaubert's mother home-schooled him until he went to the prestigious Collège Royal of Rouen in 1832.[4] Well-to-do, with servants, she had time to devote to his education. A dreamy child, Flaubert sometimes appeared lost in thought, occasionally so much so that he would fall off his chair; he may have been already showing signs of the temporal-lobe epilepsy that was to afflict him severely during his mid-twenties. But despite Jean-Paul Sartre's claim that Flaubert was dyslexic, from the time that he was ten he directed and staged plays by classical authors such as Molière, and later, by himself, with his sister Caroline, their friends Ernest Chevalier (1820–87), Alfred Le Poittevin (1816–48), and his sister Laure Le Poittevin (1821–1902). The two brother-sister pairs were constant companions. In the close-knit family, Flaubert's father was Alfred's godfather, and Alfred's father was Flaubert's godfather. Later, Laure married Gustave de Maupassant but separated from him to raise her two sons, Guy and Hervé, alone. She and Flaubert remained in touch, and her son Guy, the future writer, became Flaubert's surrogate son and literary protégé.[5]

As Flaubert's childhood theatricals, his plot summaries of all Voltaire's plays in 1845, and his persistent attempts at dramaturgy later in life suggest, he had an abiding fascination with the theater. As entertainment, that medium was more important, until the twentieth century, than we can imagine today. It had to fill the role of our radio, movie, and television dramas as well as of our stage plays. Flaubert was exposed to it early: Rouen had two active playhouses, to which his parents would take him occasionally. There, in 1840, he saw Rachel (the pseudonym of Elisa-Rachel Félix), the greatest actress of her generation. When Flaubert's parents were passing through Paris on their way to visit relatives, they also frequently took him to see plays in the capital. Throughout his life, he wrote scenarios to help him imagine living people enacting his stories. But he never succeeded in writing sustained, lively dialogue; his need to maintain satiric control over his characters precluded their speaking "freely" "among themselves." In 1857 and 1858, however, Flaubert refused two offers to have *Madame Bovary* dramatized. He mistrusted transpositions from one literary genre to another.[6]

Gustave's strong vocation as a writer persisted during his secondary school years. His history teacher, Pierre-Adolphe Chéruel, a former pupil of the great historian Jules Michelet and soon to become a distinguished historian himself (one can still find eight or nine books by him in major libraries), inspired Flaubert with a lasting passion for history and also encouraged him to write stories. The combination of amateur historiography and narration would characterize several of Flaubert's mature novels: *La Tentation de saint Antoine*, *Salammbô*, and *L'Education sentimentale.* During the fall term of 1834, probably with the indulgent support of a new teacher of composition, Henry Gourgaud-Dugazon, Flaubert began to compose his own literary journal, *Art et progrès.* Only volume 2 survives. It contains the "Voyage en enfer," modeled on satiric works such as Alain-René Lesage's *Le Diable boîteux* (1707; revised 1726). The "Voyage" "borrows the first two cantos of Byron's semi-autobiographical *Childe Harold's Pilgrimage* (1812), and is indebted to Edgar Quinet's *Ahasvérus* (1833), whose hero thirsted for knowledge."[7] Flaubert's Satan takes the author on a tour of this world, and after forcing him to witness manifold cruelties and injustices, the devil reveals that this world itself is Hell. In Lesage's work, a devil takes a young man on an aerial tour of Madrid (read: Paris), lifting the rooftops to reveal the folly and corruption of human society. If you suppress Flaubert's melodramatic indignation and intensity and Lesage's playful, supernatural narrative frame, you will be only one step away from the omniscient, impersonal perspective of Flaubert's mature satiric works: his narrator can see into people's hearts as well as spying on their behavior and overhearing their conversations.

FLAUBERT'S VOCATION AS A WRITER

In November 1839, Flaubert led a student protest against the arbitrary, harsh treatment of three of his classmates and was expelled from school. Thenceforth he studied for the *baccalauréat* at home. His letters to his friends at that time show he was deeply depressed, probably because he knew his father would insist that he study for the bar, a profession for which he felt absolutely no vocation: he was sure he wanted to write.[8] In 1842, Flaubert completed *Novembre*, the most polished of his juvenilia and his most nearly autobiographical work (although the *Mémoires d'un fou*, in 1838, had already used many of the same stories). The fine opening pages express the narrator's delight in autumn; his ecstatic sense of union with nature—a leitmotif throughout his career—recalls an opening scene in Goethe's *The Sorrows of Young Werther* (1774).[9] He longs for love but has been disillusioned by his experiences in a Paris brothel. Then he meets the prostitute Marie there. Their lovemaking is described with a keen, daring sensuality inspired by Théophile Gautier's scandalous descriptions of the bisexual Mademoiselle de Maupin. The narrative shifts from autobiography to fantasy when Marie falls in love with him and says he is the man for whom she has been searching. But Flaubert's protagonist does not embrace the rescue fantasy.[10] He can find no satisfaction even with her. A relay narrator reports that the hero had considered and then rejected suicide but had died shortly after anyway.[11]

Because he showed no signs of a medical vocation and because his father did not consider literature a viable career, Flaubert was sent to Paris to study law. At the time, the bar was the default career choice for well-to-do young men who could decide on nothing else. (Frédéric Moreau, the antihero of *L'Education sentimentale*, will also drift unwillingly into law, where he is unsuccessful until freed by an unexpected inheritance.) As today, law could often lead to a career in finance or in politics. But the law bored Flaubert, who experienced it only as a hindrance to his vocation. He seldom dared to protest directly to his father, instead using his sister as an intermediary. He did pass his first-year law exams. But after that, instead of studying, he read Homer in the original Greek every morning, composed fiction, and frequented literary circles and cafés. He had already published in a little magazine, *Le Colibri* (The Hummingbird), edited by his friend Le Poittevin, himself a serious writer.

A sudden onset of grand mal seizures (or epileptiform hysteria, according to some) in January 1844 and the six months of severe nervous disorders that followed freed Flaubert from his unwelcome law studies. Both Emma Bovary's visions shortly before her suicide and some of Saint Anthony's visions may have been inspired by their author's lived experience.[12] But epilepsy was considered a disgrace in those days, and Flaubert's family tried to conceal it. From then on, owing to his occasional attacks, Flaubert was no longer expected to hold a regular job; he could write at home, travel, or visit Paris as he pleased. Consciously, his father accepted the situation; unconsciously, he must have been furious: while treating his son, he accidentally poured boiling water on Gustave's right arm. The burns took months to heal. The premature death of Flaubert's father from a thigh infection in 1846, a month before Gustave's beloved sister Caroline died in childbirth, left the young man with a comfortable inheritance; he would live mainly in the family house at Croisset, on the banks of the Seine about two miles outside Rouen, for the remainder of his life.[13] He was devoted to his protective, hypochondriacal mother, who let him live with her until her death eight years before his.

FLAUBERT'S SEX LIFE

Before venereal disease further compromised his health, Flaubert was a strikingly handsome, slender young man, just under six feet tall (equivalent to 6'4" today), with golden brown hair and large gray eyes. He had had his sexual initiation with his mother's maid, and a more memorable affair in Marseilles in 1840, as his family was passing through on a vacation trip.[14] At his hotel, he smiled at an exotic Creole woman, Eulalie Foucaud, fifteen years older than he; she came to his room that night. They had sex several times before his departure and maintained a passionate correspondence for a time. According to the Goncourts' journal, Flaubert later felt disgusted with the flesh; yearning for some mystical purification, he did not have sex for four years—between 1842 and 1846. He then met the writer Louise Colet, and their tempestuous liaison lasted from 1846 to 1848 and resumed, on Flaubert's return from the Orient, between 1851 and 1854.

The evidence of Flaubert's reported life and his letters suggests that he was predominantly if not exclusively heterosexual. Because of his crudely sexual language in letters to a few close male friends, however, a few critics have speculated on Flaubert's emotional androgyny. Replying to Louis Bouilhet from the Middle East, for example, Flaubert writes: "This morning at noon, my poor dear old man, I received your fine long letter that I had longed for so much. —It moved me right down to my guts. *I creamed* [emphasis in original]. How much I think about you! You priceless bugger! How many times a day I think of you, and how much I miss you!" (January 15, 1850, *CORR* 1:567). It is not surprising, then, that critics find "signs and indications of at least potential bisexuality and (latent) homosexuality" in Flaubert's novels. If we are to believe his account of a visit to the Turkish baths in Beirut, he had sex with a fourteen-year-old male prostitute in 1850.[15] In any event, Frédéric and Deslauriers in the 1869 *L'Education sentimentale* and the title characters of *Bouvard et Pécuchet*, as well as some of the barbarian mercenary warriors in *Salammbô*, seem to have had latent homoerotic relationships that lasted a lifetime—and for which Homer's *Iliad*, for example, offers a model.[16] The first two works clearly value male friendships above the love of women.

But despite Flaubert's devotion to Alfred Le Poittevin (1816–48) or to Louis Bouilhet (1821–69) and his nearly lifelong dependency on his mother, women (often somewhat older than he) seemed to excite him as men did not. He believed he contracted his syphilis from a Maronite woman in Constantinople— "or perhaps it was a little Turkish woman" (letter to Louis Bouilhet, November 14, 1850, *CORR* 1:707). His account of his encounter with the courtesan Kuchuk Hanem is a famous rendering of the sexual fascination of the romantic Orient, embodied in the exotic female Other. The dream dissolves into reality when he hears her snoring and finds bedbugs when he awakes. Nevertheless, he obviously admired her and enjoyed her company. During the last two decades of his life, Flaubert also had sporadic sexual encounters with Juliet Herbert and with the actress and singer Suzanne Lagier. But most of his life was his work. He spent the better part of each year in the country, where he researched and wrote passionately nearly every day until he died.

Flaubert's androgyny appears not only in male homosocial bonding but also with at least equal force in many close friendships with women and in his lifelong infatuation with Elisa Schlésinger (1810–88: a model for Maria in the *Mémoires d'un fou*, Marie in *Novembre*, and Sophie Arnoux in *L'Education sentimentale*). He also had a prolonged, tempestuous liaison with Louise Colet (1810–76), his closest confidante while he was composing *Madame Bovary*, and on whom he tried repeatedly to impose a "virile," sinewy style.[17] She was a prize-winning poet and popular novelist who had arranged an open marriage. Unlike most women of the time, she freely frequented male-dominated writers' salons as an equal, had her own salon, and supported herself—albeit precariously—with her writing. Flaubert's epistolary exchanges with her during the composition of *Madame Bovary* reveal much concerning his evolving concept of that novel.[18] She encouraged him to record and discuss his ideas, and he called her his Muse.[19]

During the latter part of his life, from 1862 on, Flaubert was strongly influenced by, and close to, the great woman writer George Sand (1804–76)—perhaps the only woman he considered fully equal. In his letters, he addressed her with the gender-bending expression *Chère Maître*—"Dear [feminine] Master [masculine—meaning, in this context, intellectual mentor]." The antihero of *L'Education sentimentale* (1869) recalls the title character of Sand's *Horace* (1842), and Flaubert wrote the uplifting tale "Un cœur simple" (1877) for her, to respond to her suggestion that he should try to alleviate his chronic depression by creating a tale with some hopeful elements. They confided in many matters: Flaubert confessed his androgynous feelings to her, and she wisely reassured him that these were normal and that society would one day recognize this truth of human nature.[20]

LEARNING THE NOVELIST'S CRAFT

By 1845, Flaubert had completed his first distinguished full-length novel. He chose not to publish it during his lifetime owing to its defects, which include an at times incoherent plot made of two separate and largely unrelated stories (split apart during composition by his illness) and heavy-handed satire. This earlier version of *L'Education sentimentale*, with the same title as the 1869 masterpiece, was a *Künstlerroman*, a novel about a young person who becomes a novelist (Marcel Proust's *A la recherche du temps perdu* or James Joyce's *The Portrait of the Artist as a Young Man* come to mind). As such, it is quasi-autobiographical. Reflecting Flaubert's experience of living in Paris for his law studies, the novel also contrasts the provinces with the capital, as Balzac and Stendhal, for example, had already done. Two lifelong friends, Henry Gosselin and Jules (whose last name is never mentioned), live out contrasting existences that the young Flaubert could imagine for himself. Jules is marooned in the country, forced by his father to pursue a tedious career as a clerk in a customs office. Henry, envied by Jules for having the opportunity to live in Paris, is bored by both the city and his law studies. He eventually flees to America with a woman twice his age, the wife of the director of his student dormitory. In time, his passion fades, and he returns to Paris to lead the empty existence of a shallow, elegant socialite. Jules, however, finds inspiration for his literary art in the mediocrity that surrounds him and transcends his circumstances.

Learning the novelist's craft by composing the 1845 *Education*, Flaubert composes a sort of sampler, in which he experiments with a great variety of literary techniques. He perfects the detached, ironic, impersonal narrative stance that will characterize most of his later work. Meaningless repetition and its verbal equivalent, the cliché, dominate the characters' experience, although only Jules intuits their humdrum destiny. Jean Bruneau speculates that Flaubert's epilepsy and prolonged convalescence during the first half of 1844 reoriented his imagination toward introspection, a development reflected by how the character portrayal of Jules alters halfway through the novel.[21]

But Flaubert's turn toward subjectivity was overdetermined. Born in the wake of French romanticism, he came too late to share that literary movement's nostalgia for the vanished grandeur of the Revolution and the First Empire, which opened careers for nonaristocrats (if they were well-to-do, middle-class men) and then went on to conquer most of Europe. That Napoleon had been a tyrant responsible for the deaths of millions of people initially did not seem to matter in the afterglow of his victories.[22] For most young Frenchmen of Flaubert's day, the disappointment at having been born too late to partake of Napoleonic glory was aggravated by the disappointment of the failed Second Republic from 1848–51, when the idealistic romantic poet Lamartine ruled briefly, only to be quickly marginalized before the coup d'état engineered by a second-rate Napoleon, the great-nephew of the first. This Louis Napoleon founded a Second Empire without grandeur (1851–70), destined for humiliation in Mexico and in the Franco-Prussian War.

A keenly felt literary failure aggravated political disillusionment for Flaubert: during the late 1840s, he had poured his inspiration into the first version of his *Tentation de saint Antoine*, a cherished project he never would totally abandon until it was finally published in 1874. This grandiose, erudite fresco of the heresies of the early Christian period was seen through the visions of a desert hermit, the future Saint Anthony, as Christianity struggled to define and consolidate itself in the era of Constantine. Flaubert arranged with his closest friends at that time, Louis Bouilhet and Maxime Du Camp, that they would listen to him read *La Tentation* to them out loud without interruption before offering comments. He spent four days sequestered with them as soon as he had completed the work in 1849. When at last he finished, a sickly silence reigned. Dismayed by the masses of static description, episodic characters, and superfluous detail, his friends retired to confer. They returned to say that he should throw his book into the fire and never think of it again. He was devastated; it had been his love child and his first full-length project. It blends extensive historical research with personal memories of his epileptic hallucinations just before and during his seizures. In it, a parade of demonic figures and false gods tries, ultimately in vain, to distract Saint Anthony from prayer. There, for the first time, Flaubert fully develops the motif of temptation—inherited from Gérard de Nerval's 1828 translation of the first part of Goethe's *Faust*—that will strongly mark nearly all his mature work. But the novel drags when it dwells on long, allegorical speeches by abstract figures such as the Seven Deadly Sins, the saint's pet pig, or the Three Theological Virtues. Like *Salammbô* (Flaubert himself confessed that he found the pedestal of that work—the Carthaginian wars with Rome—too large for its statue, the heroine), "Hérodias," and "La Légende de saint Julien l'Hospitalier," *La Tentation* overwhelmed and bored a reading public that wanted action and characters with whom they could identify.

What criticism of Flaubert's erudition overlooks is the synthesizing power of his imagination. Seeking new subjects in order to renew neoclassical literature, French romanticism had opened four vast domains for literary exploration: the spatial exoticism of distant lands, the temporal exoticism of history, the mental exoticism of altered states of consciousness, and the supernatural exoticism of revelations foreshadowing the evolution of Creation and society toward eventual absorption in the spiritual essence of God. Trying to outdo Goethe's *Faust*, Flaubert had combined all four of these new modes in *La Tentation*: third-century Egypt, where a saintly hermit struggles against his dreams, hallucinations, and tempting illusions created by the Devil before winning through to a vision of Christ and the omnipresence of the divine. Anthony finally realizes that the spiritual is not what remains when the material has been taken away: the spiritual is anything that is in a right relationship to God.

But in 1849, his work came a generation before its time. It would have harmonized perfectly with the decadent movement, permeated with unrequited religious longing, that Joris-Karl Huysmans inaugurated and culminated at the same moment when he published *A rebours* in 1884. Eighty years later, in 1930, the *Tentation*'s swarming, ever-changing visions of monsters and temptations could have been compellingly brought to life by a Surrealist film director, and a hundred twenty years later, in 1970, by television. Victor Hugo, who like Flaubert possessed an acute visual sensibility, became fully known as an artist only when his historical dramas such as the play *Torquemada* were filmed with the new special effects available to television. But Flaubert's friends were, above all, sensitive to the nascent movement of realism in literature—stories of ordinary middle-class people trapped in routines, in the here and now—and they could experience *La Tentation* only as an aberration resulting from overindulgence in the imagination.

THE JOURNEY TO THE MIDDLE EAST

To find relief from his obsessive work on the novel and his keen disappointment at its outcome, Flaubert agreed to take a twenty-month journey through the Middle East with Maxime Du Camp (1822–94), from late 1849 till 1851. Du

Camp wanted to make a photographic record of the Nile, Egypt, and the Holy Land. This important pioneering compendium of images, little-known in Europe in his time, was to be published as *Egypte, Nubie, Palestine et Syrie* in 1852. About then, following the precedents of the Napoleonic expedition into Egypt in 1799 and of Chateaubriand, painters and writers such as Delacroix, Fromentin, Gautier, and Nerval were just beginning to explore the region.[23] Flaubert himself had an official government assignment to gather agricultural statistics, but soon abandoned that project. (Du Camp had a government commission to investigate the area and probably wangled another for Flaubert.) He and Du Camp reached Alexandria, Egypt, in January 1850, after a voyage from Marseilles. After six weeks in Cairo, they chartered a boat for a five-month excursion on the upper Nile, as far as the Second Cataract. He and Du Camp successfully set the broken leg of a crew member, as Charles Bovary was to do for his future father-in-law in *Madame Bovary*. Planning some day to return to the *Tentation*, Flaubert visited the holes in the cliffs above the Nile where desert hermits like Saint Anthony had lived, and he questioned Coptic bishops closely to learn more about the lives of those hermits. He was electrified by the sight of the Sphinx and awed by the ancient palaces of Thebes and Karnak. These sights were to enrich *Salammbô* and "Hérodias" as well as later versions of the *Tentation*.

Flaubert had hoped to find faith in the Holy City; as he entered, he had a vision of Christ. But he was soon dismayed by the local commercialism and exploitation of tourists. Moreover, rival Christian sects fought so fiercely over the Holy Sepulcher that the local pasha had to keep the keys to it. Flaubert became profoundly disillusioned.

WRITING *MADAME BOVARY*

On his return, Flaubert set himself to the dreary, self-corrective task of chastening his overactive imagination by treating a contemporary subject. He used the Delamare case as his historical prototype. Eugène Delamare, a medical student of Flaubert's father, had entered a rural practice in the Norman village of Ry as an *officier de santé*, a "public health officer," trained somewhat less well than a licensed practical nurse. This humble profession had been created by the French government to ensure at least minimal medical services for underserved regions. The public health officer could practice only in the region where he had been licensed and could not perform major surgery. After a first marriage to an older widow, who died, Delamare married a farm girl, Delphine Couturier. She, like Emma Bovary, committed adultery with a law clerk (like Léon) and then with a local squire (like Rodolphe), while spending extravagantly and falling ever deeper into debt. At length, allegedly, her debts drove her to suicide.

On September 19, 1851, Flaubert began writing his novel.[24] Many of his reminiscences of country life in Normandy crystallized around his female protagonist (named Marie in the first scenario), as they would later crystallize around the servant Félicité in "Un cœur simple." In the novel, her first name, Emma—probably chosen by her mother, of whom we learn nothing except that she was well-loved by her husband—reflects the vogue of English romanticism during the Napoleonic empire; her married name, Bovary, suggests bovine stupidity and rural calm in both French and English. Flaubert worked on this project so assiduously for the next five years that his little niece, Caroline, who lived with him and his mother, thought that *la Bovary* was the way to say "work."

In all his fiction, Flaubert uses three main character types: stolid grotesques who mindlessly, endlessly repeat the selfsame acts without reflecting on them (Binet, Hippolyte, Bournisien, or Lestiboudois in *Madame Bovary*); unscrupulous opportunists, perfectly adapted to whatever place they find themselves and highly successful because they concentrate only on exploiting others (Homais, Lheureux, Rodolphe, Monsieur Bovary *père*); and dissatisfied dreamers who—idealistically or selfishly—cherish unrealistic visions of a better world. To describe Flaubert's best-known fictions as realistic is misleading—*realistic* is always a misleading way to describe literature if we understand realism only as literally true-to-life. The material circumstances of *Madame Bovary, L'Education sentimentale,* and "Un cœur simple" are indeed unusually true-to-life; the stories are set in the here and now of the author and his contemporary readers. The leading characters in such stories are severely limited by their circumstances: modest or humble social status; restricted income; ordinary intelligence, resolve, and imagination; and the weaknesses of their bodies, which—unlike the bodies of heroes—become tired and ill, need to pause for food and rest. At last the protagonists falter and resign themselves to their fate or are destroyed by forces stronger than they, which they understand only dimly. But no realistic plot can occur unless the main characters' attitudes are somehow unrealistic. Fictional realism depends on the characters' fantasies. In order to become entangled in their punishing plots, they need to hold unreasonable hopes and expectations, which lure them into disastrous schemes and commitments. Like romantic heroes, they consider themselves superior to others and entitled to love, wealth, and fame. But unlike romantic heroes, they cannot express themselves grandiloquently: they cannot even enjoy the verbal beauty of their own swan songs. Even at the point of death, unlike Kafka's prisoner in "The Penal Colony," they remain fundamentally mistaken about their world.

The romantic novel had dwelt on frustrated claims for special consideration, made by a self-glorifying narrator-protagonist. Other people have only a shadowy presence in such stories; their social density (that is, the numbers and the range of secondary characters depicted to make up the world of the novel) is thin. The realist movement that began to supersede romanticism as early as 1830, at the very moment when romanticism triumphed, turned aside from the dramatic contrasts of crime and innocence, city and country, in order to mine the rich ground of mediocrity. Balzac and Stendhal, protorealists, remained tempted by aristocratic and urban chic. Stendhal's *Le Rouge et le Noir* uses its depictions of some working-class people in its initial small-town setting and in its sordid descriptions of political infighting in a seminary only as springboards to the world of Paris and the aristocracy, although the story then falls back ironically into the small-town milieu where it began. But Balzac and Stendhal treat several kinds and conditions of people that had previously passed unnoticed, and they multiply their dramatis personae by experimenting with contrasting variations on the same character type.[25] Although their heroes often fail, nevertheless their passion and lust for life make them stand out against a backdrop of petty, narrow-minded secondary characters.

Even these lesser characters, however, often do not have a job. Despite its small-town setting, the Delamare story that Flaubert used as an initial reference point for the plot of *Madame Bovary* is dramatic enough, with two adulteries and a suicide. But to fill in his novelistic frame, Flaubert unlike the romantics begins paying attention to the neglected petite bourgeoisie, people who don't have to work with their hands but who earn a living in the humbler professions and the service trades. *Madame Bovary* (published in book form in 1857) depicts teachers, doctors, lawyers, bankers, merchants, a priest, innkeepers, a tax collector, and a pharmacist. This best-known of French novels satirizes small-town life in Normandy, the predominantly agricultural province that Flaubert knew best. As Jonathan Culler pointed out years ago, Flaubert really rubs it in, as if he experienced a kind of morbid delectation from wallowing in rural stupidity.[26] Many of his characters have faintly pejorative names (see chapter 5).

Unlike many satirists, however, Flaubert was even-handed. The French language distinguishes Paris from *la province*, "the provinces," meaning every place in mainland France that is not Paris. The nearest American equivalents might be "out state" in states dominated by a large metropolitan area such as New York, Chicago, Boston, or Detroit, or "hick" referring to a town or person. But for Flaubert, who overturns the *beatus ille* topos (the conventional idea that life is better in the country), although small-town or rural life was a hell of vindictive scheming, greed, and petty intrigue, city life was no better. His next realist novel, *L'Education sentimentale* (1869), will mock the clichés and corruption of city life, while showing that, beneath a thin veneer of sophistication, the Parisians are just as ordinary—and often, contemptible—as the provincials. Finally, twelve years later still, Flaubert's third and last realistic novel, *Bouvard et Pécuchet* (1881), ridicules two Parisian copy clerks who retire to the country, which they initially idealize just as foolishly as Emma Bovary idealizes the big city she will never see. At length the clerks become enlightened critics of human folly and misguided intellectual structures, but no one will listen to them.

Scarcely any one of his characters, self-satisfied or dissatisfied, finds favor with Flaubert. In *Madame Bovary*, he ridicules both those vague dreamers such as Emma, or Léon in part 1, who long for the glamour of Paris, and those energetic entrepreneurs such as the pharmacist Homais or the merchant and usurer Lheureux, who are complacently content with life in a small town. The latter two figures form a subplot of the triumph of practical, avaricious mediocrity that contrasts with the disastrous failures of Emma's impractical life, while illustrating the rise of the bourgeoisie after the French Revolution, when the fortunes of the landed nobility slowly declined.[27]

Leaving aside the changes in their character caused by growing experience and resulting self-confidence (in Léon or Homais, for example), most of the characters in *Madame Bovary* are flat characters, types who do not evolve. The unchanging attributes of the secondary characters highlight the dramatic changes undergone by the major character, Emma. She is first charmed by the trappings of religion, then disrespectful of it, then a bored farm girl, then a new bride hoping to find love—whatever that is, then a mother, then platonically in love with another man, then adulterous and dominated by her lover, then devout, then adulterous again but dominating her new lover, and at last, despairing and suicidal. In contrast, Madame Homais is always a happily married woman with four children; Léon, despite his velleities for a more glamorous life, is always a law student and apprentice; Rodolphe, an unattached womanizer; Charles, a pitiable butt and dupe. At the end, corrupted by Emma's pseudoromantic ideas after her death, Charles is no longer a social being, but a recluse whom the author extinguishes for aesthetic reasons—in order to bring the novel to an end by exterminating his family.[28]

The crux of Flaubert's irony, especially in *Madame Bovary*, is to present as "live themes" from the characters' point of view—as controversial affirmations of value that make the characters feel passionate, intense, courageous, and original—the "dead themes" of cultural cliché. A few lucid, manipulative characters such as Rodolphe or Lheureux use dead themes deliberately, as traps for the others who cannot see through them. Others—Bournisien or Homais, for instance—need to convince themselves of the validity of their dead themes because their sense of selfhood depends on them. Emma's richness and special interest as a character depend on her ambivalence toward clichés: despite her inexperience, her intelligence and common sense eventually allow her to see through some of them, but her desperate will to imagine some escape from her dreary life leads her eventually to accept clichés anyway. Then she suppresses her superior awareness and limits it to keen but indecisive moments of lucidity. Flaubert excels at analyzing human beings' half-formed desires to improve, to reform, to use common sense instead of acting self-destructively. For having resisted an imprudent or immoral impulse, Emma feels authorized to compensate herself for her virtue by yielding to that impulse next time. Her abuse of credit and her constantly living beyond her means are rooted in her frustrated sense of entitlement. Believing herself a superior person, she thinks she deserves better than her lot.[29]

AFTER *MADAME BOVARY*

Having completed *Madame Bovary*, a great success, Flaubert felt that he had adequately chastened his imagination. He plunged back into historical exoticism.

His next project, *Salammbô* (1862), was nourished by his long journey to the Middle East a decade earlier and by his outstanding training at the elite Collège Royal of Rouen. Drawing on the Greek historian Polybius's *Histories,* Flaubert treated the revolt of the mercenaries hired by the city-state of Carthage, which refused to pay them after the Roman Republic defeated Carthage in the First Punic War of the third century B.C. Over five years he read hundreds of sources, researching the rivalry between ancient Carthage and Rome and the Carthaginian cult of the sun god Moloch and the moon goddess Tanit, with its human sacrifices. He invents the blindly passionate characters Mâtho, a Libyan chieftain of the mercenaries, and Salammbô, priestess of Tanit and the daughter of the Carthaginian general Hamilcar. In a daring raid, Mâtho steals the goddess's veil from her temple, demoralizing the Carthaginians, and Salammbô goes to his camp at night to take it back, after having sex with him.[30] At length, when Hamilcar Barca (the father of Hannibal) returns to Carthage and takes command, the mercenaries are exterminated to the last man. Mâtho is crucified before cheering crowds; witnessing his death, Salammbô dies suddenly at the same moment. Flaubert deliberately preserved his characters' mystery; he tells us little of their inner life. The tragic hero and heroine each believe that the other is a god.

Flaubert recreates the myths of ancient Carthage in great detail and indulges in elaborate descriptions and set pieces such as the initial banquet scene. In many scenes, he preserves ambiguity regarding the reality and power of the gods; deadpan, the last sentence of the novel announces, "Thus perished the daughter of Hamilcar for having touched the veil of Tanit," representing the superstitious viewpoint of the assembled crowd. Although George Sand's favorable response initiated an important friendship that lasted until her death, other reviewers were generally unsympathetic. But the opera composer Reyer (pseudonym of Ernest Rey, 1823–1909) was immediately attracted to the splendid possibilities for spectacle that the novel offered. Camille Du Locle, a skilled librettist who later worked with Verdi, was engaged, and Flaubert wrote an ingenious, perceptive scenario for him, suggesting which eight scenes should be kept. For various reasons, the opera was not staged until 1890. Critics praised the adaptation.[31] Meanwhile, the example of Flaubert's exotic novel contributed substantially to the birth of the decadent movement with Joris-Karl Huysmans's novel *A rebours* (1884).

With his next and second-greatest novel, *L'Education sentimentale,* Flaubert returned to modern times. He had originally thought of a picaresque novel like Alain-René Lesage's *Gil Blas* or Voltaire's *Candide,* but—unlike those novels— set in Paris to expose all the political and social follies of the Second Republic (1848–51) and the Second Empire (1851–70). Autobiography formed the nucleus of his inspiration: notably, memories of his youthful infatuation with the older married woman Elisa Schlésinger (see Bart, *Flaubert,* 474 –75).[32]

Some have objected that the title is ungrammatical, that it should be *L'education des sentiments.* But such an objection is mistaken. In French, *l'education*

emphasizes upbringing and socialization, learning to cope with other people and
the world in general. It is not the antihero Frédéric's feelings that receive an education; instead, he undergoes a flawed initiation into adult life by means of feelings—specifically, through his relationships with the four women to whom he
is sporadically attracted in various ways and who at times find him attractive.
The country girl Louise Roque offers Frédéric the pleasures of a Pygmalion who
might be able to shape a naive, passionate younger admirer in his own image.
Madame Arnoux promises a deep, maternal tenderness. Rosanette Bron em-
bodies the excitement of a relationship with a promiscuous, lascivious, sexually
experienced woman. And Madame Dambreuse is a success object, a wealthy, elegant woman whose lover would occupy a prominent place in society. None of
these relationships offers happiness beyond a brief ego gratification or the pleasures of expectancy.

In art, business, and politics as well, Frédéric repeatedly misses opportunities
through his weakness, laziness, lack of talent, and lack of conviction. A fortune
falls into his lap when a curmudgeonly old uncle, who does not particularly care
for him and who sees through the occasional attentions of his nephew, dies in-
testate with no other living relative. "*A Sentimental Education* is a gray catalog of failure. The lessons of the novel are that illusions alone are beautiful and
that life itself, by being lived, will destroy them" (Bart, *Flaubert*, 479). With the
sole exception of the idealistic Dussardier, shot for nonviolently supporting the
Republic, all the characters are shallow, cowardly, and selfish. Frédéric in particular exemplifies belated romantic *mal du siècle* or anomie, except that unlike
the romantic authors, Flaubert never identifies himself with his protagonist. Historical events—the collapse of the Second Empire—were soon to bear out his
diagnosis of the insignificance and moral bankruptcy of his age.

Flaubert's strongest political conviction was his opposition to socialism. In his
day, socialism was associated primarily with the impractical utopian visions of
an ideal community according to Charles Fourier, Père Enfantin, or Claude-
Henri de Saint-Simon, although the French revolutionary tradition, protofem-
inism, the quest to form an enduring republic rather than a monarchy, and the
struggles for workers' rights and unionization also contributed to the loose con-
geries of ideas that constituted left-wing politics in the mid-nineteenth century.
An organized French Socialist party would be formed only in 1905, thanks to
Jean Jaurès.

Flaubert delighted in satirizing the authoritarian, regimenting tendencies of
this supposedly liberal movement, although he equally deplored the brutal repression employed by the conservative forces of the day and the bourgeois wor-
ship of money and property. His scathing political comments appear most mem-
orably in *L'Education sentimentale* (1869 version), the play *Le Candidat*, and
Bouvard et Pécuchet. In the first, Old Roque and Sénécal (a tag-name evoking
the Stoic, ancient Roman Republican virtues of Seneca) each shoot an unarmed,
nonthreatening man point-blank and kill him. Flaubert's dry mockery of the
conservatives and liberals alike occurs pungently in part 3, chapter 2 of *L'Edu-*

cation: "Then [reacting against the alarming establishment of the Second French Republic through the Revolution of 1848] the principle of the sanctity of private Property rose in people's esteem to the level of Religion, and was confused with God. The attacks on this ideal seemed sacrilegious, almost as savage as cannibalism." On the other side, the procuress La Vatnaz becomes a rabid propagandist seeking revenge for her lowly social status: "The liberation of the proletariat, according to her, could be achieved only by liberating women. She wanted all jobs to be open to women ... that wet nurses and midwives be salaried state employees ... that there be special presses for women, a technical high school for women, a national guard for women, everything for women." In 1848 or 1869, these commonsense ideas seemed utterly mad to Flaubert and his contemporaries.

Similarly, chapter 6 in *Bouvard et Pécuchet* will expose the absurdities of the opposite extreme views of divine-right monarchy and of the sovereignty of the people. Flaubert rightly observes that left-wing systems proposed by Jean-Jacques Rousseau's *Social Contract* and by Charles Fourier's utopianism are both tyrannical and archconservative at bottom. Like Flaubert, his title characters in *Bouvard et Pécuchet* become disgusted with politics and lose all desire to seek public office.

THE FRANCO-PRUSSIAN WAR

Despite his apparent cynicism and pessimism, Flaubert never totally lost his idealism. The Prussian invasion of 1870 reignited Flaubert's patriotism, but he still could find no compatible political party. With the outbreak of the Franco-Prussian War on July 19, 1870, he was forced to become a minor player in history as well as a spectator. Opposed to Prussia's expanding its sphere of influence, which it was doing actively, France had demanded that Leopold, a member of the Prussian ruling family, withdraw from consideration for the kingship of Spain. He did, but King William of Prussia would not accede to Napoleon III's further demand never to allow another member of his family to become king of Spain. The minister Otto, Prince of Bismarck, skillfully maneuvered so that France seemed the aggressor and then crushed the French armies in six weeks. Flaubert understood that France was being lured into disaster but could do nothing to prevent it. Foreign troops invaded French soil in force for the first time in over half a century. Fleeing relatives disrupted Flaubert's life by seeking refuge in his beloved retreat at Croisset. Although he was nearly fifty years old, Flaubert volunteered to serve as a lieutenant in the National Guard to help defend Rouen. But all the guard units promptly surrendered when the Prussians arrived. Flaubert was dismayed and devastated when the invading Prussians commandeered Croisset as a barracks.

On September 2, Napoleon III, who had joined his troops at the front, was captured at Sedan, an industrial town on the border between Champagne and Lorraine in northeastern France. The French provisional government was required to pay heavy indemnities and to cede the coal- and iron-rich provinces of Alsace and—in part—Lorraine. Prussian troops were to occupy Paris until the indemnity was paid. The situation was envenomed when the City of Paris refused to accept the treaty with Prussia and to surrender. A revolutionary government called the Commune was formed; it ruled the city between March and May 1871. Opposing propaganda presented the Communards as bloodthirsty socialists, but in fact nearly all of them were republicans, who feared that France might now attempt to restore a monarchy—a suspicion reinforced by the move of the capital from its traditional site, Paris, to Versailles. Instead of negotiating with the Communards, government troops attacked them, and the retreating Parisians burned their city. Between May 21 and 27, more people—including women and children—were killed by the government troops than had been guillotined during the Reign of Terror in 1793. Flaubert was disgusted by the brutal repression. His comic play *Le Candidat* in 1874 may represent a final exorcism of any lingering desires for political office.

THE FINAL YEARS

The last decade of Flaubert's life, the 1870s, was frustrating and depressing. He dedicated much time and energy to futile attempts to commemorate his late, beloved friend, Louis Bouilhet (1821–69), who throughout his life had helped Flaubert revise everything that he published.[33] The two men wrote each other weekly. After Bouilhet's death, Flaubert looked through his papers in hopes of finding works that might be published—partly to celebrate his friend's memory and partly to help Bouilhet's surviving mistress and son financially. He wrote a preface for Bouilhet's posthumous volume of poetry. Once he had completed *L'Education sentimentale* in 1869, he also rewrote Bouilhet's last work, the *féerie* (staged fairy-tale) *Mademoiselle Aïssé*. He finally persuaded the Odeon theater to produce *Mademoiselle Aïssé* in 1871, but the play failed miserably. Flaubert found the manuscript of another play, *Le Sexe faible,* which appealed to his misogyny. The sarcastic title refers to domineering women. On vacation in 1872, Flaubert strove to improve the plot and dialogue. When he returned to Croisset in the fall, he tried to interest theatrical directors in the work. None of them would even consider the play until, in the spring of 1873, Flaubert made a special trip to Paris to read selections to Carvalho, who directed the Vaudeville theater. At first, Carvalho was enthusiastic. He did request further revisions, which Flaubert undertook with vigor, postponing work on his own satire *Bouvard et Pécuchet*. But then Carvalho began to have doubts; he repeatedly delayed the start of rehearsals and finally returned the play to Flaubert. No other theater would consider it when Flaubert circulated the revised version. Only in the fall of 1875 did the Cluny express interest—but the actors they were willing to use were so inept that Flaubert thought it wiser to stop trying. His efforts had consumed nearly six years.[34]

Meanwhile, he once again attempted, during 1873, to write a play of his own. Entitled *Le Candidat,* it was intended to satirize corrupt Third Republic politics, stupid industrialists, and the greedy masses. First Night was March 11, 1874. But the dialogue was awkward, the humor was crude, and the characters were stereotypes. After four performances, the play had to be withdrawn. Shortly after, Flaubert's lifelong enthusiasm, *La Tentation de saint Antoine,* appeared in print. The author had withheld it from publication for over a year so as not to be contractually obligated to give it to the publisher Michel Lévy, with whom he had had a falling out and to whom he thenceforth referred with ugly anti-Semitism, forgetting Lévy's longtime past support and generosity. The reviews were uncomprehending and unfavorable. Typically, Flaubert reacted by plunging back into his work: during the summer of 1874, he took a long trip through Normandy to seek an appropriate setting for his satiric project, *Bouvard et Pécuchet.* After intensive preliminary work, he began to write in August 1874. All the bitterness of his recent and imminent disappointments would be poured into this work.

Flaubert's trust in his unscrupulous nephew-in-law, Ernest Commanville (1834 –90), had led him to financial disaster. Commanville had married Caroline, the beloved niece for whom Flaubert and his mother had taken responsibility because she was an orphan, in 1864. Commanville had concealed his own illegitimacy, the social stigma of which probably would have prevented the marriage, which Caroline had entered dutifully but without enthusiasm and which proved unhappy. A businessman who imported wood and owned a sawmill, Commanville took over the management of Flaubert's finances in 1867. From then on Flaubert found difficulty in drawing on his funds or knowing how much money and income he had. He sacrificed half his fortune in vain to try to prevent Commanville's bankruptcy in 1875.[35] During his last years, he endured the humiliation of having friends seek sinecures for him, only to learn that the salary had been reduced to an unacceptable low or that he had lost out to other candidates. As for Commanville, he was probably both a bad and a dishonest manager. At Flaubert's wake he behaved ignobly: he played cards for money, cheated, and openly speculated how much money he might make from the sale of his uncle's manuscripts and unpublished love letters.

In the late 1870s, Flaubert found some consolation in the company of admiring friends. He and four younger writers who had also failed as playwrights formed a literary discussion group they called *les Cinq*—Emile Zola, Alphonse Daudet, Edmond de Goncourt, the publisher Georges Charpentier, and Flaubert. Moreover, Guy de Maupassant (1850–93), the son of Flaubert's beloved childhood friend Laure Le Poittevin, was trained by him as a writer. "He is *my* disciple," Flaubert said, "and I love him as a son."[36] Flaubert inculcated in him the cult of art, faith in hard work, and a deep skepticism toward social hypocrisy and egotism (see, for example, Maupassant's novel *Pierre et Jean,* 1888). Flaubert encouraged Maupassant to publish the story "Boule de Suif" (1880), about a kindly prostitute rejected by those self-righteous bourgeois she has just rescued: its success made it possible for Maupassant to quit his job and devote himself to creative writing. Flaubert also introduced Maupassant to the naturalist circle and to the Russian expatriate Ivan Turgenev, a well-connected author who was to publicize Maupassant's work out of friendship.

From the depths of despair, Flaubert experienced a brief, glorious period of creativity. Between the fall of 1875 to the spring of 1877, he composed three short masterpieces, three saint's lives called *Trois Contes,* inspired in part by his friendship with the idealistic female novelist George Sand and by his recent experience of sacrificing much of his personal fortune and financial security to help his only niece. The stories are set in antiquity, in the middle ages, and in modern times. The first story to be completed, inspired by a dream of Flaubert's youth and by a stained-glass window in the Cathedral of Rouen, was the medieval "Légende de saint Julien l'Hospitalier." When Julian, an avid hunter, killed a great stag, the animal spoke and cursed him, saying Julian would murder his own parents. Like Oedipus before him, he fled his homeland to evade the prophecy. When it came true anyway by accident, to expiate his involuntary crime Julian became a hermit who ferried travelers across a dangerous river. Late one evening, a hideous leper demanded passage, then hospitality, and finally, that Julian warm him in bed with his own body. When the saint did so, the leper embraced him, transformed himself into Christ, and carried Julian to heaven.[37]

The second story, "Un cœur simple," is widely taught in introductions to French literature. It tells of a devout, simple, illiterate, unattached peasant girl abandoned by the man who had proposed to her. She flees the area, blinded with grief, happens on Madame Aubain, who takes advantage of her desperation by offering a low wage, and for half a century, serves her cold, ungenerous mistress. She slowly matures spiritually through the idealistic love she seeks continually to offer others. Flaubert masterfully depicts her dim, distorted awareness of the outside world and of religious dogma. As she dies of pneumonia, she experiences an ecstatic vision during which, as with Julian, the skies open to welcome her. Flaubert had written the story for George Sand, but she died only a few weeks before it was finished.

Finally, aided by books borrowed from his friend Ernest Renan's vast library on the history of religion, in four months Flaubert composed "Hérodias," the story of the dance of Salomé for King Herod and the beheading of John the Baptist that Salomé's mother Hérodias has her daughter demand in return—because the queen wants to silence a critic who vehemently denounces her corruption and immorality, even from his prison cell. John knows that he must die before Christ's mission can begin. By treating this subject, Flaubert found an opportunity to depict a Roman orgy and three lascivious dances similar to those he had seen long ago in Egypt. He thus redid some of the most exotic scenes from *Salammbô* on a more manageable scale. The motifs of sacrifice and resignation that run through all three stories reflect Flaubert's acceptance of his old age, and the tales partially recapitulate Flaubert's career as a writer, while allowing him a format for recollecting his childhood and youth. They were published in periodicals in March 1877 and in book form the following month. The first two enjoyed great success and helped alleviate Flaubert's financial troubles.

Flaubert's last project, uncompleted at his death, had long been nurtured in his imagination. Two volumes were planned: the first, a satiric encyclopedia in novel form. Two middle-aged, recently retired Parisian copy clerks meet, like each other immensely, and resolve to live in the country. There they attempt to master all branches of human knowledge in its practical applications, discipline by discipline. Eventually they must acknowledge the failure of the intellect to organize or guide experience. The authorities that they read contradict each other, give faulty information, or express themselves too vaguely and ambiguously to be helpful. Their new neighbors mistrust them and fear their radical ideas. Their servant girl gives one of them a venereal disease, and a local widow flirts with the other, mainly in hopes of being able to purchase his land at a bargain price. All their enterprises, culminating in raising two abandoned children, fail miserably. But they attain the lamentable ability to be able to see through human follies. Eventually they return to their former occupation, copying text, as a diversion—although the final line, "copions comme autrefois," was an addition by Flaubert's niece, Caroline, just after he died.

Before about 1990, critics tended to treat *Bouvard et Pécuchet* as centered on the library and therefore to assimilate Flaubert to his characters as attempting to realize an encyclopedic overview of human knowledge. The image of an excessively bookish Flaubert, finally overwhelmed at the end of his career by a growing, absorbing mania for reading and note-taking and out of touch with the lived experience that might have provided a basis for a legitimately interesting novel, yielded in Eugenio Donato's compelling but misleading essays to the concept of curatorial characters organizing life like a museum.

To reinforce the conventional impression that the hapless protagonists are cut off from reality, Donato characterizes them as "asexual" (207). Sex, however, is the joker in our characters' deck, the one experience besides spontaneous combustion that forces itself on them without warning, starting with the homoerotic bonding that unexpectedly unites the odd couple and continuing with their heterosexual infatuations. Bouvard is enthralled by Madame Bordin's body; Pécuchet "felt a commotion to his very marrow" when he first kisses Mélie (*Bouvard and Pecuchet*, 210). Elsewhere he experiences a polymorphously perverse, Flaubertian pantheistic ecstasy (3). In many other passages, we realize that the two men like the country because they can run around there naked. They get into trouble not because they systematize, but because as sensual beings they enter into direct contact with the physical world. They jump from one discipline to another haphazardly, owing to their distractibility and short attention spans. But Pécuchet eventually wins through to a totalizing vision of geological cataclysm and of entropy death, "[e]nd of the world through cessation of heat" (345). Because "they undermined all foundations," they become master deconstructivists, suspect, unwelcome, and objects of "a vague terror" among their acquaintances (237, 258).[38]

The second volume was to be a compendium of what they had copied, as they sought to collect statements illustrating the absurdity of consecrated opinions on every subject. About one hundred pages of notes and excerpts survive in what is known today as Flaubert's *sottisier,* or compendium of idiotic sayings.[39] His attempt to satirize all human strivings toward knowledge and understanding, in his global satire, does not make engaging reading. Postmodern writers, however, have found great interest in the work, because it challenges and deconstructs conventional notions concerning the art of the novel and of cognition in general—as do Miguel de Cervantes' *Don Quixote,* Lawrence Sterne's *Tristram Shandy,* Julio Cortázar's *Rayuela* (Hopscotch), or Georges Perec's *La Vie mode d'emploi.* In brief, *Bouvard et Pécuchet* is a novelist's novel, whereas *Madame Bovary* is a reader's and critic's novel that reflects the irresistible fascination of adultery for the general public.

Shortly after noon on Saturday, May 8, 1880, Flaubert died suddenly but peacefully, probably from a brain hemorrhage caused by his tertiary syphilis. Guy de Maupassant kept vigil over the body for three days and readied it for burial. The Parnassian poet José-Marie de Hérédia and the novelists Edmond de Goncourt, Emile Zola, and Alphonse Daudet also attended the burial, described at length in the Goncourt *Journal.* Flaubert's niece, Caroline, promptly sold Flaubert's beloved home, Croisset. The house was razed, and a distillery was built on the site.

But Caroline also became the guardian of her uncle's papers and his memory. In 1887 she published the first version of her *Souvenirs sur Gustave Flaubert* (Paris: Ferroud, 1895) as the preface to the first edition of Flaubert's general correspondence. She calls him a fanatic who made art his God, but she suppresses much information about his sexual affairs. To her credit, she kept most of Flaubert's manuscripts intact. Three years after her husband died in 1890, she moved to Antibes, a winter resort on the Mediterranean Sea near the Alps and Italy. She named her new house there the Villa Tanit, after the moon goddess in Flaubert's novel *Salammbô.* In 1900, she proposed to and married Dr. Franklin-Grout, a childhood friend and the son of one of her father's students. He died in 1921. Generations of Flaubert scholars made pilgrimages to the Villa Tanit to consult Flaubert's manuscripts. In later years, she herself became an active Flaubert scholar. On her death in 1931, Flaubert's manuscripts were sold at auction. Many were kept together in library collections, but Flaubert's notebooks for *Madame Bovary* and the *Trois Contes* have disappeared.[40] Today, Flaubert has become the most widely studied nineteenth-century French author, and his *Madame Bovary,* despite its depressingly mediocre characters, dour realism, and deep pessimism, has become a landmark in the history of the novel. Only Faulkner's work, perhaps, rivals its influence on writers around the world.

NOTES

1. To be precise, Flaubert's mother was born September 7, 1793, in Pont-l'Evêque, Normandy, about thirty miles east southeast of Rouen, and christened Anne-Justine-Caroline Fleuriot. Her mother died a week after her birth; her father, January 30, 1803.

2. Dr. Flaubert's conservatism in this respect was natural, because phlebotomy was a commonly accepted practice at the time (it probably weakened and killed President George Washington). In a case that may have inspired Flaubert's later depiction of the clubfooted stable boy Hippolyte in *Madame Bovary*, he treated a patient, Céline-Stéphanie Martin, with the traditional splinting.

3. Despite the publication of later biographies by Herbert Lottman (1990), Jean-Paul Sartre (1971–72), and Enid Starkie (1967–71), the best remains Benjamin F. Bart's monumental *Flaubert* (Syracuse, NY: Syracuse University Press, 1967). It adopts a searching but restrained psychological approach and is weak only in the section that interprets *Madame Bovary*. For cultivated general readers, the revised edition of Francis Steegmuller's *Flaubert and Madame Bovary: A Double Portrait* (New York: Farrar, 1968) offers engaging reading. Further studies of Flaubert's life, with evaluations, are listed in Eugene F. Gray and Laurence M. Porter, "Gustave Flaubert," David Baguley, ed., *A Critical Bibliography of French Literature*, vol. 5, *The Nineteenth Century*, vol. 2. (Syracuse, NY: Syracuse University Press, 1994), 801–66, esp. 805, 808–16.

4. Today, the Collège Royal de Rouen has been renamed the Lycée Corneille (the playwright Corneille was born in Rouen). Corot, Maupassant, and Maurois as well as Flaubert studied there; the philosopher Alain taught there.

5. Rumors that Guy was Flaubert's biological son have never been convincingly supported.

6. See Jean Canu, *Flaubert auteur dramatique* (Paris: Ecrits de France, 1946); René Descharmes and René Dumesnil, *Autour de Flaubert*. 2 vols. Paris: Mercure de France, 1912. 1:200–62; and Marshall C. Olds's *Au pays des perroquets: La Féerie de Flaubert* (Amsterdam: Rodopi, 2001).

7. Robert Griffin, ed., *Early Writings: Gustave Flaubert* (Lincoln, NE: University of Nebraska Press, 1991), xiii.

8. See his protest petition of November 11–14, 1839, in Bruneau, ed., *CORR* 1:56–57, and three letters to Ernest Chevalier (April 21, 1840, *CORR* 1:63–64; January 10, 1841, *CORR* 1:76–77; and December 31, 1841, *CORR* 1:88–91).

9. Benjamin F. Bart has traced throughout Flaubert's career the motif of pantheistic ecstasy, of the sense of fusing one's identity with nature, in "Psyche into Myth: Humanity and Animality in Flaubert's *Saint Julien*," *Kentucky Romance Quarterly* 20 (1973): 317–42.

10. In classical psychoanalysis, "the rescue fantasy" refers to the enduring influence of the Oedipus or Electra complex in our unconscious life, when childhood desires to claim the other-sex parent from his or her "unworthy" partner for ourselves lead us unconsciously to enter a relationship with the intention of "saving" a debased parent-surrogate such as a prostitute, criminal, or substance abuser.

11. See Shoshana Felman's outstanding "Modernity of the Commonplace" in Laurence M. Porter, ed., *Critical Essays on Gustave Flaubert* (Boston: Hall, 1986), 29–48, and Michal Peled Ginsburg's *Flaubert Writing: A Study in Narrative Strategies* (Stanford: Stanford University Press, 1986), 16–45.

12. Compare Fyodor Dostoevski's epilepsy and its depiction in his novels. See James L. Rice, *Dostoevsky and the Healing Art: An Essay in Literary and Medical History* (Ann Arbor, MI: Ardis, 1985).

13. Flaubert had felt that his father's wealth was sufficient to support him as a writer, whereas his father wanted him to be able to make his own living. The death of his disapproving, disappointed father and the release of his inheritance undoubtedly fulfilled a suppressed wish. One can speculate that in consequence, Flaubert suffered Oedipal guilt that emerges in his tale "La Légende de Saint-Julien l'hospitalier" (1876; first conceived 1856).

14. The Goncourts mention the maid in their *Journal* 1:709 (4 vols. Paris: Flammarion, 1959).

15. See Lawrence R. Schehr, "Homosexuality," 172–73 in Laurence M. Porter, ed., *A Gustave Flaubert Encyclopedia* (Westport, CT: Greenwood, 2001). Jean-Paul Sartre believes that Flaubert was making up his report of a homosexual encounter with a fourteen-year-old male prostitute in a Lebanese bathhouse in 1850 (*L'Idiot de la famille*. 3 vols. Paris: Gallimard, 1971–72, rev. 1988). Enid Starkie finds his friendship with Alfred Le Poittevin romantic, if not frankly sexual. His use of expressions such as "old bugger" or (once) "old pederast" in letters to a few close friends such as Louis Bouilhet probably was facetious (see Jean Bruneau and Yvan Leclerc, eds., Flaubert, *CORR* [5] vols. [Paris: Gallimard, 1973–(98)], 3:116 and passim). Mary Orr has recently pioneered with her book on ambiguous sexuality in Flaubert's fiction, *Flaubert: Writing the Masculine* (Oxford, UK: Oxford University Press, 2000).

16. On homosociality as sublimated eroticism in Flaubert, see Roger Kempf, "Flaubert: Le double pupitre" in Roger Kempf, *Mœurs: Ethnologie et fiction* (Paris: Seuil, 1976), 69–95.

17. Janet Beizer, who is preparing a book on the subject, has studied this masculinism and its crude, graphic stereotypes in Flaubert's correspondence.

18. See Roger Bellet, ed., *Femmes de lettres au XIXe siècle, autour de Louise Colet* (Lyon: Presses Universitaires de Lyon, 1982).

19. See Jean Bruneau, ed. *CORR 2 (juillet 1851–décembre 1858)* (Paris: Gallimard, 1980), 134–507, passim. Flaubert says he began writing *Madame Bovary* on September 19, 1851 (letter to Louise Colet, September 20, 1851, p. 5), but his most substantive comments on that novel, in his letters to Colet, occur between July 18, 1852, and January 13, 1854, printed in the range of pages noted previously.

20. See Renée Winegarten, *The Double Life of George Sand, Woman and Writer* (New York: Basic Books, 1978).

21. For my discussion of the 1845 *Education,* I am particularly indebted to Scott D. Carpenter, who treats the work succinctly in Laurence M. Porter, ed., *A Gustave Flaubert Encyclopedia* (Westport, CT: Greenwood, 2001), 108–12. See also Benjamin F. Bart, *Flaubert* (Syracuse, NY: Syracuse University Press, 1967), 105–21, and Jean Bruneau, *Les Débuts littéraires de Gustave Flaubert* (Paris: Colin, 1962).

22. Stendhal debunked the myth of military glory in *La Chartreuse de Parme* (1839), and Victor Hugo, himself once an enthusiast for Napoleon, later dramatized the contrast between illusion and reality in *Les Misérables* (1862), when his enthusiastic young Marius (some ten years older than Flaubert), who idolizes Napoleon, exclaims to his skeptical friends, "'To strike like thunder; vanquish; dominate; to be among the European nations the one gilded by glory; to sound a titanic fanfare in history; to conquer the world twice, first by conquest and then by dazzling all others, that is sublime; and

what could be more splendid?' 'To be free,' said Combeferre." Victor Hugo, *Les Misérables*, ed. René Journet. 3 vols. (Paris: Garnier-Flammarion, 1967), vol. 3, book 4, chapter 5, pp. 202–3.

23. See François-René de Chateaubriand's *Itineraire de Paris à Jérusalem*, 1811; Alphonse de Lamartine's *Souvenirs, impressions, pensées et paysages pendant un voyage en Orient*, 1835; Maxime Du Camp's *Souvenirs et paysages d'Orient*, 1848; Gérard de Nerval's *Voyage en Orient*, 1851; Théophile Gautier's *Constantinople,*1852 (reissued 1990); Guy de Maupassant's *Lettres d'Afrique: Algérie, Tunisie*, 1990; and Eugène Fromentin's *Between Sea and Sahara: An Algerian Journal* (Columbus, OH: Ohio State University Press, 1999). Edward Said's important *Orientalism* (1978) surveys much of this literature, but he overvalues the cultural awareness of Flaubert and Nerval in contrast to other French travelers.

24. Letter to Louise Colet, September 20, 1851. *CORR* 2:5.

25. See Laurence M. Porter, "Nuance in the Novel," in Michal Peled Ginsburg, ed., *Approaches to Teaching Balzac's* Old Goriot. (New York: MLA, 2001).

26. Jonathan Culler: *Flaubert; The Uses of Uncertainty* (Ithaca, NY:, Cornell University Press, 1974, rev. 1985).

27. The *bourgeoisie* refers to those town dwellers who own their own shops and tools *(la petite bourgeoisie)* or to those nonnoble but wealthy people who own factories or land and live off the surplus value of the labors of others *(la grande/haute bourgeoisie)*. For a long time, the landed gentry preferred to preserve their traditional quasi-aristocratic status by collecting from their tenant farmers fees fixed as far back as in medieval times rather than renegotiate a more lucrative but less so-called noble arrangement of sharecropping *(mettre les terres de moitié)*. As late as 1948, for example, the paterfamilias of Hervé Bazin's *Vipère au poing* agonizes over whether to accept such an arrangement. More generally, the *bourgeoisie* means "the middle class," to which most of us teachers and college students belong.

28. The fate of its members, sketched rapidly in two pages of the conclusion, is as arbitrary as that of the several characters in *Jurassic Park* who each injure a leg, sprain or break an ankle, and thus become vulnerable each to a different species of dinosaur—introduced for variety.

29. On the relationship between a frustrated sense of entitlement and self-destructive behavior, see Laurence M. Porter, "Le faux fantastique de *La Peau de chagrin*," in Didier Maleuvre and Catherine Nesci, eds., *L'œuvre d'identité: Essais sur le romantisme de Nodier à Baudelaire (Paragraphes:* Département d'Etudes françaises, l'Université de Montréal, 1996), 29–38.

30. The *zaïmph*, or goddess's veil, seems inspired by the palladium (generically, a sacred object that can protect the city or state that owns it), the statue of Pallas Athena that ensured the safety of Troy provided that it remained within the city.

31. See Joseph-Marc Bailbé, "*Salammbô* de Reyer: Du roman à l'opéra," *Romantisme* 38 (1982): 93–103. On decadence, see Laurence M. Porter, "Decadence and the *Fin-de-siècle* Novel," in Timothy Unwin, ed., *The French Novel from 1880 to the Present* (Cambridge, UK: Cambridge University Press, 1997), 93–110, and Jean Pierrot, *L'Imaginaire décadent (1880–1900)* (Paris: Presses Universitaires, 1977).

32. Bart draws in turn on Marie-Jeanne Durry, *Flaubert et ses projects inédits* (Paris: Nizet, 1950).

33. See Benjamin F. Bart, "Louis Bouilhet, Flaubert's accoucheur," *Symposium* 17 (1963): 183–201.

34. See Benjamin F. Bart, *Flaubert* (Syracuse, NY: Syracuse University Press, 1967), 621–22.

35. The Commanvilles—Flaubert's niece and her husband—were ungrateful as well. According to the Goncourts, they criticized him for spending money on cigars, and his niece supposedly said, "My uncle is a peculiar man; he doesn't know how to endure hardships" (*Journal* 2:1275).

36. See Charles J. Stivale, *The Art of Rupture: Narrative Desire and Duplicity in the Tales of Guy de Maupassant* (Ann Arbor, MI: University of Michigan Press, 1994), 214 n. 25.

37. Benjamin F. Bart offers a particularly fine analysis of this tale and its possible psychoanalytical interpretations in his *Flaubert* (670–86).

38. Quotations from Flaubert come from the translation by T. W. Earp and G. W. Stonier, with a brilliant introduction by Lionel Trilling (New York: New Directions, 1964). See also Stephen G. Brush, "Thermodynamics and History," *The Graduate Journal* 7 (1967): 477–566—more accessible than Michel Serres's *Hermes III* (Paris: Minuit, 1974); Eugenio Donato, "The Museum's Furnace: Notes toward a Contextual Reading of *Bouvard et Pécuchet*," in Laurence M. Porter, ed., *Critical Essays on Gustave Flaubert* (Boston: Hall, 1986), 207–22; and Laurence M. Porter, "The Rhetoric of Deconstruction: Donato and Flaubert," *Nineteenth-Century French Studies* 20.1–2 (Fall–Winter 1991–92): 128–36.

39. In 1870, the "Comte de Lautréamont" (Isidore Ducasse) had made a similar compilation of maxims, which he ironically entitled *Poésies* and which distort the thought of the seventeenth-century *moralistes* often by changing only one key word in their aphorisms. Flaubert may not have known this work, but, like Flaubert's, it reflects a skeptical attitude toward the Second Empire and its supporters.

40. See, however, Yvan Leclerc, ed., *Plans et scénarios de* Madame Bovary (Paris: CNRS-Zulma, 1995).

ABBREVIATIONS FOR FLAUBERT'S WORKS

BP: Bouvard et Pécuchet
CORR: Correspondance (ed. Jean Bruneau)
ES (1845): *L'Education sentimentale* (1845 version)
ES: L'Education sentimentale (1869 version)
MB: Madame Bovary
SAL: Salammbô
TC: Trois Contes
TSA: La Tentation de saint Antoine
UCS: "Un cœur simple" (in *TC*)

Chapter 1

Content

Emma Bovary's story, twenty-seven chapters long, is nested inside her husband's (five chapters at the beginning and three at the end). Charles Bovary, an only child, is neglected by his father and dominated by his mother. His mother chooses his profession of public health officer, the town, Tostes, where he shall work, and his first wife, Héloïse Dubuc, an older, unattractive, but supposedly well-to-do widow. Charles meets Emma and falls in love with her without realizing it. After Héloïse dies, he marries Emma, a pretty, intelligent, self-centered girl who is bored on her father's farm. She too is an only child, although she once had a brother, of whom nothing more is said. She thinks she loves Charles, who is devoted but stolid; but marriage, like farm life, also bores her soon.

Emma nurtures a psychosomatic illness, possibly centered on anorexia, so that Charles will move to another town.[1] That town, Yonville, is no more interesting than Tostes. In part 2, Emma distracts herself through a platonic friendship with a young law clerk, Léon Dupuis. After he leaves to pursue his career in Paris, Emma is seduced by an unscrupulous, experienced womanizer, the country squire Rodolphe Boulanger. When she becomes too demanding, insisting that he flee abroad with her, Rodolphe abandons her, and she becomes seriously ill. To distract Emma during her long convalescence, Charles takes her to the opera in Rouen. There she again meets Léon, who has moved there to study Norman business law. In Paris, the clerk has become sexually experienced and more self-confident. He seduces Emma, who ruins her husband financially with extravagant, secret expenditures for the affair. When the bailiff is about to seize the Bovarys' effects to pay Emma's debts and when she can obtain no more money, she poisons herself with arsenic. Charles sinks into deep depression and dies quietly. No money remains. His daughter, Berthe, will be doomed to work in a cotton mill, where her incipient tuberculosis will most likely kill her promptly as well.

PART 1: CHILDHOOD AND MARRIAGE

Chapter 1: The New Boy in School

We first see Charles Bovary from the viewpoint of anonymous schoolboys in study hall. Because of his drunken, promiscuous father's neglect, Charles is older than his classmates. Several motifs converge in this scene to foreshadow his future. His experience of life is belated; he will always be the last one to catch on. He is ill-prepared for school, as he will be for life: the old priest who gave him Latin lessons often dozed off during them and never demanded much of Charles. As a schoolboy, he appears ridiculous because he has been both neglected—he has outgrown his clothes—and overindulged: his mother, a haberdasher's daughter, has bought him a ludicrous, elaborate visored cap, which the other boys hide from him. He has no friends: his social life and his happiness will later depend almost entirely on his contemptuous, unfaithful wife.

Flaubert creates a vivid image of the classroom with his schoolboy slang and rituals and with frequent mentions of the gestures and postures of his characters. The motif of awkward artificiality predominates. Charles is dressed *"en bourgeois"* (emphasis added) *as if* he were a boy from town, although he has been allowed to spend his childhood running barefoot in the country. Flaubert's description of him includes only his physical appearance. He seems to have no inner life. Like many other characters, he has trouble communicating or asserting himself. When the teacher asks Charles's name, first he mumbles, and then, overcompensating, he shouts too loudly, provoking a general uproar but still failing to be understood until he has repeated his name several times. His helplessness appears in his repeated failures to pick up his cap, which the other boys knock onto the floor. His passive attitude contrasts with the other students': they wage a guerilla war against their education, whereas he submits to it, learning everything by heart.

Next, a flashback describes the lives of Charles's parents. His father, after whom he was named, unlike Charles was handsome, loquacious, and dishonest, discharged from the army for (unspecified) recruiting irregularities. He anticipates Charles's future, however, by having been a second-rate health worker—an *aide-chirugien-major* in the army—not a real doctor himself, but an assistant to one. Similarly, Charles will not be a real doctor, but rather a county health officer, who is not himself allowed to perform major surgery. Like Emma with Rodolphe, Charles's mother loves her husband so slavishly for his good looks and dashing demeanor that he becomes disenchanted with her. By creating such unstated but obvious parallels in behavior among quite different people, as he will do throughout the novel, Flaubert implies that human beings possess a limited repertory of coping strategies, mostly ineffectual, just as they possess a limited vocabulary and capacity for self-expression in language. Thus he tacitly conveys his pessimism concerning the human condition.

Charles's father vainly tries to transform his peaceable son into a hard-drinking, hard-boiled blasphemer, whereas his mother projects all her own dreams onto him, in compensation for the heartbreaks of her marriage. Protective and possessive, she teaches him to read—as he will later, unsuccessfully, try to teach his own daughter—but little else. Her choice of a paramedical profession for him, like her choice of his first wife and of the town where he shall practice medicine, is made without consultation. At school in Rouen, Charles goes through a period of lazy self-indulgence, frequenting bars, playing dominoes, and learning about sex—so he fails his professional qualifying examinations on his first attempt (an autobiographical echo of Flaubert, a reluctant law student, failing his own exams) but then learns all the answers by heart and is passed. When he marries, he dreams of being free after leaving his controlling mother. However, "sa [Charles's] femme fut le maître" (69). Both women join in bullying him to dress more warmly and spend less. Emma's later domination of Charles, then, will be no surprise.

Chapter 2: The Broken Leg

One night at eleven P.M., a rider comes to summon Charles to treat a broken leg on a farm fifteen miles away. It is hard to realize today how isolated country life was before paved roads, telephones, telegraphs, radio, television, e-mail, and the like. Emma, inexperienced, alone with her father, and bored, would have been predisposed to escape to town by marrying almost any acceptable suitor. Presumably, he impresses her in turn by splinting her father's broken leg without difficulty—it is the simplest possible fracture.[2]

Emma is the more talkative of the two, taking the initiative in self-disclosure. When Charles prepares to leave, he accidentally brushes against the kneeling Emma's back as they both are looking for his riding whip (a phallic symbol, if you like), and she blushes. He will return the next day, and twice a week thereafter, as if by accident. His pleasure at seeing Emma is innocuous, but Charles's jealous wife soon investigates, discovering that her husband's patient has a daughter who was well-educated in the convent school; Charles's behavior indicates he is infatuated with her. Angry allusions that Charles does not understand give way to direct remarks, then accusations and denunciations of Emma's ancestors, her vanity, and her father's mismanaged financial affairs. Héloïse's aggressiveness leads Charles to feel entitled to love Emma and to compare her favorably with his own wife.

Now Flaubert moves the plot with happenstance. Charles's wife's estate manager and lawyer runs off with her money (as Madame Aubain's financial manager, also a lawyer, runs off in "Un cœur simple"). Charles's parents investigate and discover that the Widow Dubuc's dowry was far less substantial than she had led them to believe. They make a violent scene, and she dies of an apparent hemorrhage a week later. Typical of Flaubert's realistic rendering of mixed feelings, he describes Charles remaining on the evening of her funeral in a "painful revery"—"She had loved him, after all," he thought.

Chapter 3: Courtship

Charles's passivity and inertia prevent him from returning to the Bertaux Farm, where Emma and her father live. But after five months have elapsed, Old Rouault comes to pay Charles and to invite him to come see them again. The Rouaults indulge him and express sympathy for his loss. One summer day, Charles finds Emma alone in the kitchen, sewing. Little beads of sweat glisten on her bare shoulders. (Flaubert often uses liquids and fluidity as symbols of arousal and sexual desire.) The scene is laden with other symbolism. Behind the shutters, the light is dim—Charles cannot see Emma clearly; she appears in a bluish haze.[3] Trapped flies are drowning at the bottom of nearly empty cider glasses (Norman cider is ordinarily lightly alcoholic), foreshadowing Charles's own fate with Emma. She offers him a stronger liqueur, a glass of curaçao. She sensuously darts her tongue in and out of her glass. "Les phrases leur vinrent," observes Flaubert, meaning that conventional remarks come to them both. Emma boasts of her musical talents, her piety, and her managerial skills and communicates her willingness to change her life. On subsequent visits, Charles begins blushing when he is around her; Old Rouault knows he will propose soon. He has been thinking that it might be desirable to marry Emma off: she is not useful around the farm. When the two men are alone together one day and Charles, helpless as ever, stammers out Old Rouault's name, Emma's father articulates the proposal for him, saying he'll talk to his daughter and signal her reply by opening the shutters of the kitchen window if she accepts Charles, who will wait behind the hedge. After nearly an hour, the shutter bangs against the wall. Flaubert leaves the details of the conversation between father and daughter indeterminate, like the wedding night later. Eventually he will report that she thought she loved him but that she might have simply been excited by the prospect of a different way of life.

Chapter 4: The Wedding Feast

The Rouaults offer a sumptuous banquet for forty people. Typically for Flaubert's pessimistic view of human nature, joy is not unalloyed. Madame Bovary *mère* resents not having been consulted about the wedding, and several guests who by chance were served less-desirable cuts of meat several times in a row gather to denigrate *le père* Rouault and the wedding. After the wedding night, the traditional gender roles are reversed: Emma shows no reaction, but Charles is cloyingly affectionate. Rouault's sad memories of his deceased wife and son, which conclude the chapter, seem a digression but anticipate the denouement by suggesting that happiness is something destined to be lost.

Chapter 5: The Newlyweds' House

The moods of the newlyweds are contrasted: their incompatibility begins with their marriage. Charles finds a tranquil happiness in little things and in Emma's mere presence: "For him, the universe did not extend beyond the silky circle of her skirt" (94). He can't keep his hands off her things or off her. She pushes him away, half-irritated, as one would dismiss a clinging child. Emma's point of view, deferred until now, emerges only in the final paragraph. Before her marriage, she had thought she loved Charles, but now she isn't happy. She must have been mistaken. She seeks to comprehend what was meant by the words "felicity, passion, and the intoxicating delights of love," which had seemed so fine in books.

Chapter 6: Emma's Twofold Education

A flashback recalls her education in convent school, a finishing school where she was sent when she turned thirteen. (Why she went there remains a mystery; such an experience was unusual for a farm girl.) She was more intelligent than the other girls, and at first the nuns thought she had a religious vocation, but at bottom her enjoyment of convent life was only nascent sensuality. She *tried* to fast for a whole day (characteristically, Flaubert sarcastically underlines the failure of a modest effort), invented sins to confess so that she could get more attention, and found "unexpected pleasures" in the religious language that referred to Christ as "a celestial lover" and a partner in "an eternal marriage."

In using Chateaubriand's *The Spirit of Christianity* to sugarcoat the pill of the religious life, the Church took a viper to its bosom: the divine viscount's Catholic sentiment was more opportunistic and sensual than devout. But shortly after the Revolution had nearly abolished French Christianity, a beautifully written, thousand-page essay by a prominent writer and statesman who claimed to defend the Christian religion was hard to resist. Moreover, because the Revolution had attacked the nobility along with the clergy, the Church assumed that the enemies of its enemies must be its friends. In sympathy for an aristocratic victim of the Revolution, the convent that Emma attended had taken in a former noblewoman from a ruined family, who did the laundry. She surreptitiously introduced the convent girls to sentimental novels from the ancien régime and to Sir Walter Scott and the medievalizing *genre troubadour*. By disguising sensuality as exalted sentiment, supported by an exotic decor, such reading experiences prepared Emma to respond to Rodolphe's seduction speeches.

For a time, Emma found sensuous pleasure in being the center of attention while she mourned her mother's death. At length, she became bored with both romanticism and religion. Her practical mind rebelled at the mysteries of the faith. When she returned to her farm, she soon became bored ordering servants about and was ready for the novelty of marriage. We must remember that she was only about eighteen. Emma's convent experience, which exposed her to girls wealthier and more aristocratic than herself, left her with an unrealistic yearning to enter such society.

Chapter 7: Emma's Marriage and Its Discontents

Emma had dreamed of an exotic honeymoon. Her fantasies emphasized her fantasy husband's clothes. Her actual husband, Charles, is boring, inexperienced, and incurious. She resents even the oblivious happiness he derives from her company. At first, she prides herself on running an elegant household; it expresses her narcissism. Her mother-in-law finds Emma too prodigal and self-indulgent and instinctively detests her as a dangerous, disrespectful rival. Emma, meanwhile, tries in vain to love Charles; failing that, she takes long walks with her greyhound and stares out over the abandoned countryside.

Chapter 8: A Weekend at the Chateau of La Vaubyessard

An invitation to a ball, which the local marquis offers to prepare his political candidacy, provides a distraction. The Bovarys were invited because Charles had created the illusion of competence, successfully lancing a boil in the marquis's mouth, and because Emma seemed to him pretty and well-bred. She refuses to dance with Charles, on the specious pretext that such an amusement would detract from his professional dignity. The peasants watching from outside the windows seem a distant reminder of her former life. Waltzing with a viscount, Emma feels a swooning surrender. This contact with luxury has left an indelible impression on her, but her memories fade and only a poignant sense of loss remains.

Chapter 9: Emma's Commodity Fetishism

Before Freud wrote on objects as sexual fetishes (items that developmentally retarded males use as a fantasy replacement for the perceived missing penis of women), Karl Marx in *Capital* had commented that we acquire some possessions as status symbols, badges of class privilege, rather than for their intrinsic utility. Flaubert anticipated and combined the insights of both Freud and Marx in his psychological analysis of Emma. During the Bovarys' return from the ball, Charles has found an embroidered cigar case containing two cigars on the road and ineptly tries to smoke one of them. Emma hides the case with the remaining cigar (suggesting a penis inside a vagina) as a fetish. She speculates that it was a love token, handmade and given to the viscount who waltzed with her. It becomes the nexus of a broad fantasy construction: the viscount has returned to Paris; Emma buys a map of the city and studies it; she subscribes to Parisian fashion magazines, "seeking in them imaginary assuagements for her personal lusts" (118). She imagines herself frequenting aristocratic and artistic milieus. In contrast, everything around her seems an unwelcome exception. She confuses sensuality with happiness, elegant manners with delicate feelings. Love must require a special climate to flourish, she thinks, as do certain plants. Emma trains a fourteen-year-old orphan (named Félicité, like the protagonist of Flaubert's tale "Un cœur simple" twenty years later) to be a lady's maid who addresses her in the third person, serves beverages on a plate, and so forth.

Meanwhile, she charms Charles with her delicate ways and carefully adjusts or replaces his clothes: in her mind, he is a narcissistic extension of herself. Consequently, she despises him for his lack of ambition. Once the anniversary of the ball passes without a second invitation, she loses hope for a change in her existence and sinks into a clinical depression, abandoning all her interests. She feigns contentment when with her mother-in-law but finds her own father crude and boring. Her psychosomatic illnesses begin, and she feigns illness to persuade Charles to move. He chooses Yonville, a town similar to Tostes. Emma finds her wedding bouquet and throws it into the fire, symbolically rejecting her marriage. When the Bovarys move, she is pregnant, Flaubert notes in a terse one-sentence concluding paragraph. She will be even more trapped in marriage than before. Divorce was illegal in France between 1814 and 1886. Even after 1886, a woman could not legally divorce in order to marry her lover.

PART 2: PLATONIC AND ADULTEROUS LOVE

Chapter 1: The New Home

Flaubert characterizes a characterless land: a bastard country lying between Normandy, Picardy, and the Ile-de-France, served by no practicable road until 1835. Even that greater accessibility doesn't help to rouse the sleepy town. Farmers would rather "watch the grass grow" (raise hay) than take the risks of truck farming. An allusion to floods in Lyon situates the action in 1840. Flaubert uses a central square—between the pharmacy and the inn Le Lion d'Or, where the coach arrives—like the stage of a theater, to motivate the meetings of the characters he wants to introduce and portray through their conversations. Madame Lefrançois, the innkeeper, is vindictively competitive with Le Café Français opposite her; Homais, self-satisfied and conventionally anticlerical; Binet, an impolitely silent automaton; the priest Bournisien, hearty and quite unspiritual; Hivert, the coachman, busy and harried; Emma, hostile toward Charles, whom she blames for her greyhound having run away during the journey; the merchant and money-lender Lheureux, ingratiating.

Chapter 2: Emma Meets a Soul Mate

For their first evening in Yonville, Emma and Charles have supper at the inn. Homais, the pharmacist, acts very friendly toward the new health officer. His conversation is long-winded and affected. Léon, a young law clerk, feels attracted to Emma and soon discovers their affinities. Both like novelty, and both express themselves in romantic clichés about things such as the sea and mountains that they have never seen. They both love to read, but Emma's marked taste for strong sensations distinguishes her from the more cautious Léon. When she enters her new house, she feels a chill but hopes for a better life in her new location, romantically believing that moving can transform one's situation.

Chapter 3: Motherhood and Platonic Love

The next morning Léon, unconsciously smitten with Madame Bovary, waits all day in vain hopes of seeing her at the inn for supper again. Homais comes to help the Bovarys settle in, with obsequious cordiality: having been officially reprimanded for practicing medicine without a license, he wants to ingratiate himself with Charles, who might otherwise denounce him. Charles feels sad because he has few patients. Emma's dowry, 9,000 francs (equivalent to two years' salary today), had been spent in two years, owing largely to the expense of her clothes and of the move occasioned by her nervous illness. But Charles delights in the prospect of being a father; Emma's pregnancy makes him feel closer to her and completely fulfilled. Emma, in contrast, loses interest in the layette and the baby because she cannot spend all she wishes. Moreover, she hopes for a son, "the anticipated revenge for all her past helplessness. A man, at least, is free." When she has a daughter, she faints with disappointment.

In Flaubert's day, well-to-do French families customarily sent infants to a wet nurse.[4] One day, Emma goes to visit Berthe on an impulse. Léon encounters her and goes along. Emma picks up the baby and sings to it, but it vomits on her dress and she puts it down, disgusted. But then she notices Léon's nails, as Charles had noticed hers when they first met. As Flaubert notes sarcastically, "one of the clerk's main occupations was to maintain them." Léon considers Emma a kindred spirit, but "he felt vague abysses, as it were, separating them" (161).

Chapter 4: Emma and Léon's Mutual Infatuation Grows

In this brief, quiet chapter, Emma vaguely thrills when Léon's shadow passes outside her curtain on his way to Le Lion d'Or each day. Homais's young assistant, Justin, a distant relation taken in for charity, spends as much time as possible offering to run errands for the Bovarys' maid, Félicité; Homais suspects that Justin is in love with the maid, but he is actually in love with the mistress. Léon joins the Bovarys and the Homais for many evenings when they play cards or dominoes; Emma sometimes looks at fashion magazines, and Léon recites verse. At length they exchange innocent presents. Léon wants to declare his love but is afraid. Emma, expecting love to be tempestuous because of the models she found in books, suspects nothing of her own feelings.

Chapter 5: Emma Plays the Good Wife

On one snowy Sunday in February, the Bovarys, Homais, Léon, Justin, and the two older Homais children stroll to a cotton mill under construction. Emma, walking arm in arm with Homais, has an opportunity to compare Charles and Léon from a distance. Charles looks stupid to her, and Léon looks idealized, with eyes like a mountain lake (a sight Emma never encountered except in books). Back home, she suddenly realizes that Léon loves her.

To avoid Charles's company, she takes supper in her room and, playing the virtuous, devoted wife, pretends to be absorbed in her sewing when Léon visits. After that evening, Emma begins to act devoted to her household chores and to religious observance. She also brings her daughter, Berthe, back from the wet nurse and lavishes histrionic effusions on her. She conscientiously mends Charles's clothes and acts obedient and affectionate until Léon abandons hope.

Everyone in town admires her, but inwardly, "she was full of lusts, rage, and hatred" (172), in love with Léon and obsessed with him, although his presence decreases her excitement. The narrator wonders whether Emma did not make advances "perhaps because of laziness, or anxiety, and sexual modesty as well" (173). She finds consolation in her pride, but Charles's oblivious happiness exasperates her. He does not appreciate her sacrifices in remaining faithful; her hatred crystallizes as she blames him for all her disappointments.

Chapter 6: Religion Fails Emma; Léon Leaves

Spring comes. On impulse, Emma seeks spiritual guidance from the local priest, Bournisien. But he is a hearty, matter-of-fact man preoccupied with the physical world and, when she approaches him, distracted with his catechism class. They speak at cross-purposes, Emma referring to her spiritual dissatisfaction, and the priest, to physical illness. When she calls him a doctor for souls, he gives the grotesque example of treating a sick cow.

Weary of his hopeless love, Léon leaves to study law in Paris. The desultory conversation between him and Emma as they say farewell conceals a great tenderness.

Chapter 7: The Substitute: Emma Meets Rodolphe

At first, Emma's memories of Léon boil into a febrile passion. Gradually, she despairs, indulges herself in needless purchases and repeatedly begins and abandons new reading projects. When she coughs blood one day, Charles desperately summons his mother, who feels Emma simply needs hard manual work as a distraction from her self-absorption. "Someone without religious faith will always turn out badly," she opines (192). She cuts off Emma's lending library subscription.

One market day, a new local resident, Rodolphe Boulanger, brings his servant to Charles to be bled. Rodolphe has just purchased a local chateau and its two farms. An experienced seducer, he immediately recognizes Emma's boredom and sexual frustration. Attracted to her, after a few moments' hesitation he resolves to begin a seduction campaign during the county fair.

Chapter 8: The County Fair

The long-awaited county fair arrives. Rival squads of national guardsmen and firemen compete in drills. Rodolphe, dressed with eccentric independence, mocks the fair and the unsophisticated country dwellers. He complains of his unhappiness to Emma, who objects with common sense that he has no reason to repine—as a man, he is free and rich.[5] But Rodolphe's posturing makes her fictional heroes come to life. And his outrageous flattery quickly overcomes her skepticism.

A municipal counselor, Lieuvain (empty place), replacing the departmental prefect (chief administrative officer), gives a pompous, clumsy closing address. The audience hangs stupidly on his words, but only fragments of phrases get through the bellowing of the animals, a satiric counterpart to the mystified humans. Flaubert cuts back and forth between Lieuvain's and Rodolphe's clichéd speeches, as Emma gazes into Rodolphe's eyes. He says he cannot live without her; he takes her hand, and their fingers intertwine.

Chapter 9: The Fall

Rodolphe deliberately waits for six weeks to whet Emma's impatience. He then seeks her out and starts a vehement seduction speech. He had absented himself through despair, he said. He can't use "Emma" with her, "that name that fills my soul," but only "Madame Bovary," the name of another. Meanwhile,

Homais suggests that Emma take up horseback riding to improve her health. Rodolphe jumps at the chance to lead her into the forest with him and offers to lend her one of his horses. Emma resists, half-sincerely, until Charles offers to buy her the riding habit she does not have. When it arrives, with unconscious irony Charles writes Rodolphe that "my wife is at your disposal."

Rodolphe's prepares his semi-rape with hypocritical reassurance: "in my soul, you are like a Madonna on a pedestal" (227). After lovemaking, Emma floats in the aftermath of what may be the first orgasm she has experienced, whereas Rodolphe, relatively unaffected, is already fixing a broken strap on the bridle, with a cigar clamped between his teeth. Returning home, Emma feels transfigured, as if she had joined a sisterhood of adulterous women in novels. She goes to contemplate herself in the mirror, meditating on the "bluish immensity" she has just entered (229). The next day, the lovers discover a hut in the forest where they can hide. They begin writing each other every day. One morning when Charles has left on his rounds before dawn, Emma goes to surprise Rodolphe in his chateau. These visits become habitual, until Rodolphe begins to feel irritated at her possessiveness. He hypocritically objects that she might be seen and compromise herself.

Chapter 10: Anxiety and Deception

Rodolphe's fears of detection gradually affect Emma, to whom his love means everything now. One early morning, on her return from Rodolphe's chateau, La Huchette, she meets Binet, who is hunting ducks illegally from a blind on the shore instead of from a boat. Both are embarrassed. Emma lies awkwardly, saying that she was going to see her little girl at the wet nurse, although everyone knows Berthe has been home for a year and although the path she is on leads only to La Huchette.

A pattern of deception begins forthwith. The next day, Emma and Rodolphe arrange a system of rendezvous that will expose Emma less. She hides the key to the gate in the back fence of the garden, and Rodolphe throws sand against the shutters to let Emma know he's there. She delays going to bed until Charles falls asleep, and then the lovers meet under the arbor, where Léon had gazed at her amorously before. Flaubert presents an ecstatic description of their lovemaking during starry nights.

When it rains, they meet in the semidetached consulting room. There Rodolphe, surrounded by the instruments of Charles's profession, cannot resist making fun of him. Emma would have liked him to be more serious. He inwardly finds her odious when she asks whether he has brought his pistols to defend himself against Charles. He has too much good sense to wound or kill someone unnecessarily, and has no fear of Charles. Her sentimentality annoys him—she says that their dead mothers, looking down from the moon, must approve of their love. But she is so pretty, so candid compared to his former mistresses, and

so exalted in expressing her love that Rodolphe is flattered even when his bourgeois common sense disdains her attitudes. But he increasingly takes Emma for
granted. She feels their great love receding beneath her like an outgoing tide
that leaves only muddy clay behind, but she is subjugated. Rodolphe, who has
directed the adulterous affair according to his whims, has domesticated it like a
marriage (238).

Emma wants Rodolphe to love her more intensely. He finds her too moody
and deliberately misses three rendezvous in a row, ignoring her sighs and tears.
Then Emma repents and wishes that she could love the devoted Charles. But he
is too placid and boring to inspire such feelings, until Homais unwittingly suggests a way that she could love him better.

Chapter 11: The Botched Operation

Homais, "a partisan of progress," has just read of a new operation for correcting clubfeet. A natural meddler, he encourages Emma to try to persuade
Charles to perform the operation on Hippolyte, the stable boy of Le Lion d'Or.
Emma has no evidence that Charles is incompetent in his profession. His reputation and fortune could benefit if he were successful; his glory would reflect on
her. "She was asking nothing more than to lean on something more solid than
love" (242). At length the unfortunate Hippolyte agrees to the operation. Everyone he knows is nagging him to get it, suggesting that it would make him
attractive to women—and it would be free. Flaubert does not specify that such
an operation, by a health officer, was illegal. Charles may not know better, and
Homais is too unscrupulous to care.

The operation itself is simple; Charles merely cuts Hippolyte's Achilles tendon (an alarming detail; one wonders whether he would ever be able to walk
again, even if all went well), and then buckles his foot and ankle into a special
box designed to straighten the foot. Emma hugs Charles and makes plans with
him. She feels happy to be able to have some affection for that poor boy, who
cherishes her. Homais writes a fulsome report for *Le Fanal de Rouen* (The Rouen
Beacon), taking, as usual, the opportunity to exalt science over religion.

But neither Charles nor Homais knows enough to loosen the compression on
Hippolyte's ankle regularly, to allow his blood to circulate. The stable boy soon
feels terrible pain and develops gangrene. All those who had been urging Hippolyte to get the operation now criticize him for having done one thing or another wrong. Finally, a well-known doctor, Canivet, must be summoned from
Neufchâtel. To save Hippolyte, he must amputate above the knee. Homais lets
Charles take all the blame, while supinely flattering the surgeon. Fearing ridicule
and liability, Charles hides in his house and blames fate for his failure.

Emma feels enraged that she imagined Charles ever could amount to anything and that she denied herself anything on his account. He didn't even suspect, she inwardly rages, "that from now on the ludicrousness of his name would

sully her as well" (253). Everything about Charles irritates Emma now, and "what remained of her past virtue crumbled under the furious blows of her pride" (253). She angrily pushes him away when he wants a comforting kiss. Rodolphe finds her waiting at their rendezvous that evening, and all their past rancor evaporates.

Chapter 12: Emma Demands Too Much

Emma soon begs Rodolphe to run off with her. He doesn't understand "why there should be so much fuss over such a simple thing as love" (meaning sex, 255). Charles has had to buy two wooden legs for Hippolyte (one for everyday, the other for special occasions), as a minor compensation for the bungled operation. Lheureux, who took care of the orders, uses the opportunity to inveigle Emma into making expensive purchases. Despising Charles, she no longer exercises any restraint in gratifying her whims. She begins embezzling money from Charles to pay for them. Her presents bother Rodolphe and hurt his pride; he refuses some until she insists. "Rodolphe finally obeyed, feeling her tyrannical and too intrusive" (258). She also begins insisting on sentimental rituals such as his thinking of her at midnight. The novelty of their relationship fades for him, and he comes to find her like all mistresses. Despite all his experience, he can't discern the depth of her feelings beneath the commonplace expressions that we all use to express devotion. But Rodolphe takes advantage of her subjection, judging that all sexual modesty is unnecessary, and "made something supple and corrupt of her" (presumably meaning that he initiated her into oral and anal sex, 259).

Emma becomes bolder and more independent, and defies her mother-in-law, who has taken refuge with them from her own conflictual marriage. After Charles makes her apologize, she summons Rodolphe. She can't stand living with Charles any more after four years. In a tender moment, Rodolphe asks what she wants: to flee with him, she repeats. Rodolphe, inwardly resolved never to subject himself to such scandal, difficulty, and expense, asks what she plans to do with Berthe. After reflecting for several minutes, Emma says she'll bring her along. Evidently, she never plans to do so, for she doesn't mention Berthe again. Rodolphe pretends to agree to go abroad with her.

After that, Emma acts much more docile toward her mother-in-law, perhaps to deceive her and Charles or perhaps fully to savor the bitterness of the existence she would soon abandon. She never had looked more beautiful than during this period of her life, Flaubert observes: "She finally blossomed into complete self-realization" (263). Charles feels renewed delight in their relationship, as if it were a second honeymoon, and dreams of his daughter's future, while Emma dreams of her flight to Italy.[6] Rodolphe postpones their departure for weeks, on various pretexts. On the beautiful, warm summer night of their last rendezvous, Emma describes a classic codependent relationship: she and

Rodolphe will live exclusively for each other, forever. Rodolphe is unresponsive, but Emma is oblivious. After he leaves her, however, he must briefly struggle against his own passion, until his common sense wins out.

Chapter 13: Rodolphe's Betrayal

To find inspiration for an appropriate farewell letter, Rodolphe looks over the letters and love tokens she sent him, mingled with souvenirs from many other women in the same tin box. As he cascades these from hand to hand like a deck of cards, he scoffs at love. "Like schoolboys during recreation, pleasures had trampled the courtyard of his heart until nothing could grow there" (270). Cynically, he invokes the same fate that he once claimed had brought them together as the reason that they must part. He claims to be acting in her best interests, helping her avoid a mistake she would regret later. He drips a false tear on his letter and sends it to Emma under a basket of apricots—an agreed-upon channel of communication. Alarmed, Emma rushes to the attic to read it. In despair, she almost yields to the temptation of suicide by hurling herself out the window, but Charles and Félicité accidentally forestall her by calling her to supper. When she sees Rodolphe's blue carriage passing her window on its way to Rouen, she faints, and she remains prostrated by "brain fever" for six weeks, while Charles remains devotedly by her side.[7] When she finally recovers and Charles leads her outside to get some air and to rest under the arbor, she collapses again as she remembers her lost loves, and the illness resumes.

Chapter 14: The Consolations of the Religious Life

Expenses mount in the invalid's household, where Charles has little time to see his patients. Finally, he borrows money from Lheureux. Flaubert reveals Lheureux's secret ambitions. He plans to underbid the delivery service offered by Hivert and his coach *L'Hirondelle,* to gather all Yonville's transport business in his hands.

During a hard winter and a long, difficult convalescence, Emma dislikes everything she used to enjoy. "All her thoughts were limited to taking care of herself" (281). Feeling sicker than usual one day, she asks for extreme unction and has a religious experience. Exhausted by her punishing pride, Emma seeks rest in Catholicism. She plans to become a saint. Charles's mother now finds little to criticize in Emma except that her excessive charity leads her to neglect household sewing. Emma often has the neighbor ladies over now, for devotional evenings. Her egotism and charity, corruption and virtue blend indistinguishably. But as she recovers her health, she sheds some of her piety.

Then, with another typically disastrous suggestion, like that of the horseback riding or the clubfoot operation, Homais suggests that Charles distract Emma by taking her to Rouen to hear the famous tenor Lagardy in a touring opera. Emma resists the frivolity of the excursion, but Charles insists.

Chapter 15: A Night at the Opera

In this famous tableau, Emma listens to the Donizetti opera *Lucia di Lammermoor* and is transported to her youthful readings of Sir Walter Scott, on whose novel *The Bride of Lammermoor* the opera is based. She can follow the plot and recognizes her own former passion in the heroine's and hero's effusions. Charles can't understand what is going on and irritates Emma with his ignorant questions. She realizes, as she watches, that art exaggerates feelings. But Lagardy's reputation as a womanizer has enhanced his artistic reputation. He seems a combination "charlatan-hairdresser-toreador" (293). Emma drifts into imagining a life with him.

At intermission, Charles meets Léon, who has returned from Paris to Rouen to serve a two-year apprenticeship in Norman business law. To have a chance to talk, Léon and Emma insist on leaving before the last act. She now can think only of their unexpressed past love. Charles encourages Emma to stay alone an extra day, to see the last act after she has rested. Léon, who had been disparaging Lagardy's performance in order to get Emma to come outside, now praises it so that she will stay in town. She hesitates but finally accepts.

PART 3: A SECOND ADULTERY AND SUICIDE

Chapter 1: The Mutual Seduction

Léon has become more self-confident and is sexually experienced after two years in Paris. Seeing Emma again reawakens his passion. He secretly follows the Bovarys to their hotel and sits up all night making plans to seduce her. The next afternoon, Charles has left for Yonville. Emma smiles at Léon's silly story that instinct had guided him to her hotel. At first she protests that she must return home; she has obligations Léon can't understand because he's not a woman. But then she begins to play Rodolphe's former part, complaining of how isolated she is from any kindred spirit. Emma's eyes glow encouragingly. She and Léon join hands, and past, present, and future flow together. Probably she didn't know herself whether her resistance to Léon's entreaties was sincere, Flaubert observes. She had never found a man so handsome. He begs for one final meeting. She agrees to eleven A.M. in the cathedral but then writes a long letter excusing herself. Not knowing his address, however, she will have to give it to him in person.

The next morning, for the first time in his life, Léon buys a bouquet for a woman. An importunate sexton offers to take him on a tour of the cathedral, but Léon can see it only as a "gigantic boudoir." Emma arrives late and then, desperately resisting her attraction to Léon, immediately goes to pray. When she finishes, she insists on a guided tour that Léon repeatedly tries to cut short. At last, he drags her to an enclosed cab. Emma agrees to join him there when he says, "It's done in Paris." The long ride that follows is described only from the outside, as the tired, thirsty driver tries to rest, only to have a furious voice urge him to keep moving. At one point, a bare hand throws torn-up scraps of paper out the window—the letter of farewell. Finally, in the early evening, a veiled woman gets out and walks quickly away.

Chapter 2: Charles's Father Dies

After waiting nearly an hour, Hivert has left without Emma. She rents a carriage and catches him in Quincampoix. As soon as she disembarks, she is summoned to see Homais for an important message. But he is distracted; it is jam-making day, and he is scolding Justin for having brought an extra basin from near his poison cupboard. He describes exactly where he keeps his arsenic, so as to dramatize the danger. Then a book on *Conjugal Love,* with engravings, falls from Justin's pocket, and the boy is scolded again. Finally, Homais blurts out to Emma that her father-in-law has died suddenly of apoplexy after a heavy meal with his fellow former army officers—although Charles had delegated him to break the news gently. She says the minimum to save appearances, but Charles takes her taciturnity for stunned sympathy and is touched. She finds him mediocre and pitiable.

The next day, Charles's mother arrives, and she and Charles are surprised how much they miss the dead man, unpleasant though he was. Emma seeks solitude to meditate on her new love. Then Lheureux insinuates himself and suggests that in this time of crisis, Emma should get power of attorney (unusual for a woman in France in those days) to manage Charles's financial affairs and help him. She does so after her mother-in-law leaves, exaggerating the difficulties of settling the estate. By expressing reservations about Guillaumin, the local lawyer who has drawn up a model document, she manages to get permission to go to Rouen to consult Léon, now a lawyer, for three days.

Chapter 3: A Secret Honeymoon

Emma and Léon take a boat ride to an island. Imitating Lamartine's semific-tive heroine Elvire in the romantic poem "Le Lac," Emma sings a musical version of that poem. Léon and Emma arrange for him to write her care of *la mére* Rollet, the wet nurse.

Chapter 4: Music Lessons

Léon neglects his work in the law office and goes to see Emma one Saturday (at the time, it was customary to have Thursday afternoons and Sundays off). They rendezvous under the arbor, as she had done with Rodolphe. Emma plots to see Léon every week: she starts playing the piano again but deliberately makes mistakes. Charles had been proud of her playing, which reflected favorably on him, and finally she gets permission to go to Rouen each Thursday for lessons.

Chapter 5: More Master than Mistress

On Thursdays, Emma arises quietly before Charles is awake and goes to wait for the coach in the inn. The crowds in the city intoxicate her. She and Léon are lost in an isolated world of love, the hotel room they rent. At evening, Emma must return. Here Flaubert introduces the blind man, a beggar with pustulent eyes who sometimes jumps on the moving coach and sticks his head in through the curtains, moaning for alms. He symbolizes Emma's own blindness and her eventual public disgrace when she too must beg for money, to pay her debts.

Sadness overwhelms Emma as she returns home each week, but she acts charming to Charles. When he meets Mademoiselle Lempereur, Emma's supposed piano teacher, in Yonville one day and that woman has never heard of Emma, Emma invents an elaborate lie and forges a receipt for the lessons. From then on, she lies for pleasure.

One day, however, Lheureux sees her coming out of the Hotel de Boulogne on Léon's arm. The merchant is too canny to allude to his discovery, but three days later, he asks Emma to repay some of her debts and suggests secretly selling a piece of Emma's father's land without letting Charles know. Thus she saves enough to pay off the first three of four promissory notes spaced a month apart, but the fourth arrives on a Thursday when Emma is not at Yonville, and Charles is consternated by it. When Emma returns, she explains the necessity of her various purchases of luxury items. Charles appeals to his mother for more money, but she will not give it over without first inspecting things herself. Emma has secured a false bill from Lheureux, which itemizes purchases at bargain prices— but Charles's mother still finds many of them unnecessary. She makes Charles promise to reclaim the power of attorney. Emma is furious, but her mother-in-law throws the document into the fire. When she leaves, Emma acts cold toward Charles until he has another, identical document drawn up and restored to her.

Increasingly, she needs to indulge herself. One Thursday night, she does not come home from Rouen. Charles desperately seeks her there until he runs into her in the street. She lies that she was taken ill but tells Charles that she can't feel free if the least delay upsets him so. She uses the incident as an excuse to go to Rouen whenever she chooses, on any pretext. Often, she interrupts Léon at work, until his employer complains. She insists that he write love poetry for her; uninspired, he always ends up copying verses from a keepsake.[8] She imposes all her tastes on him until he becomes more her mistress than she is his. Léon wonders at the deep, hidden corruption revealed in her skill in lovemaking (presumably, the "kisses that ravish his soul" include oral sex).

Chapter 6: Financial Disaster

When Léon comes to see Emma in Yonville (these visits, except for the first, are not described), Homais often invites him to a meal. The pharmacist, like Emma, has become fascinated with life in Paris, questions Léon closely about it, and adopts Parisian slang to be chic. Out of politeness, Léon feels obliged to return the invitation; one Thursday, therefore, Homais unexpectedly arrives in Rouen and keeps Léon at table in a restaurant for hours, while Emma waits. When he finally appears in their hotel room, she is furious. He is about to win her forgiveness when Homais has him summoned, believing that Léon actually wants to get free of the appointment he claimed to have. Léon pleads the pressure of work but is too weak and indecisive to resist being dragged off by Homais again. Emma leaves in disgust.

At first she detests him; then her anger abates. "But our disparagement of those we love always detaches us from them somewhat" (355). Emma tries to reanimate her passion but must fuel it with fantasies of an ideal lover; she always feels disappointment when she sees Léon again. In desperation, she feels increasingly lustful and demanding sexually, which somewhat alarms and frightens Léon, while he increasingly resents her domination. With a classic codependent demand, she seeks to separate him from his friends: "Don't see them, don't go out, think only about us, love me!" (356). She even thinks of having him followed. One day she happens to pass by her convent school and recalls the joys of that calm life and her past attractions to men. She'd never been happy, she concludes: "Where did that inadequacy of life come from, the way things decayed instantly when she depended on them?" (357). Her passions absorb her.

One day, in Yonville, a shabby little man brings a bill for 700 francs from Vinçart, the moneylender who supplies Lheureux with funds. Emma can't pay. She asks for help from Lheureux, who claims he can do nothing. Finally, he has Emma sign four 250-franc promissory notes dated a month apart (to postpone repayment of the 700-franc debt for a month and to spread it over four months, Emma agrees to pay interest of over 125% a year). We must assume that Lheureux—who knows Emma's financial resources better than she—is gambling that Emma in her desperation may be able to extract some additional money from her lovers. If not, Lheureux realizes he has now extracted from the Bovarys all the usurious interest charges he can and that it is time to foreclose and move on to other victims. Flaubert was not particularly expert in financial matters—he never made a living from writing (in fact, his trip to the Middle

East in 1848–49 cost him more than he ever earned as a writer until his death in 1880), and he asked his nephew-in-law, Ernest Commanville, to manage his affairs later in life. By itself, the imminent seizure and sale of some of the Bovarys' effects would scarcely be worth Lheureux's while. We must speculate that he will secure a lien on the Bovarys' house and, consequently, on their estate, in compensation for their nonpayment of debts.

Emma desperately tries to raise money. She has already spent the annual 600 livres (francs) annual income from Charles's father's estate. She secretly sells her possessions and collects bills from his patients for herself. Her debts are so massive that she can't face them. She takes out her frustration on Charles, refusing to share a bed with him any more and making him sleep on the third floor. She reads orgiastic novels in her bedroom all day.

At length, an anonymous denunciation reaches Léon's mother: he's "ruining himself" with a married woman. His employer lectures him benevolently. Léon begins to feel his mother and boss are right: he should settle down. He is about to become a head clerk in his law firm. He abandons his vague dreams of an artist's life. "Within every lawyer you can find the debris from a poet" (364). Emma and he have become tired of each other. "In adultery, Emma rediscovered all the platitudes of marriage."[9] But she still needs Léon; her love letters to him are addressed to a vague, ideal phantom that she imagines in his absence.

One day she stays overnight at Rouen for a masked ball and dances all night with Léon and his friends. When they go out to a third-rate restaurant early in the morning, she realizes that most of the other women with her are whores. Implicitly, this degrading evening contrasts horribly with the exhilarating aristocratic ball at La Vaubyessard. Emma leaves early, detesting everything. On her return to Yonville, she finds a notice posted on her door. Her household furnishings will be seized unless she pays 8,000 francs within twenty-four hours. Lheureux, when appealed to, hypocritically lectures her, threatens to tell Charles of her embezzlements, and hints that she should try to get money from her lovers.

Chapter 7: A Desperate Quest

Charles, out on his rounds, has not yet learned of the disaster. A bailiff and two witnesses come to inventory the Bovarys' property. Emma goes to Rouen to seek money from bankers and, finally, from Léon. She suggests that he steal it from his office. He pretends to be seeking the money from friends and finally gets rid of her by saying that a wealthy acquaintance who is returning that evening might lend him money. "She felt herself lost, rolling at random in indefinable abysses" (374–75).

The next morning, an official announcement is posted on the Bovarys' door: (most of) their furniture and effects will be sold. Emma's maid, Félicité, advises her to see Guillaumin, who is sexually attracted to her. Emma makes an appeal as Guillaumin sidles closer to her and at last offers 3,000 francs for her body. Emma recoils. She storms out, despising all men. Because of her pride, she can't endure the thought of having to accept Charles's forgiveness. When she sees him return, she runs to Binet's house. The point of view switches to that of the mayor's wife. From a distance, Emma's and Binet's gestures and one shocked exclamation—"Madame, y pensez-vous!" (Madame, what *could* you be thinking!)—suggest that she is trying to seduce him. Rejected, she runs off to the house of Berthe's former wet nurse and her current go-between in the affair with Léon, Madame Rollet. She confuses the sound of the spinning wheel with the fateful sound of Binet's lathe, symbol of a limited, routinized world where she has no place. Léon does not arrive with the promised money when *L'Hirondelle* returns from Rouen. Suddenly she remembers Rodolphe and goes to appeal to him, "without in the least suspecting this prostitution" that had so angered her with Guillaumin not long before (382).

Chapter 8: Emma's Last Hope Vanishes; Her Suicide

Emma finds Rodolphe at home; he has been avoiding her for three years, "owing to that innate cowardice characteristic of the stronger sex" (383). She recalls their past love. Rodolphe is charmed until she tells him she needs money, 3,000 francs. He really doesn't have them at the moment. Emma's underlying resentment at his earlier betrayal emerges: "you're not worth any more than the others" (386). According to the sexual double standard, she betrays and condemns herself. A man may have all the affairs he chooses; a woman who has had more than one (justified by an unhappy arranged marriage, a predestined passion, and so forth) is a worthless whore. She becomes sarcastic about Rodolphe's luxurious possessions, contrasts her selfless devotion with his egotism, and storms out.

Returning home, she has a hallucination; as after her and Rodolphe's first sexual act, she is conscious only of the beating of her heart, and then, blurred memories fill her vision like fireworks, and the land seems to roll, wavelike, beneath her feet. For the moment she is aware only of her lost love and not her financial problems. Suddenly, reality opens before her like an abyss. With a surge of heroic resolve, she runs to Homais's pharmacy. He and his family are at dinner. She orders Justin, whom she intercepts in the kitchen, to give her the key to the lab, goes directly there, and eats arsenic straight from the bottle. She silences Justin by telling him his master will be blamed if her act becomes known. Then she writes a letter of farewell, tells Charles to wait until tomorrow for explanations of their financial debacle, and lies down.

After a time, a horrible taste of ink fills her mouth; she becomes terribly thirsty and begins to vomit. Charles does not know what is the matter and feels helpless. When Emma's symptoms develop into severe abdominal pain, a weak pulse, and convulsions, she finally shows Charles the letter. Homais sends for Dr. Canivet and for the renowned Dr. Larivière but ignorantly fails to induce vomiting to purge Emma of some of the poison. Canivet arrives and foolishly administers an emetic, which sends the poison through Emma's intestinal tract, aggravating her condition. Soon she vomits blood and curses the poison. Canivet is nonplussed. When Larivière arrives, he realizes that Emma is doomed, but he is moved by Charles's despair.

The trivial, self-interested reactions of the townspeople contrast grotesquely with the tragedy of Emma's suicide. Homais wants to evade blame for the poisoning and to impress Larivière. He seeks free medical advice for his entire family; the townspeople crowd around to do the same.

Bournisien comes to administer extreme unction. Emma gives the cross "the greatest kiss of love that she had ever given" (399). Reverting to her narcissism, she asks for a mirror but cries after contemplating herself. Her death agony begins. When she hears the blind man's song outside and finally recognizes all the words, which are a metaphorical counterpart to her own story—a country girl initiated into sex outside marriage—she hallucinates his hideous face in the shadows like the threat of an eternal punishment, desperately cries out "the blind man!" and dies in a final convulsion. This episodic, symbolic character, who reappears several times in part 3, represents both the figurative emotional blindness of love and the punishment of illicit love by syphilis, which can cause literal blindness.

Chapter 9: The Wake

Charles throws himself on Emma's body; Homais and Canivet restrain him. Homais returns to his shop, to spread the lie, in Yonville and in a news item for *Le Fanal de Rouen*, that Emma mistook arsenic for sugar. Charles insists on an extravagant funeral, with three nesting coffins and a green velvet cloth over the body. He curses God. Homais and Bournisien come to watch over Emma's body and argue vehemently about religion when they are not dozing. For a moment, Charles hopes to revive Emma with the force of his will. His mother arrives at dawn and objects in vain to the expense; Charles has become much more stubborn. When Félicité, Charles's mother, and Madame Lefrançois lift Emma's head to place a crown of flowers around it, a black liquid gushes from her mouth. Charles is horrified when he takes a final look at her. At his request, relayed by Félicité, Homais clumsily cuts a few locks of her hair. In a striking contrast of science and religion, the priest Bournisien sprinkles holy water around the room, and Homais sprinkles bleach. They make peace over the food and drink that is brought to them; the priest observes: "We'll end up understanding each other!" (409). Emma's father arrives, having received an ambiguous message from Homais thirty-six hours late, and faints when he sees the black cloth draped over the coffin.

Chapter 10: The Burial

In a flashback, Flaubert describes *le père* Rouault's frantic ride to Yonville, during which premonitions, hallucinations, and hope alternate. The father and the husband fall sobbing into each other's arms. It is an ironically beautiful day. Charles feels despair and tries to crawl into the grave. Then, calmer, he may have felt, like everyone else, "a vague satisfaction at having finished with the business" (413–14).

Binet doesn't attend; Lheureux offers hypocritical solicitude. Old Rouault can't stand to stay longer, even to see his granddaughter, but he tries to comfort Charles by telling him he'll still receive a turkey every year. Charles's mother affectionately plans to live with him, inwardly rejoicing to recapture his love, which had eluded her for so many years. Rodolphe and Léon sleep peacefully— although Rodolphe has had to take a long walk in the woods to calm himself. That night, Justin sobs uncontrollably over Emma's grave.

Chapter 11: Victimized Again, Charles Dies

Berthe soon forgets her mother. Lheureux extracts exorbitant interest from Charles for Emma's old debts—real and invented. Charles sells much of his furniture but will never part with Emma's. He has become willful. At last his mother becomes exasperated and leaves. Everyone starts taking advantage of Charles with false or inflated bills from the past. He shuts himself up in Emma's dressing room with some of her clothes. At Pentecost, Félicité runs off with Theodore and the rest of Emma's wardrobe. Léon marries a Léocadie Lebœuf. "How happy my poor wife would have been," Charles writes him (417).

One day, Charles finds Rodolphe's farewell letter in the attic. He tells himself Emma's and Rodolphe's love must have been platonic; how could any man not desire her? He tries to please Emma posthumously: "She was corrupting him from beyond the grave" (418). He leaves her room intact. Berthe's presence consoles him, but her clothes are shabby, and therefore Homais won't let his children play with her anymore.

The blind man denounces Homais for having failed to cure him with an anti-inflammatory cream. Humiliated, the pharmacist places false, anonymous denunciations in *Le Fanal de Rouen:* it's disgusting to allow a loathsome beggar to roam the roads and importune travelers; he has startled horses and caused several accidents. Finally Homais manages to have the blind man interned in a hospice—at first temporarily and then permanently. Next, he begins a publicity campaign against the church: "He was becoming a force to be reckoned with" (419). He starts writing more ambitious works than newspaper articles, including a statistical guide to and history of Yonville.

Despite his best efforts to remember her, Charles has trouble preserving a clear mental image of Emma, except in a horrible nightly dream: he takes her in his arms only to have her suddenly become a rotten corpse. He briefly flirts with re-

ligion but then abandons it. Meanwhile, Bournisien becomes steadily more fa-
natical, every other week telling the story of how the archenemy of the church,
Voltaire, died insane, eating his own excrement. Charles needs to ask his mother
for money, and they quarrel when he won't give her one of Emma's shawls in return. They finally are estranged for good when he cannot bear to send Berthe to
her. He worries, however; Berthe seems to have early signs of tuberculosis. In
contrast, everything prospers for Homais and his flourishing family—except his
campaign to be awarded the Legion of Honor. He secretly prostitutes himself to
help the prefect of his *département* (one of a hundred administrative units in
France, halfway between a U.S. county and state) in the elections.

Finally, Charles opens a last drawer in Emma's desk and finds Léon's sexually
explicit letters. He cannot deny her affair any longer. Searching frantically
through the rest of the house, he also finds Rodolphe's letters. Demoralized, he
will see no one. At length, having to sell his last valuable possession, his horse,
he encounters Rodolphe at a market. Embarrassed at first, Rodolphe recovers
and brazenly invites Charles to have a beer. Charles listens vacantly to
Rodolphe's empty talk, as he remembers Emma. After a moment of silent rage
that frightens Rodolphe, he forgives his rival: "Fate was to blame" (424).
Rodolphe, who had directed that fate, feels contempt for Charles. The next
evening, a beautiful day like that of Emma's burial, Charles dies quietly while
sitting under the arbor, with a lock of Emma's hair in his hand.

When the estate is liquidated, only 12 francs and 60 centimes remain. Berthe
goes to Charles's mother, who dies within the year. Because Emma's father has
become paralyzed, Berthe must go to live with a poor aunt and work in a cotton
mill. (The hard work and her incipient tuberculosis will probably soon kill the
child). In an ironic coda underlining the triumph of unscrupulous mediocrity,
Homais is esteemed and protected by the authorities. He continues giving illegal medical consultations with impunity. His popularity grows. Three doctors in
succession cannot compete with him and are forced to abandon Yonville. A final
sentence notes that he has just received the Legion of Honor award for distinguished public service.

NOTES

1. All page references to *Madame Bovary* refer to the Garnier-Flammarion edition,
by Bernard Ajac (Paris, 1986). All translations are ours.
On Emma's anorexia, see Lilian R. Furst, "The Power of the Powerless: A Trio of Nineteenth-Century Disorderly Eaters," in Furst and Peter W. Graham, eds., *Disorderly Eaters:
Texts in Self-Empowerment* (University Park, PA: Pennsylvania State University Press,
1992), 153–66.

2. There is a biographical reminiscence here: Flaubert and Maxime Du Camp treated
a boatman's similar injury on the Nile when they were traveling in Egypt. The confi-
dence that Charles and Emma gain from this successful treatment of a damaged leg implicitly leads them to be willing to have Charles perform an (unknown to him) illegal op-

Chapter 2

Texts

THE TOPIC OF ADULTERY

What drew Flaubert to adultery as a subject for his "third attempt" at a novel, after the 1845 version of *L'Education sentimentale* and the 1849 version of *La Tentation de saint Antoine?*[1] His imagination seems torn between a despairing sense of monotony and a frenetic escapism. Each of these extremes generates paradoxes. Henry, in the 1845 *Education*, impetuously flees to America with an older, married woman, only to become bored with her and to escape back to France, into an empty, elegant life of socializing and cliché. His friend Jules, a would-be novelist stuck in the provinces, successfully escapes at last to the world of his art. In the *Tentation*, the deluded, ascetic hermit sees wondrous exotic visions that emerge, unrecognized, from his own memories and imagination. As distractions from God, these visions humiliate him; as temptations of sex, luxury, and power, they make him confront his own moral weaknesses.

That Flaubert reworked and published both these works twenty-five years after completing the original versions illustrates how persistently certain motifs obsessed him, becoming the nuclei of future stories. His choice of female adultery as the subject of his first successful novel was overdetermined personally, socially, and literarily, without, of course, being predictable. When only fourteen, Flaubert had conceived a strong crush on a married woman, Caroline-Augustine-Elisa Schlésinger.[2] He had to settle for platonic adoration but saw her and her supposed husband socially. The fantasy of having sex with her preoccupied him intermittently for years. He would write to Elisa tenderly more than thirty years later. Obviously, that Flaubert himself never married meant that all his sexual experience took place outside of marriage, but as a novelist, he still found troubled marriages useful as a device for creating plot twists and obstacles that prolonged and complicated the action. Fictive adultery afforded an ideal way for him to blend his personal experience with the storyteller's art. More generally, in a world that offered women few opportunities and where divorce was illegal between 1814 and 1886, marriage was nearly the only option that allowed women to enjoy some sort of respectable social existence. But marriage itself often proved a trap for women, while their extramarital affairs could prove just as tedious and constraining as legitimate unions. Because men had more freedom of action (Emma Bovary compromises herself by being seen taking an innocent country walk with Léon to visit her baby; there is no talk of Léon's being compromised), even a mediocre man such as Frédéric Moreau in the 1869 *Education sentimentale* could enjoy the sadistic control inherent in juggling two or more affairs at once. Only wealthy, financially independent women could openly have affairs and still maintain their social standing. So adulterous women of Flaubert's time tended to be more desperate than their male counterparts; their resulting extravagances made them more newsworthy. Throughout the 1840s, several of them who murdered or committed suicide with poison were much in the news. The irony that the apparent rebellious triumph of adultery in such real-life situations was short-lived for women, often leading to situations worse than the original marriage, fit Flaubert's pessimistic views of life. He added a literary dimension to the topic of adultery when he parodied the morbid delectation of romantic literature, which encouraged unrealistic schemes such as Emma's, by showing how she had been seduced and betrayed by such literature before being seduced and betrayed by her lovers.

Flaubert creates a sense of inevitability in his plots by devising such a multistranded causality. In his great novels of the distant past, *Salammbô* and *La Tentation de saint Antoine,* he merges history with myth to create a fictive determinism. In his great novels of the near present, *Madame Bovary* and *L'Education sentimentale,* he merges social conditions with individual psychology.

HOW FLAUBERT DEVELOPED HIS PLOT OUTLINES

Flaubert's careful record keeping lets us trace the development of his creative process. He habitually laid the groundwork for his novels and short stories with great care. He claimed, "I never discard any piece of paper. It's a mania of mine." When his niece, Caroline Franklin-Grout, left the manuscripts of *Madame Bovary* to the Rouen town library in 1914, where they were catalogued as Manuscript gg 9, there were 1,793 pages of rough drafts, 3,400 pages of fair copies bound into six volumes, a final draft of 470 pages, and the copyist's manuscript showing the objections of the editors for Maxime Du Camp's *Revue de Paris*—they feared suppression by the royal censors—and the last-minute rewritings before publication in serial form. In addition, 62 pages of scenarios, notes, and sketches survived. From the first, Flaubert planned a narrative frame featuring Charles Bovary at the beginning and the end, before Emma's appearance and after she had died.[3]

Conceding that Flaubert often backtracked, returning to earlier phases of composition—"je refais un nouveau plan" [I'm redoing a scenario all over again] is a typical remark to his friends—we can nevertheless identify five main phases in his creative process. First, a gestation period: Flaubert often mentions a possible subject months or years before developing it. His life experience generated the setting from his earliest childhood onward. He situated *Madame Bovary* in the regions of Normandy he knew best: Bray and Caux. The imaginary composite town (Yonville) is sited roughly at Forges-les-Eaux, six miles from the western edge of the Bray region. In the Parisian basin north of the Seine, this small, fertile rectangular valley in Normandy, about twenty-five by thirty miles, has Beauvais near the southeast corner. The Caux, a chalky plateau, descends stepwise to the valley of the Seine in the south, to the English Channel in the northwest, to the borders of Bray and Picardy to the northeast, and to the valley of the Andelle to the east. It extends from about fourteen miles east of Rouen to Dieppe and east to Le Havre, forming a triangle bounded by the English Channel and nearly forty miles on a side. It was a recognizable region even before the Roman conquest. Flaubert observed his surroundings closely, characterizing the local terrain with a precision that even a professional geographer might envy.[4]

Visual observation was essential to Flaubert. He allegedly trained his beloved pupil Guy de Maupassant to write by assigning him the exercise of going down to the train station, studying all the coachmen there, and describing the features and physique of each in such detail that their identity would be unmistakable; he supposedly advised writers to study the trees around them until they could clearly perceive all the differences. He was not a naturalist, like, say, Victor Hugo in *Les Travailleurs de la mer*, a great regional novel of the Isle of Guernsey, but he did possess a keen visual sensibility to space, form, and colors. So it seems unfair to claim that he could not appreciate nature.[5] But just as he most delighted in the sounds and rhythms of words rather than their spellings, when describing the outdoors he does not name the flowers: he responds instead with keen sensuality to the sounds of nature, light, and temperature.[6] Critics have insisted, "For Flaubert the starting point for the conception of every story is a place— more accurately, is a graphic carving out of an area in space"; indoors, particular rooms serve as a point of departure for the action.[7] Without his long trip through the Middle East and down the Nile, he could not have completed *Salammbô* or *La Tentation de saint Antoine*.

Next, Flaubert developed scenarios that summarize the overall plot, its transitions between episodes, and the general emotional effect he wishes to produce. He may exploit more than one possibility at a time. In *Madame Bovary*, for instance, he probably combined a project about Don Juan (in his depiction of the seduction techniques and attitudes of Rodolphe) with the Delamare adultery-profligacy-poisoning scenario derived from a news item (for details, see the introduction and chapter 3). His literary sources were surprisingly few. "Once you have said that *Madame Bovary* borrows its scene of the sacrament of extreme unction [as Emma dies] from [Charles-Augustin de Sainte-Beuve's novel] *Volupté*, that Charles Bovary's first appearance in secondary school somewhat resembles a passage from Maxime Du Camp's *Livre posthume*, that Flaubert may have inherited his taste for ironic amplification and alliterative lists from Rabelais, and that M. Homais is a relative of Joseph Prudhomme, you have surveyed all the literary sources for *Madame Bovary*," with the exception of Honoré de Balzac's *La muse du département* and his *Physiologie du mariage*. In his "Smarh" (1839), Flaubert explicitly recommends the latter as a source for information on the psychological phases of a marriage relationship, starting with the disillusioning experience of a honeymoon for a romantic young woman, and on how too much education in literature and the arts can make her dissatisfied with the routines of marriage.[8] *Don Quixote,* one of Flaubert's favorite readings, may have distantly inspired his depiction of Emma Bovary's romantic delusions, but it seems misleading to add that the pharmacist Homais serves to contrast with her as Sancho Panza does with his master. Homais plays a much more dominant role than Sancho, as a major dramatic mover and the representative of the crass materialistic optimism that triumphs at the end of the novel—and he was not even present in Flaubert's first scenario.[9] A corollary of realism in literature, as opposed to romanticism, is that direct observation and nonfictional documentation become far more important than the literary tradition. Here, the "Mémoires de Madame Ludovica," a long handwritten manuscript in a crude style, supposedly written by a servant and confidante of the famous Parisian beauty Louise Pradier, provided details on the latter's adulteries and persistent financial problems. These would inspire many details of Emma Bovary's dealings with the merchant Lheureux. Flaubert frequented the Pradiers' salon in Paris and may have had sex with the hostess. The memoirs were found among his papers.[10]

Third came the rough draft, interrupted periodically by weeks or months of serious research to make Flaubert's depictions of places and professions more authentic. He took extensive reading notes (he may have read one hundred fifty works on history and religions to prepare for *Salammbô*), wrote descriptions of sites he visited, and interviewed experts in various subjects such as surgery, business law, and archeology—all in the interest of vivid, accurate portrayal.

Fourthly, Flaubert rewrote most sections at least twice. He might recast a key sentence ten or twelve times. During composition, he tested his prose for rhythm and euphony by reading it aloud to detect and eliminate undue quantities of *quis* and *ques*, strings of prepositional phrases, or repetition of sounds, words, or syllables too close together. He strove for a style that would have a compelling, hypnotic effect on the reader.

Finally, before final revisions, Flaubert consulted other writers. When possible, he read aloud to his friends when asking their opinion. One memorable reading, of the 1849 version of his *Tentation de saint Antoine,* lasted four days. He arranged regular consultations with his best friend Louis Bouilhet as he was completing *Madame Bovary.* Otherwise, he would write. In his letters, he frequently commented at length on his ideals for style and structure and on the progress of his writing. Consequently, we have ample material for studying the evolution of his texts. Since the 1970s, with the development of genetic criticism—the study of how a text comes into being through a series of *avant-textes*—the workings of the author's creative process have been seen as supremely important.[11]

FLAUBERT'S LETTERS LET US TRACE THE DEVELOPMENT OF HIS NOVEL

Flaubert's correspondence allows us to trace roughly half the composition of *Madame Bovary.*[12] On August 8, 1851, still smarting from his friends' condemnation of the 1849 version of *La Tentation de saint Antoine,* he writes to Louise Colet, "I have nothing [no creative writing] to show you. It's been more than two years now that I haven't written a single line of [fiction in] French.... Besides, I'm so disgusted with myself right now that this is not the time to start" (*CORR* 2:4). But six weeks later, he tells her "I started my novel yesterday evening. Now I'm glimpsing stylistic problems that terrify me. It's not an easy matter to be simple. I'm afraid of lapsing into the style of Paul de Kock or of doing Balzac flavored with Chateaubriand" (*CORR* 2:5, September 20, 1851).[13]

Most of the pertinent letters concerning the development of *Madame Bovary* were addressed to only two people. Between August 1851 and April 1854, Flaubert's mistress, Louise Colet, received nearly five hundred pages. To help her become a serious writer, he comments tactlessly but devotedly on her works in progress—of which the most ambitious are stories in decasyllabic verse—and bemusedly encourages her efforts to win the literary prizes that he himself scorns. He praises both her mind and body with real enthusiasm but insists on controlling the schedule of their meetings in Paris or, more often, in a hotel at a halfway point, in Mantes, making their time together contingent on his having finished a section of his novel. He insists on absolute peace and isolation in the country in order to write and habitually postpones their meetings when his work is not progressing well. But he writes long letters at least every few days, and his remarks to Colet about his novel obviously represent a way of being with her in spirit. These reports take us from part 1, chapter 6, of *Madame Bovary* through the botched clubfoot operation in part 2, chapter 11—53 percent of the novel. After Flaubert's breakup with Colet his comments—now much briefer—are nearly all addressed to his best friend, Louis Bouilhet, between August 2, 1854, and September 8, 1856. Four earlier letters to Bouilhet that mention *Madame Bovary* also survive.

Flaubert's surviving comments in the letters omit the narrative frame (part 1, chapters 1–5, and part 3, chapters 9–11), which presents Charles Bovary before he has married Emma and after her death. Flaubert also passes over the long middle section between when Emma demands too much of her lover Rodolphe (she wants him to flee the country with her; he promises to do so, but then betrays and abandons her instead) and the end of her second adulterous liaison, with Léon, who had loved her platonically earlier (part 2, chapter 12, through part 3, chapter 5).

To juxtapose Flaubert's life with the history of the composition of *Madame Bovary* suggests some speculative connections with the sections of the novel that he does not discuss in his letters. Flaubert's comments about women, when he writes Louise Colet, display a shockingly insensitive gender stereotyping and misogyny.[14] Frequently he says that these comments do not apply to her, because she has a virile mind, but he also—sounding like Professor Henry Higgins in George Bernard Shaw's *Pygmalion*—says often that she should write more like a man. At length, he begins addressing her condescendingly as "chère sauvage." In other words, he labels her conventionally as a creature governed by impulse and instinct, more primitive than a male. In his mind, as his neglect made her more and more demanding, she must have served increasingly as a model for the hysterical Emma Bovary. As Flaubert composes part 2 of his novel, Rodolphe's growing disaffection with and final rejection of Emma, who from his point of view wants to complicate unduly "such a simple thing as love" (meaning sex), parallels Flaubert's progressive rejection of Louise Colet. Rodolphe's flight anticipates Flaubert's farewell letter of March 6, 1855. "I've been told that you came to my apartment three times to try to talk to me," he writes, brusquely. "I wasn't in, and I shall never be in for you again" (*CORR* 2:572).

A timetable correlating Flaubert's letters with the creation of the novel follows. He averaged just over six completed pages a month (counting those in the published Garnier-Flammarion edition): 364 in fifty-eight months. Page numbers, when provided, refer to volume 2 of the *Correspondance* edited by Jean Bruneau.

9/20/51: writing begins (5).

3/3/52: reading girls' romance novels to prepare for I.6 on Emma's education (55–56). *9% done in 10% of the time of composition.*

4/4/52: women mistake their cunt for their heart [*sic*] and think the moon was made to light their boudoir (refers to Emma's disillusionment with marriage in I.7; 80–81).

9/9/52: eight pages of description of the couple's new home, Yonville-l'abbaye (II.1; 150). *20% done in 20% of the time.*

9/13/52, 10/9/52: struggling to create the conversation at the inn, where Emma and Léon meet and discover their affinities (II.2).

12/16/52, 1/15/53: their unspoken platonic love (II.3–5).

rhythm of life in his depiction of his heroine by alternating long periods of frustrated waiting with brief bursts of action, providing gratifications that often were
illusory or pernicious. (Again, one thinks of his long-distance relationship with
Louise Colet.) The first surviving scenario, only two pages long, clearly follows
Emma from her marriage to her suicide, characterizing her as an avid reader of
romance novels, as needing luxury, and as a debtor to Lheureux for fabrics and
furnishings. Flaubert imagines Emma as silently frustrated, hungry for adventure, a sensualist but not a creator. He depicts Charles as gentle, sensitive, and
fair-minded, but unimaginative and of only average intelligence. (The representation of Charles's inner life was sacrificed to make room for the thoughts of
the developing characters Homais and Emma.)[16] The latter resembles Charles
in being weak and malleable but is more intelligent and more selfish. Flaubert
initially planned a sexual relationship rather than a platonic friendship between
Emma and Léon at the beginning, but he later decided to make the experienced
Rodolphe responsible for Emma's first affair and for her sexual awakening. He
increased her vulnerability by giving her a keen sense of missed opportunity
with Léon, nourishing the feeling that she deserves compensation for having
been so virtuous as to resist her desire for him. Flaubert masterfully depicts how
Emma's moral resistance gradually erodes under the tedium of her isolated
small-town life and the impetus of her histrionic need for attention.

Flaubert later sacrificed a scene at the chateau of La Vaubyessard, written in
April 1852, in which Emma takes a walk on the grounds at dawn and then looks
through the varicolored panes of a summerhouse in the gardens, while the narrator remarks on the transformations of the colors and the mood they create.
The final pane seems to bathe the scene in blood, an ominous premonition inspired by two scenes in Le Rouge et le Noir part 1, chapters 5 and 28, where
Julien finds himself in churches draped with crimson cloth (he will later shoot
Madame de Rênal, his former and future mistress, inside a church, and, eventually, be decapitated). Both by being digressive and by presenting a vague but
accurate intuition of Emma's fate, this scene enhances and validates the authenticity of her subjectivity more than Flaubert cares to do: he wishes to depict her as always blind and deluded. In the event, Rodolphe's wish for fleeting
pleasures clashes with Emma's possessive desire to hold him forever, according
to the ideas of love she has derived from the vague endings of novels; later, her
desire for an intense codependent relationship with Léon eventually drives away
that weak, cowardly man.

Homais was a later addition, a pompous clown whose rhetoric of science and
progress create "a constant counterpoint" both to Emma's passionate senti-
mentalism and to the priest Bournisien's simple-minded Catholicism. This counterpoint is played in the parallel conversations between Homais and Charles,
Emma and Léon during their first meeting in Le Lion d'Or when the Bovarys
arrive at Yonville. It climaxes in the scene of the county fair (Les Comices), bring-
ing nearly all the characters on stage and orchestrating their remarks like a sym-
phony, where Rodolphe's cynical seduction speech invoking ethereal elective

affinities is interwoven with justifications for bourgeois materialism. Flaubert researched this scene by attending the fair of Grand-Couronne on July 18, 1852, and Homais's distorted report in *Le Fanal de Rouen* closely follows the account Flaubert read in *le Nouvelliste de Rouen* on July 19. In both the fictional and the real fair, an old servant received a prize for many years of service (Gothot-Mersch, *La Genèse*, 199). The scene took Flaubert the latter half of 1853 to compose.[17]

Once he had drafted the scenarios, Flaubert wrote full versions of the scenes he had in mind, making serious attempts to articulate each to its neighbors organically, according to a verisimilar, complex, but unstated progression of cause and effect. His simplest device is to announce, in the final sentence of a chapter, the essence of what will happen in the next. See, for example, in part 2, the endings of chapters 3, 4, 7, and 9–14.

HOW FLAUBERT REFINED HIS PROSE STYLE

Finally, Flaubert would polish his prose carefully. Nearly all this effort consisted in sacrificing material, creating a lean, economical narrative purged of what he considered the flowery, diffuse habits of romantic writers—long descriptions, distracting ornate comparisons, abundant adjectives, otiose details. Simultaneously, he tried to suppress his ribald Rabelaisian verve, which tended to the grotesque.

A compilation of many discarded vignettes can be found in the two volumes edited by Gabrielle Leleu in 1936. Jeanne Goldin has devoted a rather plodding study to the scenes and variants for the county fair at which Rodolphe begins to seduce Emma.[18] The Nouvelle Version of *Madame Bovary*, which blends into a coherent narrative the words of the final version, together with some passages Flaubert thought of using and then sacrificed, exemplifies what occurs during the final stage of his creative process. In the two paragraphs that follow, the words shown in regular type were preserved in the published novel; the words in italics were cut during revision. Here is Charles's first appearance in the novel, on his first day in school.

C'était un *gros* gars de la campagne, d'une quinzaine d'années environ, et plus haut de taille qu'aucun de nous tous *et qui commençait presque à avoir de la barbe.* Il avait les cheveux coupés droit *et peignés* comme un chantre de village. *La couleur en était d'un blond sale, entre le brun et le châtain, de même que les longs poils clairsemés, qui garnissaient ses mâchoires, calmaient la violence de son beau teint rose et donnaient à l'ensemble de sa tête un ton général gris, indécis et comme poussiéreux.* [Printed version: Les longs poils fins qui veloutaient ses joues comme une moisissure blonde, tamisant l'éclat vif de ses pommettes, estompaient d'un duvet incolore sa figure tranquille.] Il *était carré* des épaules, *avait de larges mains,* qui *sortaient* de son habit-veste vert à boutons noirs. *Son* pantalon *purée de pois,* très tiré, *d'où sortaient* comme d'un *étui deux* jambes en bas bleus, *chaussées de gros* souliers *à* clous, mal cirés, *souliers d'un cuir dur, avec lesquels il marcha précautionneusement, sur le parquet de l'étude, pour aller s'asseoir près de la fenêtre, à la place qu'on lui désigna pour sienne ... (134)*

[He was a *big* boy from the country, about fifteen, taller than any of us, and *just about to have a beard*. His hair was cut straight across *and without a part*, like a village choir-boy. *It was a dirty blond color, between brown and chestnut, as were the long, sparse hairs that garnished his jawbone, moderating the violent pink color of his agreeable complexion, and giving his head, overall, a generally gray, ambiguous, and, as it were, dusty tone.* (The long, fine velvety hairs that covered his cheeks like a blond mold, filtering the vivid brightness of his cheekbones, blurred his calm face with a colorless down.) He had *square* shoulders, *and wide hands, that were sticking out of* this three-piece green suit with black buttons. *His* pea-soup colored *trousers* were very tight on him; *and from them, as if from a sheath,* stuck out two legs in blue stockings, *shod with heavy* hobnailed shoes, clumsily polished, *shoes of a hard leather, on which he walked cautiously, on the wooden floor of the study hall, in order to go sit near the window, at the desk that had been pointed out to him as his.*]

As Flaubert revised, he eliminated the extraneous detail that comes from a scrupulous concern with the full reporting characteristic of realism. Of course Charles would walk on the floor, Flaubert would think to himself, not on the walls or the ceiling; and of course he would sit at his assigned seat, not somewhere else.

To depict how awkward Charles is and how he sticks out among his classmates, Flaubert heavily uses the mimetic device of hypotyposis (vivid description), ordinarily deployed to represent a person or object that is feared or scorned. Such descriptions may depict their objects as (1) larger than life; (2) garish, with clashing colors; often, (3) excessively marked or covered with coarse or curly hair, facial hair or tattoos, scars and other disfigurements, parasites, birthmarks and blotches, and so forth; and (4) clumsy, ill-dressed, and unkempt, calling attention to themselves by gracelessness of movement as well as dress and grooming. But as he revises, Flaubert attenuates his satiric exuberance and abridges a description whose length and detail call attention to the author at the expense of verisimilitude. In the earlier versions, Flaubert depicts Charles as quite tall, with square shoulders, broad hands, big shoes, and arms and legs that stick out of his clothes. But in the final version, he deprives Charles of physical features that might suggest superior strength; he wants to deny Charles any attributes that might allow him to master a situation—even through brute strength. So he suppresses any allusions to a strong body: build (Charles is no longer *gros*), square shoulders, and broad hands. (Later, Old Rouault will find his future son-in-law *un peu gringalet*—rather puny.) To prevent Charles from seeming monstrous or caricatural, Flaubert also reduces from eight to four the mentions of color in the young man's description, omitting the gray, pink, and pea-soup, while leaving the black, green, blond, and blue. And he eliminates the pejorative "dirty" blond as a hair color. The codes of clumsiness and of excess combine in details of the coarse hobnailed shoes (more suitable for farm work

than the classroom), the long, scattered hairs that "garnished" Charles's jawbone (softened, in the final version, to a colorless down that blurs his face), and
the arms and legs protruding from his outgrown clothes. The clumsiness code
also persists in notations of Charles's rustic appearance, but his gait no longer
seems faintly ridiculous. Flaubert prefers to show rather than tell, and he will
bring out Charles's clumsiness richly in the ensuing scene when the new boy
does not know what to do with his hat and when he first mumbles and then bel-
lows his name—making both marked choices for telling the schoolmaster his
identity, two opposite extremes rather than the appropriate middle way.

Shortly after, in the description of Charles's grotesque cap, the trace of his
mother's loving, hyperprotective, and ineffectual domination, a comparison between the full possible version culled by Leleu and Pommier from the drafts,
and the final text, again shows how stringently Flaubert disciplined his ebullient
imagination:

C'était une de ces coiffures d'ordre composite, où l'on retrouve *réunis* les éléments du
bonnet à poil, du chapska, du chapeau rond, de la casquette de loutre et du bonnet de
coton, *synthèse des disgracieusetés et des incommodités de toutes les autres, une monstruosité en fait de chapellerie, l'une de ces ineptes créations de l'homme, qui sont dé-
plorables à voir,* une de ces pauvres choses, enfin, *où la matière elle-même semble triste,
et* dont la laideur *silencieuse* a des profondeurs d'expression *misérable* comme le visage
d'un imbécile. (134–35)

[It was one of those composite pieces of headgear where you can find, *reunited,* features
of the fur bonnet, the shako, the bowler hat, the visored otter-skin cap, and the cotton
nightcap, *a synthesis of the ill-favorednesses and incommodities of all the others, a mon-
strosity of haberdashery, one of those inept human creations that are deplorable to see,*
in brief, one of those wretched objects *whose very material appears sad, and* whose *silent*
ugliness conveys depths of *misery* like the face of an imbecile.]

As Flaubert's playful creativity carries him away, he begins to write a pastiche
of Rabelais (as he once did in a letter to a friend), stuffing the passage with heavy,
Latinate, archaic polysyllabic nouns from the Renaissance such as *disgracieusetés, incommodités, monstruosité,* and *chapellerie;* he then reinforces the
impression of *le grotesque triste* (the lugubriousness of a freak show) with a
string of adjectives within a single sentence: "inept, deplorable, sad, silent,
wretched"—all of which, on reflection, he regretfully sacrifices to achieve (we
may assume) a taut, economical style.

As Flaubert revises his first portrait of Emma in part 1, chapter 6, he dimin-
ishes her superiority. Initially, she fasts for an entire day (185); in the final version, she merely *tries* to do so. The ruined aristocrat who does the laundry in
the convent is, in the first version, drawn to Emma and a few others among the
girls because they seem "inherently distinguished" (187). And in her first
incarnation, Emma does serious reading: not just vague novels in the *genre
troubadour* (conventional romantic medievalism, like diluted Walter Scott), but

real classics: Madame de Staël's *Corinne* (ironically, about a superior, artistically gifted woman who falls in love with a less sensitive and duller man) and Ann Radcliffe's Gothic novels. On the other hand, when Emma returns from the convent school to her father's farm, the first version spells out her ineptitude in creating or performing high culture: her awkward drawing and clumsy piano playing (191, 195). Charles, in contrast, is depicted more favorably than later, content because he has "healthy organs working in harmony with a pure soul" (194).[19]

After Emma's marriage, her lonely walks with her whippet are treated at much greater length in the earlier version (200–202). She confides in the dog because she feels she has nobody to talk to, and her grandiosity flourishes in the hothouse of her imagination. Flaubert signals her attitude equivocally in part 1, chapter 7, when Emma's mother-in-law finds in her "un genre trop relevé pour leur position de fortune," a lifestyle too pretentious for people with their income. But Charles's mother is jealous of her son's blind devotion to his wife. Can we trust her perceptions? The remainder of the novel will bear them out only too well.

The ball at La Vaubyessard (part 1, chapter 8) that follows offers an interlude of ecstatic fulfillment, during which Emma can imagine herself one of the elite. Flaubert's less realistic treatment of the episode in revisions produces a more realistic result in terms of his purpose. Faithful to Emma's viewpoint, he shows her dazzled by a sumptuous display of wealth such as she has never seen. Flaubert suppresses half the descriptive detail of the drafts in the final version because Emma is a less acute observer than he; moreover, her fantasies of romance and glamour distract her. Owing to the gender transposition, Flaubert's most probable models for Emma's bedazzlement have passed unnoticed—scenes of a young provincial seeing a luxurious Parisian townhouse for the first time, in Stendhal's *Le Rouge et le Noir* (1830) and Balzac's *Le Père Goriot* (1834).

In the drafts, Flaubert had analyzed at length the boredom of the noble *fils de famille* among their social inferiors at the ball and the impossibility of serious communication between the nobility and the bourgeoisie beyond the merely pragmatic. The marquis hosts the ball because he seeks election to political office. At the same time, Flaubert equitably satirizes the petite bourgeoisie's apparently irremediable admiration for the old aristocracy's dissolute, parasitical lifestyle. The strongest affirmation of Emma's blindness is the juxtaposition, in both drafts and final text, of the deaf, drooling ruin of a man, the old Duke of Laverdière, at table, with Emma's enchanted reaction to tales of his adventurous, self-destructive life of debauchery, duels, gambling, and elopements. She translates the rumor that he had been Marie-Antoinette's lover into "He had lived at Court and slept in the beds of queens!" (drafts 206, text 109). The blind beggar of the final chapters, who may be syphilitic, is a degraded doublet of the duke: both display the consequences of an existence lived all for "love," meaning sexual gratification. Later, in both versions, Emma overhears a conversation about Italy. The drafts (212) associate that country with the elopement of a married woman, but the ending of the story becomes inaudible. This narrative fore-shadowing of Emma's plans for escape with Rodolphe does not conclude in the novel, both because those plans will not be realized in fact and because the outcome would have been disastrous if they had been carried out. Thus the anecdote resembles the tale perused by Dante's Paolo and Francesca in the *Inferno* and interrupted by their lovemaking—"We read no more that day"—before they reach the admonitory conclusion of their book. In the drafts, the first section of the novel (part 1, chapter 9) concludes with Emma's growing distaste for Charles, her orgy of expenditures on a pleasure trip to Rouen, her nervous tics, and her manipulativeness (228–36), explicitly associated, here, with her wish to have been born a man.[20]

Like the ball scene, Emma's first encounter with her future lover Léon simultaneously emphasizes two contradictory elements: subjective affinity and objective incompatibility. The published version of her conversation with Léon when she first arrives at Yonville notes one gesture or posture by him; the drafts remind us of their physicality by noting ten—four each by Emma and Léon, and two mutual moves, when they steadily draw nearer to each other and when he takes her arm. But just before this moment, the original text, through commentary by the omniscient author, emphasized the contrast between Emma's passionate nature and Léon's more timid, temperate one (256, 257–59).

The draft version of the April evening when Emma goes to the priest Bournisien to seek spiritual help (part 2, chapter 6) greatly expands the portrayal of her subjectivity and its frustrations. An impressionistic style adds fourteen adjectives and some adverbial intensifiers, plus a hallucinatory experience during which Emma wishes "que l'existence pût disparaître" (that her existence might vanish, 301). The tragicomic dialogue of the deaf between the young woman and the priest, in which he relentlessly mistranslates her appeals for spiritual help into physical terms, accumulates nine *quiproquos* instead of only four as in the final text (303–5).

The next chapter (part 2, chapter 7) shifts from Emma's platonic love for Léon (who has finally left, despairing of winning her, to pursue his law career in Paris) to her seduction by Rodolphe. Here Flaubert marks time; he wants to suggest that a decent interval has elapsed between Emma's involvements with two men so that we will not simply judge her as an undiscriminating nymphomaniac. Her inner life and complex motivation must be portrayed. But then Flaubert confronts a dilemma: the more such psychological analyses are expanded, the more we become aware of the omniscient author who alone, within the text, would be capable of making them. Thus he spoils the austere, impersonal tone he has sought throughout the novel. The outcome reflects the considerable, and in this instance perhaps regrettable, sacrifices Flaubert made to preserve an aura of impersonality. The original included a much richer analysis of Emma's despair after the fall; her idealization of Léon crystallizes (in a manner that suggests Flaubert's close reading of Stendhal's *De l'amour* and his novels) and then gradually modulates into a deeper hatred of Charles; she compensates by indulging in expensive purchases, and she alternates pathologically between excessive animation and torpor (319–23).

Flaubert sketched two other possible solutions in the drafts for this chapter. He tried to use the pause in the action, which occurs nearly halfway through the text, as an opportunity to develop social satire of bourgeois mediocrity and hatred of the talented and exceptional. So he introduces a three-page discussion between Homais and Charles's mother, who is visiting, on the importance of religion as a guarantor of morality. (The reader here recalls how ineffectual the priest Bournisien has proven in this role, in the previous chapter, and the "macrotext" of Flaubert's entire career reinforces this irony by associating religion—in *Salammbô* and "Hérodias," for example—with sadism and bloody sacrifice.)[21] They agree that romance novels such as those Emma reads are pernicious because they embellish reality, only to lead to more painful disappointments afterward (327). Then the omniscient author intervenes at length to associate Homais and Charles's mother in a blanket condemnation. They join in criticizing Madame Bovary because

[t]here was in Emma's mannerisms, her language, her glance, and even in her clothes, something exceptional that disturbed their ideas. They vaguely saw there a higher form of disorder, and so they hated it, they pursued it with the relentless fury that provokes governments and families to oppose all forms of originality. (327)

Unfortunately, this reflection distracts us by calling attention to the privileges of omniscience; it also weakens the consistency of characterization by implying that the self-absorbed, self-satisfied Homais is momentarily much more insecure and more alert and sensitive to others than normally; it implausibly unites the Voltairean pharmacist and the pious mother-in-law; and it transforms the selfish, mediocre antiheroine into a martyr to conformity, bathing her in an unwonted aura of authentic superiority. So Flaubert abandoned the scene.

A third section of the drafts for part 2, chapter 7, develops the motif of the pharmacist's assistant, Justin, as a Cherubino figure hopelessly infatuated with Emma and seeking every pretext to be close to her. And the fourth topic, interwoven with the third, seeks to reinforce the transition to Rodolphe's seduction in part 2, chapter 8, at the agricultural fair. When he tells an anecdote about a duel of honor where he presumably served as a second, Emma looks him up and down.[22] Rodolphe's expanded musings about her allure conclude the chapter. In other words, Flaubert originally motivates their mutual attraction with a conventional gender-based code: brave man, attractive woman. Eliminating some elements of this code in the final text leaves more to the imagination of the reader.[23]

After the botched clubfoot operation and Emma's reconciliation with Rodolphe, Flaubert greatly develops, in the drafts, the future chapter 11 of part 2. There, in contrast to the published novel, Emma again takes three horseback rides a week with Rodolphe; the latter often has dinner with the Bovarys; she plays romantic songs after dinner, shamelessly staring at him and stressing the words "heart" and "happiness" when she sings (414). The lawyer Guillaumin, an occasional guest, also seems to lust after Emma and to be seeking to exchange confidences with Rodolphe. Flaubert experiments here with depicting her as more thoroughly integrated into Yonvillais society—and not just the pious society of church ladies—while scandalizing that society at the same time. In the drafts, her man's vest seems a shocking gender inversion (424).

Regarding Rodolphe's preparations to write a farewell letter to Emma before he leaves town, successive drafts deepen the analysis of the negative crystallization that both results from and reinforces his resolve. When he contemplates the miniature portrait of herself that she has given him,

[t]he colors [seemed to him] abominable, the drawing distorted, and the fit of her clothes, ridiculous; her complexion was coarsely ruddy like a peasant's; her [flirtatious sidelong glance], shameless ... and Rodolphe confessed to himself that, after all, she was not exceptionally pretty. (part 2, chapter 12: 436–47)

Originally, Rodolphe's attitudes in this scene were even more fatuously self-satisfied than in the final version. As he rereads letters from three former lovers, "Rodolphe day-dreamed of them as nonchalantly as a pasha ogling his harem, and he complimented himself on having had more mistresses than any of his friends" (437–38). In contrast, Emma's shock and anguish on receiving his letter of rejection are intensified, as is the hallucinatory experience, inspired by Flaubert's epileptic attacks, that anticipates the moments just before her suicide. The drafts emphasize Charles's uncomprehending, stolid obtuseness. At supper, while he obliviously eats one of the apricots that had concealed Rodolphe's letter in a basket, the juice runs grotesquely down his cheeks (in a variant, down his *babines,* a word used for an animal's muzzle). Thus Flaubert implies that Emma could have no hope of achieving emotional communion with him.[24]

Much of the remainder of the novel, although still extensively retouched, was not changed nearly so much during composition as were the earlier sections. When Emma seeks desperately to raise money to prevent seizure of her household effects, the drafts make her more calculating and less pitiable than does the final version. As she goes to ask money of the lawyer Guillaumin, who she has learned is attracted to her, she smiles at the thought of seducing him; his proposition was originally much more detailed and explicit, mingled with protestations of love; and the major impediment to her prostitution is that she wants the money in hand first, while he first wants the sex (582–86). Thus her approaching Binet a few minutes later becomes more plausible.

In the drafts, one finds more frankly physical details of Emma's death and dying. One moment, recognizing Charles's kindness, she strokes his hair while he thinks that all his happiness has depended on her (603); seeing Emma's bare feet during extreme unction, he recalls when he first undressed her (611); and after she has died, he bares her breasts and kisses them (614). Emma may at times seem contemptible and Charles pitiable, but eliminating such homely details from the final version further distances us from the two main characters. In contrast, in both the drafts and the final version, the physicality, confusion, fatigue, pain, and fear in minor characters such as Old Rouault allow us to identify with them as fellow human beings. Homais, however, a grotesque but nearly allegorical figure, strikes one as disembodied, achieving a certain abstract grandeur because his unscrupulousness thus comes to seem transcendent.

Flaubert cannot resist adding some grotesque details, later suppressed, to the drafts of the final chapter, emphasizing the fatuousness of several characters. Léon imagines that Emma may have killed herself from frustrated love for him (632); he becomes vain, self-confident, and a dangerous seducer. Charles's mother says that Emma "was born to be a kept woman in Paris," a remark the narrator approves as "a deep insight" (633). The development of Homais's writing career, starting with journalism, is traced; the text notes that the pharmacist likes to compare himself, as a polymath, to Goethe and to Michelangelo (636). Flaubert notes that Rodolphe, the main dramatic mover of the novel, could never have understood Charles's all-consuming love and devotion. Although eventually suppressed, this playful profusion of ludicrous and pitiable detail—*le grotesque triste*—contrasts starkly with the immaculate aridity that later characterizes the conclusion of *L'Education sentimentale* when all emotion evaporates, leaving only the perfectly economical, dismissive sequel to the adventures of the antihero Frédéric Moreau: "Il voyagea"—He traveled. Thus Flaubert adopts Baudelaire's conclusion to *Les Fleurs du Mal*.

THE LOST POSTMODERN ENDING TO *MADAME BOVARY*

Having completed *Madame Bovary*, Flaubert could not resist experimenting with a postmodern ending worthy of the Theater of the Absurd. In a section entitled "Epilogue," Homais stands alone in front of his mirror, contemplating the newly awarded cross of the Legion of Honor on his chest.

Doute de son existence. *délire. effets fantastiques. Sa croix répétée dans les glaces, pluie foudre de ruban.*—ne suis-je qu'un personnage de roman, le fruit d'une imagination en délire, l'invention d'un petit paltaquot [*sic*] que j'ai vu naître et *qui m'a inventé pr [pour] faire croire que je n'existe pas.*—Oh cela n'est pas possible. Voilà les fœtus. *Voilà mes enfants/voilà.voilà.*

Puis se résumant il finit par le gd [grand] mot du rationalisme moderne Cogito; ergo sum. (Folio 39 recto, in Leclerc)

[Doubt concerning his reality. delirium. hallucinatory effects. His decoration reflected in multiple images in the mirror panels, the ribbon like rain and lightning—am I only a character in a novel, the product of a fevered imagination, the invention of a little pipsqueak [*paltoquet*] whose birth I witnessed and who invented me to create the impression that I don't exist.—Oh that's not possible. There are the fetuses [preserved in glass bottles in his pharmacy]. There are my children. There they are. There they are.

Then, summing himself up, he concluded with the definitive slogan of modern rationalism: "I think; therefore I am."]

Thus the all-triumphant bourgeois character Homais acquires an independent existence at the end, denying that he could possibly have had a creator. Flaubert chose not to add this postmodern ending to his novel, but—like Victor Hugo in the hyper-experimental "Théâtre en liberté"—he was easily capable of imagining it. He knew his public was not ready for such a radical innovation.[25]

COMPARATIVE RATINGS OF AVAILABLE TEXTS

After the initial publication of *Madame Bovary*, all editions have suffered from inaccuracies, deficiencies in documentation, excessive cost—or a combination of these defects. A national survey of college and university instructors a few years ago asked their preferences among both French and English-language editions for research and for teaching. In courses, where reducing costs for students is a major concern, two-thirds of the survey respondents use the 1986 Garnier-Flammarion edition by Bernard Ajac, which includes a chronology and an introduction. An appendix reproduces the lawyers' and judge's speeches at the trial of Flaubert and his publisher Maxime Du Camp (as editor of *La Revue de Paris*) for subverting public morals (see chapter 6 of this volume on the reception of the novel). Based on the 1873 Charpentier edition, this version unfortunately does include a few annoying errors, although Ajac's choice of it conforms to the widely accepted scholarly practice of using the latest text version that appeared during an author's lifetime and that was reviewed by the author prior to publication. Nearly all the remaining instructors have adopted the Folio or the Classiques Garnier editions. For the research library, Claudine Gothot-Mersch's edition is considered definitive.

Half the instructors who teach in English use the Norton Critical Editions, which combines the old translation by Eleanor Marx Aveling, Karl Marx's daughter, with some modifications by the late Paul de Man. It still contains errors. De Man added translations of a few scenarios and preliminary versions of scenes, sixteen critical essays, and three letters by Flaubert in addition to a critical bibliography. An updated translation recently appeared in this series. The remaining instructors' preferences were distributed rather evenly among translations by Lowell Bair (Bantam Classics), Gerard Manley Hopkins (The World's Classics edition by Terence Cave, at Oxford University Press), Francis Steegmuller (Random House's Modern College Library), and Alan Russell (Viking Penguin). Those who compared translations found Lowell Bair's version less stilted than Aveling and De Man's and more accurate than Steegmuller's.[26]

NOTES

1. Flaubert uses this phrase in his letter of January 16, 1852.

2. Actually still Foucaut, she passed as married to Schlésinger and would be after her first husband died. Some claim Flaubert had a lifelong crush on her, but the evidence of their contacts suggests not (see Bruneau in *CORR* 1:894–95).

3. *CORR* 2:315, letter to Louise Colet, April 26, 1853. Further references to the letters come from this edition. For basic information on the manuscripts as well as a diplomatic transcription of the scenarios, notes, and outlines, see Yvan Leclerc's indispensable edition of *Gustave Flaubert: Plans et scenarios de* Madame Bovary (Paris: CNRS/Zulma, 1995).

4. Jean Canu, "La 'Couleur normande' de *Madame Bovary*," *PMLA* 48 (1933): 167–208 (167–68). Charles is a country boy ill at ease in the city of Rouen; Emma longs only to leave the country to go to Rouen or to Paris (169–70). Canu gives many examples of Norman local color manifested through landscapes, weather, buildings, language, food, crops, and behavior. See also René Herval, *Les Véritables Origines de* Madame Bovary (Paris: Nizet, 1957), 91, 109–10, 113. Canu situates the action in the Caux—accurate for Rouen. Herval situates the action in the Roumois—which lies along the Seine south of the scenes in *Madame Bovary*—and in the Bray. Yonville's fictive setting appears to be on the border between the Bray and the Caux, some six miles west of its main model, Forges-Les-Eaux.

5. "Flaubert aimait peu la nature, et tout de même, ça lui a manqué." Jules Renard, *Journal*, Léon Guichard and Georges Sigaux, eds. (Paris: Gallimard, 1960), 1038. Visiting the Cauchois region, André Gide went so far as to say, "Pas de plus assoupissante atmosphère qui celle de ce pays. Je me doute qu'elle contribua beaucoup à la lenteur et difficulté du travail de Flaubert. Où il croyait lutter contre les mots, c'était contre le ciel." *Journal 1889–1939* (Paris: Gallimard, 1960), 1025.

6. Emma Bovary shares with her creator an acute sensitivity to temperature and humidity. Jean Starobinski has analyzed this important physical trait, which reflects her primary narcissism, in his excellent "L'Echelle des températures: Lecture du corps dans *Madame Bovary*," *Le Temps de la Réflexion* (Paris: Gallimard, 1980), 145–83.

7. Isabelle Daunais, *Flaubert et la scénographie romanesque* (Paris: Nizet, 1993), 9, 68 (translation mine). See also Jacques Neefs, "La Figuration réaliste: L'exemple de *Madame Bovary*," *Poétique* 4.16 (November 1973): 466–76.

8. See Claudine Gothot-Mersch, *La Genèse de* Madame Bovary (Paris: Corti, 1966), 51.

La Physiologie du mariage, although written by a lifelong bachelor over 170 years ago, should not be dismissed lightly. Dr. Laurence Pernoud, the French pediatrician equivalent to Dr. Spock in the United States, cites Balzac's novel at length to describe the experience of pregnancy, in her often-reprinted *J'élève mon enfant.*

9. On Balzac's influence, see Gothot-Mersch, *La Genèse*, 50–58, and "Balzac, Honoré de," in Laurence M. Porter, ed., *A Gustave Flaubert Encyclopedia* (Westport, CT: Greenwood, 2001), 20–21, including a bibliography supplementing the older references provided by Gothot-Mersch.

10. See Benjamin F. Bart, *Flaubert* (Syracuse, NY: Syracuse University Press, 1967), 267–68, and Jean Pommier and Gabrielle Leleu, "Du Nouveau sur *Madame Bovary*," *Revue d'histoire littéraire de la France* 47 (1947): 216–26. The manuscript is preserved as Ms g 226⁴, folios 233 ff., in the Bibliothèque de Rouen.

11. See Eric Le Calvez, "Genetic Criticism" and "Genetic Editions," in Laurence M. Porter, ed., *A Gustave Flaubert Encyclopedia* (Westport, CT: Greenwood, 2001): 145–48.

12. See Vincent Kaufmann, *L'Equivoque épistolaire* (Paris: Minuit, 1990).

13. Paul de Kock (1793–1871) was an immensely popular writer of humorous light novels and comedies, which provide valuable insights into everyday life between 1815 and 1848. To write like Balzac with a Chateaubrianesque flavor probably means to treat the contemporary scene in novels that would combine melodrama with grandiloquence and grandiosity. In other words, in his depiction of ordinary people in everyday life, Flaubert will try to navigate between the Scylla of pomposity and the Charybdis of frivolity.

14. See Martine Fisher, "L'Art des sacrifices: La correspondance de Flaubert avec Louise Colet de 1851 à 1854," 75–85 in *Les Femmes de lettres: Ecriture féminine ou spécificité générique?* (Montreal: University of Montreal Press, 1994). Several other studies of this correspondence have recently appeared or are in progress: one should check the latest bibliographies to identify them.

15. "Scénarios, esquisses et plans de *Madame Bovary,*" 1–129 in Gustave Flaubert, Madame Bovary: *Nouvelle Version précédée des scénarios inédits; textes établis sur les manuscrits de Rouen avec une introduction et des notes,* eds. Jean Pommier and Gabrielle Leleu (Paris: Corti, 1949).

16. For many examples from the sketches and drafts, see Pommier and Leleu 158, 165, 175, 179–81, 269, and 508–9.

17. For some details in this paragraph and the previous one, I am indebted to Rosemary Lloyd's succinct presentation in her *Madame Bovary* (London: Unwin Hyman, 1990), 47–51.

18. Gabrielle Leleu, ed., Madame Bovary: *Ebauches et fragments inédits, recueillis d'après les manuscrits,* 2 vols. (Paris: Conard, 1936); and Jeanne Goldin, ed., *Les Comices agricoles de* Madame Bovary *de Flaubert: Transcription intégrale et genèse,* 2 vols. (Geneva: Droz, 1984). Unfortunately, Madame Goldin presents the 323 pages of this scene in an arbitrary order established by the library rather than according to the order of composition.

The lengthy drafts presenting the agricultural fair contain several mentions, later suppressed, of ironic repetition and anticipation: at the beginning, the fourteen lamps hung on the town hall above a gaping crowd anticipate the fireworks display that concludes the festivities.

19. An illuminating article by Graham Falconer, "Flaubert assassin de Charles," shows how Emma's husband was originally more independent and had a livelier imagination in the early notes and drafts, where his inner thoughts appear more often than in later versions. See Michael Issacharoff, ed., *Langages de Flaubert* (Paris: Lettres Modernes, 1976), 115–41.

20. The drafts return to these motifs later. During the stroll to look at the cotton mill under construction in part 2, chapter 5, the drafts greatly develop Charles's hateful appearance and Léon's appeal from Emma's viewpoint (285–86). The moment when her hatred crystallizes is dramatized in the drafts (299). Léon's idealization of her is explored (296–97). And Flaubert mentions that Charles, as a mother, would have nursed a baby and is surprised that Emma doesn't want to (269).

21. The term *macrotext* has been recently introduced and explored by Eric Le Calvez in *"Le Père Goriot* and *La Comédie humaine:* from Text to Macrotext," in Michal Peled Ginsburg, ed., *Approaches to Teaching Balzac's* Old Goriot (New York: Modern Language Association of America, 2000), 23–31.

22. Flaubert would later use a similar motif in *L'Education sentimentale:* at a dinner party attended by three women who are attracted to the antihero, it is revealed that he has fought a duel with an opponent who collapsed from fright. The detail hints that the women would become more attracted to Frédéric Moreau because they were impressed by his courage.

23. Flaubert's skepticism concerning the authenticity of Emma's feelings surfaces at the beginning of the next chapter of the drafts, as he describes at length her letters to Rodolphe: "Thus Emma expanded her feelings, by passing them through the roller press of style" (part 2, chapter 9, 383–84).

24. Flaubert endowed Charles with clothing (clogs, padded gloves), habits (cutting corks at the table), and a type of beard (clipped short all around the face) that he particularly detested (see Gothot-Mersch, 131).

25. For a fine speculative study of Flaubert's flirtations with a postmodern aesthetics, see Marshall Olds, *Au pays des perroquets: Féerie théâtrale et narration chez Flaubert* (Amsterdam: Rodopi, 2001).

26. The findings from this survey and the names and affiliations of the respondents are reproduced in Laurence M. Porter and Eugene F. Gray, eds., *Approaches to Teaching Flaubert's* Madame Bovary (New York: Modern Language Association of America, 1995), 3–8. Full facts of publication for the editions cited are provided in chapter 7, the bibliographical essay.

Chapter 3

Contexts

Restricting supposed influences on Flaubert's intellectual development to just a few would be imprudent. The broad categories, besides his reading (well-nigh encyclopedic in post-Renaissance writers in literature, history, biology, medicine, philosophy, and religion as well as the classics), would have to include his family life (the second son of an austere but respected surgeon), his friends and acquaintances, personal experiences (his travels in France, Italy, Greece, and the Near East), historical events (the revolution of 1848 and the Second Republic), and the political and intellectual currents of the day.

POST-NAPOLEONIC FRANCE

Gustave Flaubert, born in 1821, came of age during that troubled transition between romanticism and realism, between the revolution of 1830 and the revolution of 1848, a period of great political and intellectual turmoil in Europe. At the Congress of Vienna (1814–15), interrupted by Napoleon's 100-day attempt at regaining his throne, the allied powers attempted to restore the old order in Europe. In France this meant the restoration of the Bourbons to the throne in the person of Louis XVI's brother, who ruled as Louis XVIII. An easygoing gourmand, he failed to check the excesses of fanatic royalists *(la Terreur blanche)* against former revolutionaries and Bonapartists, especially in the south. He was succeeded in 1824 by his younger brother, the comte d'Artois (Charles X), whose reactionary policies led in 1830 to the July Revolution *(les Trois Glorieuses,* July 22, 23, 24), which induced him to abdicate in favor of his grandson. The radicals (i.e., center-left) wanted the marquis de Lafayette as president of a new republic, but the liberals (i.e., capitalists) managed to have the duc d'Orléans, a member of the younger Bourbon line and son of Philippe-Egalité, accepted as *roi des Français* (as opposed to *Roi de France*) by a rump Assemblée. The lower classes, dreaming of a republic, woke up to find another aristocrat on the throne. They felt that their revolution had been *escamotée* (spirited away). It was during the reign of Louis-Philippe that Flaubert's early intellectual development and the action of *Madame Bovary* take place.

The political reforms after 1830 were timid, leading to continued dissatisfaction among those ineligible to vote. The electoral law of 1831 reduced the amount of property tax necessary to be on the voter list, which increased the all-male electorate from 100,000 to 168,000 out of a population of about 30,000,000. To those who complained about not being able to vote, prime minister Guizot replied: "Enrichissez-vous!" [Get rich!]. This was not a viable option for the increasing numbers of unskilled laborers who flooded the major cities to work in the factories. On the other hand, Catholicism was no longer the state religion, although the Guizot law of 1833 gave the Church control of elementary education, and the peerage was no longer hereditary—the king appointed peers for life (essentially a victory for the upper bourgeoisie). All in all, the king and the upper bourgeoisie had a political system made to order for them.

As a result the so-called July Monarchy was far from tranquil. Riots over low pay for textile workers broke out in Lyons in 1831 and in Paris and Lyons in 1834 (Daumier's lithograph of the massacre in the rue Transnonain is famous). Attempts at overthrowing the regime by la duchesse de Berry in 1832 and by Louis-Napoleon Bonaparte in 1836 and 1840 were easily squelched, however. There were ten attempts on Louis-Philippe's life between 1830 and 1840, the most spectacular one by the Corsican Giuseppe Fieschi in 1835 by means of his *machine infernale.*[1] The inevitable reaction led to the passage of the infamous September Laws, which severely restricted the freedom of the press, which the regime accused of contributing to the insurrectionary mood of the population. Opposition to the regime increased, particularly among the lower classes. Finally in 1848, unrest led to the end of the regime and to the establishment of the Second Republic.

Although the Industrial Revolution came late to France and evolved slowly, a great many technological advances occurred during Flaubert's formative years, profoundly affecting people's lives. The use of the steam engine as a source of power led to the establishment of factories for the production, for example, of cloth, using mechanical spinning machines and looms invented in England. (Rouen was an important cloth-making center. When Charles and Emma go to the opera they overhear people discussing cotton and indigo dye.) Workers began to crowd into insalubrious tenements near their places of work. The development of railways, encouraged by prime minister Guizot's bill of 1842, improved the transport of people and heavy goods and stimulated the iron and coal industries. The introduction of gas lighting in Paris in 1829 made the streets safer and furthered the development of cafés and evening entertainments. The

Eh ! mon cher, ne te plains pas ! tu seras médecin, je serai procureur du roi : quand tu seras obligé d'avoir du talent, je serai forcé d'avoir des mœurs. C'est ça qui sera dur !

Gavarni, *Les Etudiants de Paris* [Paris University Students]. "Ah, my good friend, don't complain! You will be a doctor, I will be a state prosecutor. While you will have to have talent, I shall be forced to have morals. That's what will be difficult!" (*Source*: Gavarni [pseud. of Sulpice-Guillaume Chevalier], *Œuvres choisies*. Paris: Hetzel, 1846.)

electric telegraph facilitated the diffusion of information (the line from Paris to Rouen dates from 1845). In 1832 the Rouen businessman Charles Havas founded an agency that supplied news items from many countries to the French press (in the twentieth century the Havas agency became Agence France-Presse). The road to riches now lay in banking (Périer, Laffitte, Rothschild) and industry (Schneider, Japy) rather than land. Industrialists and bankers, many of them self-made men, played an important role in the government of Louis-Philippe—both Casimir Périer and Jacques Laffitte served as prime ministers, while many members of the upper bourgeoisie served in the legislature. Being rich became a virtue along with the standard bourgeois virtues of thrift, hard work, prudence, and a preference for order and doctrines associated with the *juste milieu*. The rich man (always a man) was a man of distinction, an elector, a member of the National Guard, and a potential member of parliament. However, with some exceptions, the wealthy bourgeois was extremely utilitarian and little interested in the arts and sciences, even less in philosophy. In Balzac's satiric play *Mercadet* (1851), Mrs. Mercadet says to her daughter that there is no happiness possible in poverty and there is no misfortune that a fortune will not relieve (Balzac, *Mercadet* 1.9).

Already during the Bourbon restoration, social reformers began advocating political reforms that would give power to the workers or at least ameliorate their living conditions. Henri de Saint-Simon, an impoverished nobleman who had taken part in the American Revolution, proposed that society be established on a scientific basis. He believed that the structure of medieval society had been good for its time but that modern society required a new, meritocratic structure implemented by scientists and industrialists. After his death in 1825, his followers continued to promote his ideas, advocating, for example, the abolition of individual inheritance rights, public control of the means of production, and the gradual emancipation of women. Charles Fourier advocated the establishment of small cooperative communities termed *phalanstères;* Louis Blanc maintained that workers had a right to a job and a decent wage; Pierre-Joseph Proudhon went so far as to declare that property was theft; and Félicité Lammenais tried to move the Catholic Church in the direction of supporting workers' concerns. His newspaper *L'Avenir* was condemned by the pope in the encyclical *Mirari Vos* in 1832, and his *Paroles d'un croyant* in the encyclical *Singulari Nos* in 1834.[2] In addition to these speculative writers, some people began to study the economy, and especially the workers, from a scientific point of view, calling attention to the appalling conditions under which they suffered.[3]

Flaubert does not strictly relate events in *Madame Bovary* to events in the outside world. Nevertheless, the passing references that he gives (to the cholera epidemic of 1832, the Polish revolt against the Russian czar in 1830–31, and the floods in Lyons in 1840 [*MB*, 136, 138]) allow us to confirm that the story's main events occur during the regime of Louis-Philippe (1830–48). Charles's father leaves military service in 1812 and marries a short while afterward, so one can conclude that Charles could not have been born before 1813. At the beginning of the novel he is about fifteen, which means that the action of the novel probably begins about 1828–29. Roger Bismut has worked out a plausible, detailed chronology of the novel's events.[4] He places Emma's marriage in 1838 and her death in 1846. These dates must be taken as approximate, but clearly the most important events of the novel take place during the July Monarchy in a Yonville about to undergo the revolutionary social changes that the railroad and industry will bring. Hints of these changes can be seen in the "chemin de grande vicinalité" [major highway] and in the linen factory under construction in the neighborhood (part 2, chapter 5). The advent of steam-driven looms destroyed the home-based spinning and weaving that had been prevalent in Normandy before then.[5] The society of Yonville-l'Abbaye was about to enter the modern world.

THE IMPACT OF SCIENCE

The rapid evolution of scientific thought in the nineteenth century had a profound impact on the intellectual attitudes of writers and other educated people. Building on the advances made toward the end of the eighteenth century, the sciences gradually became *experimental* and *quantitative*, shedding the metaphysical presuppositions that had hindered progress in earlier centuries. Gone were the explanations based on the postulate of subtle substances (phlogiston for combustion, caloric for heat, corpuscles for light). The growing importance of steam power led Nicolas Léonard Sadi Carnot (1796–1832) to study the efficiency of heat engines. He showed, among other things, that it is impossible to construct an engine (e.g., on a ship) whose only function would be to draw heat from a reservoir (e.g., the ocean) and convert it into energy. He thus stated the second law of thermodynamics in one of its many forms and demonstrated that it is impossible to construct a perpetual motion machine.

The problems of explaining electricity and magnetism attracted the attention of many scientists. André-Marie Ampère (1775–1836), father of the literary historian Jean-Jacques Ampère, studied the interactions of electric currents and magnets, founding the science of electromagnetics. His friend, Augustin-Jean Fresnel (1788–1827), investigated the wave properties of light and invented a powerful, lightweight lens for lighthouses, known as the Fresnel lens.

In biology, the slow advent of the theory of evolution had the greatest impact. Jean-Baptiste de Lamarck (1744–1829) believed that species changed over time in reaction to their environment, but his contemporaries were unwilling to consider such a possibility. The nineteenth century was a battleground between conservatives and adherents of scientific progress in the life sciences. The former were wary of any attempt to subject living beings, and a fortiori humans, to scientific law, maintaining that there is an essential difference between organic and inorganic matter. Friedrich Wöhler's (1800–1882) synthesis of the organic compound urea in 1828 and Darwin's (1809–82) publication *On the Origin of Species* in 1859 (French translation, 1862) added fuel to the battle. Flaubert, although partial to science as a disinterested study of nature, deplored many of technology's consequences.[6]

FLAUBERT AND MEDICINE

As mentioned in the introduction, Flaubert's father was the distinguished chief surgeon of the hospital in Rouen. According to contemporary accounts, he was highly respected; Maxime du Camp wrote that Dr. Flaubert was devoted to his patients; the Goncourt brothers related in their diary that Flaubert told them how his father would travel at his own expense to the far reaches of Normandy to perform an operation, on one occasion accepting a dozen herrings as payment from a fisherman's wife.[7] Because of his position, Dr. Flaubert and his family occupied an apartment in a wing of the eighteenth-century hospital building. It was in this apartment, now a museum dedicated to the family's memory, that Gustave was born in 1821 and lived until 1846, when the death of Dr. Flaubert forced the family to vacate the premises. The young Gustave attended school at the still-existing lycée Corneille, passing each day through the medieval streets of Rouen, some of which are described in *Madame Bovary*, such as the picturesque Eau-de-Robec, so named because of the stream that flowed (and still flows) down one side of the street. Flaubert's early enthusiasm for Gothic romanticism was undoubtedly reinforced by the facades of the Gothic churches and old timbered houses that he passed on his way to school or by sites such as the Aître Saint-Maclou, an ancient burial site for those who died from the plague, decorated with wooden friezes sculpted in the shapes of skulls and tibias and with columns depicting the *Danse Macabre*.

Growing up in a wing of the hospital had a profound effect on the young Flaubert, as he himself remarked to George Sand in 1869. Dr. Flaubert trained future *officiers de santé* (a sort of paramedic, an office created during the Revolution to bring medical care to rural areas) and the dissection hall looked out onto the Flauberts' garden where Gustave and his sister played. In a letter to Louise Colet, Gustave tells of climbing the trellis and looking into the dissection room where his father was working, and his morbid turn of mind adds this detail: "les mêmes mouches qui voltigeaient sur nous et sur les fleurs allaient s'abattre là, revenaient, bourdonnaient!" [The same flies that flew over us and over the flowers would land there and come back, buzzing!] (*CORR* 2:376). About the 1832 cholera epidemic he wrote: "une simple cloison, percée d'une porte, séparait notre salle à manger d'une salle de malades où les gens mouraient comme des mouches" [A mere partition with a door separated our dining room from a patient ward where people were dying like flies]

(*CORR* 3:173). Growing up literally in a hospital, Gustave must have observed much more and overheard numerous anecdotes of medical cases such as the story of Eugène Delamare (1812–46) and his ill-fated wife Delphine Couturier (1821–48), a story on which Flaubert probably drew as a source for the plot of *Madame Bovary*. In addition, two of Gustave's best friends had medical connections: Louis Bouilhet had studied medicine with Dr. Flaubert, and Maxime du Camp was the son of a physician. So it should come as no surprise that Flaubert chose a medical background for his novel *Madame Bovary*—Charles, the *officer de santé*, Homais the local druggist, and scenes such as Rouault's broken leg, the phlebotomy of Rodolphe's servant, the operation on the club-foot Hippolyte, and Emma's agonizing death by poison.

The clubfoot operation is solidly anchored in the medical science of that day. The progress of the experimental sciences as applied to human beings, begun essentially in the seventeenth and eighteenth centuries in the face of strong opposition (the character Dr. Canivet asks, e.g., "Redresser des pieds-bots! est-ce qu'on peut redresser les pieds-bots? c'est comme si l'on voulait, par exemple, rendre droit un bossu!" [Straighten out clubfeet! Can you straighten out clubfeet? It's as if you wanted, for example, to straighten a hunchback!] [*MB*, 250]), continued at an accelerated pace throughout the nineteenth century. Flaubert's lack of knowledge of the mathematical and physical sciences (not uncommon among artists) meant that he was unable to follow recent advances in those areas; he freely admitted that he knew nothing about chemistry, but he had a solid grasp of developments in medicine and biology. Moreover, when gathering documentation for his novels, Flaubert did not hesitate to consult experts such as Dr. Jules Cloquet, an old friend of Dr. Flaubert and a distinguished surgeon in Paris, or Professor Pennetier of the Jardin des Plantes. And just as Charles Bovary consulted Vincent Duval's *Traité pratique du pied-bot* (1839) to learn how to perform the surgical procedure, so did Flaubert in order to document the scene; he also consulted his brother and his friend Bouilhet.

Flaubert's notes show clearly that he followed Dr. Duval's exposition closely.[8] Clubfoot (or talipes) is a congenital deformity caused by retraction of the tendons or muscles of the lower leg. There are several types, depending on which tendons or muscles are involved, and it is Charles's misfortune to be faced with one of the more complicated cases, for Hippolyte "avait un pied faisant avec la jambe une ligne presque droite, ce qui ne l'empêchait pas d'être tourné en dedans, de sorte que c'était un équin mêlé d'un peu de varus, ou bien un léger varus fortement accusé d'équin" [had a foot that was in almost in a straight line with his leg, but it also turned inward, such that it was an equinus combined with a little bit of varus, or rather a slight varus with a strong equinus component] (*MB*, 243). Hippolyte is afflicted with the equinovarus type, in which the heel is turned inward and the rest of the foot is bent downward and inward.[9] Having completed the course of *officer de santé* with difficulty, Charles naturally finds Duval's groundbreaking book hard slogging, in which barbarous neologisms such as *stréphopodie, stréphocatopodie, stréphen-dopodie,* and *stréphexopodie* only add to his distress and incomprehension. The traditional treatment was the use of splints (in his book Dr. Duval mentions Dr. Flaubert's failed attempt at curing a young girl's clubfoot by this method); Duval's procedure consisted in cutting the appropriate tendon and then fastening the foot in a device to allow the tendon to grow back in its proper position.

Although Charles proceeds cautiously, daring to cut only the Achilles tendon to correct the equinus deformity, he nevertheless will inevitably commit several errors that will lead to disaster. Flaubert listed in his notes four "bêtises du chirurgien," and Charles may have committed all four. His diagnosis could have been totally wrong; the incision could have been too small, which would cause ecchymoses, erisypelas, and edema; the incision could have been done improperly, leading to convulsions; and the device could have been tightened too much, producing a great deal of pain. Hippolyte experiences all of these symptoms and finally develops gangrene, necessitating amputation of the leg. One should note that this was an *elective* operation, performed in an era before anesthetic and antisepsis. People at that time generally avoided surgery unless it was absolutely necessary (war wounds, severe accidents, life-threatening illnesses such as kidney stones).

Another scene that reflects medical practice of that day is the bleeding of Rodolphe's workman (*MB,* 193). Bloodletting (phlebotomy) is an ancient practice that persisted well into the nineteenth century, especially in France under the influence of François Broussais (1772–1838), who attributed all disease to gastroenteritic inflammation and in spite of Pierre Louis's (1787–1872) refutation of the efficacy of the practice.[10] George Washington died after excessive bloodletting for a septic sore throat, and Gustave Flaubert in 1844, when hit with a seizure while riding with his physician brother, was bled three times before he recovered consciousness. Bloodletting was a common therapy for many illnesses—one of the duties of hospital interns was to bleed the patients every day. Oliver Wendell Holmes, who studied medicine in Paris in the 1830s, wrote of the physician Lisfranc (1790–1847): "I remember his ordering a wholesale bleeding of his patients, right and left, whatever might be the matter with them, one morning when a phlebotomizing fit was on him."[11] Charles Bovary learned that lesson well, for "il vous saignait les gens largement, comme des chevaux" [He bled people unsparingly, as if they were horses] (*MB,* 121). Phlebotomy was also used to reduce sexual drive; compare Homais's remark: "Envoyez donc vos filles en confesse à des gaillards d'un tempérament pareil! Moi, si j'étais le gouvernement, je voudrais qu'on saignât les prêtres une fois par mois" [Sure, send your daughters to confession with strapping fellows like him! If I were the government, I would require that priests be bled once a month] (*MB,* 141). Flaubert's father, a conservative practitioner, stubbornly continued this therapy with his own patients.

LITERARY MOVEMENTS ·

Romanticism

The official artistic doctrine in the schools and academies during the Restoration and the July Monarchy was classicism. The school curriculum was heavily weighted toward Greek and Latin classical writers, as well as French seventeenth-century writers, a small selection of eighteenth-century works, such as Voltaire's epic poem *La Henriade*, his neoclassical tragedies (but not his philosophical works, of course), and Fénélon's *Télémaque*. Boileau's and Malherbe's precepts of order, restraint, and stylistic description, reiterated in La Harpe's influential *Le Lycée, ou cours de littérature* (1799), held sway.

But such works held little interest for the petite bourgeoisie and the general population. They (and some aristocrats as well) flocked to the boulevard theaters to see the melodramas of Pixérécourt and Ducange. These works placed their emphasis on a simplistic plot involving the struggle between good and evil, in which the hero and (usually female) victim are morally pure, whereas the villain has no redeeming virtues. Virtue wins; evil is banished as Eden is recreated. Stage sets became ever more elaborate, in contrast to the simplicity of classical sets. Language was direct, gestures were important, and frozen scenes, or tableaux, became popular. These devices of melodrama would later become elements of romantic drama, a genre toward which the young Flaubert was strongly attracted, as was Balzac, his closest precursor as a realist novelist.

Many of the exiled aristocrats who returned to France after the fall of Napoleon also felt, if not exactly antipathy for classical forms, at least a certain dissatisfaction with them. They had become familiar with other cultural traditions (especially in Germany and England) and sensed the need for something new. Madame de Staël visited Goethe and Schiller in Weimar and advanced a theory that explained cultural traditions according to climate, a theory already evident in Montesquieu and one that would later form the basis for Hippolyte Taine's positivistic analyses of art. Northern literatures (of England, Scandinavia, and Germany) she characterized as imbued with melancholy, enthusiasm, imagination, the mysterious, and the awe-inspiring. Great accomplishments result from the "sentiment douloureux de l'incomplet de sa destinée" (the painful feeling of the incompleteness of our fate) that characterizes the northern literatures.[12]

Chateaubriand illustrated the feelings of the "vague des passions" in *René*, which became the main sentimental guidebook of the young romantic generation, including Flaubert, who, the day before his twenty-fifth birthday, told Louise Colet, in words reminiscent of Chateaubriand's character: "Sous mon enveloppe de jeunesse gît une vieillesse singulière. Qu'est-ce donc qui m'a fait si vieux au sortir du berceau, et si dégoûté du bonheur avant même d'y avoir bu?" [Under my youthful exterior lies a strange senescence. What made me feel so old while still young and so disgusted by happiness before having even tasted it?] (*CORR* 1:420). One can easily recognize similar feelings in Emma Bovary.

Shakespeare's plays, criticized by Voltaire, and hissed in 1822 when an English company performed them in Paris, for many years were considered too crude for French tastes. But in 1827 an outstanding English troupe (consisting of Harriet Smithson, Edmund Kean, Charles Macready, et al.) came to Paris and scored a considerable success, prolonging their tour into 1828. Flaubert's youthful enthusiasm for Shakespeare, which he was able to read in the original, lasted all his life. Byron, Scott, Cooper, Schlegel, Goethe, and Schiller were translated into French and provided the younger generation with new ways of viewing the world. Not only did Flaubert and his friends plunge into these works with all their adolescent enthusiasm, they tried to live the romantic ideal: "Je buvais du cidre dans une coupe de vermeil. J'avais une tête de mort dans ma chambre, sur laquelle j'avais écrit : 'pauvre crâne vide, que veux-tu me dire avec ta grimace?'" [I drank cider from a gilded silver cup. I had a skull in my bedroom, on which I wrote: "poor empty skull, what are you trying to tell me with your grimace?"] (*CORR* 2:279). Flaubert slept with a dagger under his pillow. But some young romantics carried the charade too far:

Nous étions, il y a quelques années, en province, une pléiade de jeunes drôles qui vivions dans un étrange monde, je vous assure. Nous tournions entre la folie et le suicide. Il y en a qui se sont tués, d'autres qui sont morts dans leur lit, un qui s'est étranglé avec sa cravate, plusieurs qui se sont fait crever de débauche pour chasser l'ennui. (*CORR* 2:15)

[In the provinces, a few years ago, we were a strange group, I can assure you. We oscillated between madness and suicide. Some killed themselves, others died in their beds, one strangled himself with his tie, several, out of boredom, killed themselves in debauchery.]

Flaubert maintained all his life that he was a *vieux troubadour, une vieille ganache romantique* (an old romantic fogy). He criticized his friend Ernest Chevalier for getting married and becoming settled in a bureaucratic job (cf. Léon in *Madame Bovary*). In his youth Chevalier had been part of Flaubert's little group; he, too, had dreamed of art, had carried a stiletto, had been a wild student in the Latin Quarter dancing the cancan, in essence living the life described in Murger's *Vie de Bohème*. Then he obtained a law degree, became serious, bought a watch, and abjured imagination (which Baudelaire called the "queen of faculties").

By the time Flaubert wrote this criticism of his friend, romanticism was losing steam. The movement had had its greatest and noisiest successes in the theater, with Dumas's *Henri III et sa cour* in 1829 and Hugo's *Hernani* in 1830 and *Ruy Blas* in 1838, and it was in the theater, too, that the movement's death rattle could be heard. According to Maxime du Camp, "Le drame, le drame romantique avec le bric-à-brac du moyen âge, les fioles de poison, les dagues de

Tolède, les drogues merveilleuses et les tirades historiques, était bien malade"
(The romantic drama, with its bric-a-brac from the Middle Ages, its poison vials,
its daggers of Toledo steel, its magic potions and historical tirades, was seriously
ill).[13] Flaubert described the same literary landscape in Emma's reading:

Ce n'étaient qu'amours, amants, amantes, dames persécutées s'évanouissant dans des
pavillons solitaires, postillons qu'on tue à tous les relais, chevaux qu'on crève à toutes les
pages, forêts sombres, troubles du cœur, serments, sanglots, larmes et baisers, nacelles au
clair de lune, rossignols dans les bosquets, *messieurs* braves comme des lions, doux comme
des agneaux, vertueux comme on ne l'est pas, toujours bien mis, et qui pleurent comme
des urnes. (*MB*, 96)

[It was nothing but love, lovers, mistresses, persecuted ladies swooning in lonely cabins,
postriders killed at every relay, horses ridden to death on every page, dark forests, troubled hearts, vows, sobs, tears and kisses, boats in the moonlight, nightingales in the shrub-
bery, gentlemen as brave as lions, as gentle as lambs, virtuous like you wouldn't believe,
always well-dressed, and whose tears flowed like fountains.]

In 1838, an unknown actress sparked a classical revival, playing Camille in
Corneille's *Horace*. Elisa-Rachel Félix (1821–58), known as Rachel, the daughter of a Jewish peddler, excited audiences in the major classical roles until her
death.[14] In 1843 Hugo's play *Les Burgraves* was a failure, while a neoclassical play, *Lucrèce*, by Ponsard, with Rachel in the lead role, was a success. Romantic themes subsequently passed into popular culture, where they live to
this day.

When Flaubert read his *Tentation de saint Antoine* to his friends du Camp
and Bouilhet in 1849, they were horrified at its unbridled lyricism, for it represented the literary values of an out-of-date romanticism. They advised him to
try a subject more down-to-earth.

Realism

With the waning of romanticism and the end of the Rachel-inspired classical revival, another literary tendency began to dominate—realism. Already
during the Restoration the public began to gravitate toward depictions of recent French history or contemporary life that often included analyses of contemporary problems (Sand, Balzac). Philarète Chasles (probably writing at
Balzac's dictation) called the period of the July Monarchy "l'époque la plus an-
alytique de l'ère moderne" [the most analytical period of the modern era].[15]
A new type of *conte philosophique* was born under Balzac's pen (Bruneau, *Les
Débuts*, 109.) Félix Davin called this genre "la physiologie générale de la destinée humaine" [the general physiology of human destiny] (Balzac, *La
Comédie humaine* 10:1209). Instead of the questions of ultimate or transcen-
dent reality that occupied the elucubrations of classical philosophers, Madame

de Staël tended to adopt a sociological penchant: "J'appelle philosophie l'investigation du principe de toutes les institutions politiques et religieuses, l'-analyse des caractères et des événements historiques, enfin l'étude du cœur humain et des droits naturels de l'homme" [I call "philosophy" the investigation of the foundation of all political and religious institutions, the analysis of historical characters and events, and finally the study of the human heart and of the natural rights of man] (de Staël, part 1, chapter 1). This will be the sense adopted by many writers of the July Monarchy and the Second Empire in works such as Balzac's "Physiologie du mariage" and *Père Goriot*, Stendhal's *Rouge et Noir*, or Flaubert's *Education sentimentale*. During the same period, authors such as [Charles-] Paul de Kock (1793–1871), with no pretensions to elevating the public's intellectual level, churned out a large number of facile novels and plays centered on scenes of daily life. People flocked to the Gymnase theater to see the comédies-vaudeville of Eugène Scribe, who exhibited the bourgeois values in a realistic setting.

Growing in parallel with novelistic depictions of modern life were newspapers and magazines, fed by a growing literate readership and a population that took a greater interest in current events, either because they had the means to participate in public life or because of a growing awareness among the disadvantaged of the possibilities for improvement preached by diverse political reformers.[16] The number of writers and performers increased enormously, the former providing copy for the innumerable small newspapers and brochures that sprang up like mushrooms, the latter providing entertainments for the crowds strolling the increasingly paved and well-lighted streets of Paris. Most of the authors and performers of that age are now totally forgotten; many enjoyed a short period of popularity, then died in obscurity and poverty, like Eugène de Pradel (1787–1857), an author of racy songs and improvisations, who amazed audiences with his ability to improvise dramas and poems on any given subject.

The newspaper was to have a huge influence on literature through most of the nineteenth century. At the beginning of the century, newspapers were published for an intellectual elite, were expensive, had a low circulation, and were closely controlled under Napoleon and the Restoration. After the July Revolution, censorship was relaxed; newspapers were born and died at a dizzying rate. Some lived only a short time—Balzac's *Revue Parisienne* published only three numbers in 1840, for example.

In 1836 Emile de Girardin created the modern newspaper with the founding of *La Presse*. His brilliant idea was to reduce the subscription price by one-half, thereby increasing circulation, and to make up the difference in revenue with advertising and announcements. In order to make this idea work, Girardin had to increase circulation, and in order to increase circulation, he had to offer a bait to attract readers.[17] His bait was to publish novels in serial form on the first page of the newspaper. Balzac's *Vieille Fille* (1836) was the first novel published in this way. Other newspapers followed suit, except those aimed at specialized readerships, and bidding wars ensued for the most popular authors. Balzac published in several different newspapers; George Sand in like fashion published *Le Meunier d'Angibault* and *François le Champi*. But the kings of the serial novel were Alexandre Dumas and Eugène Sue, the former with, for example, *Le Comte de Monte-Cristo* (1844–45) and the latter with *Les Mystères de Paris* (1842–43) and *Le Juif errant* (1844–45). *Les Mystères de Paris* ran for 147 installments in the *Journal des débats*. Sainte-Beuve deplored the coarseness that this innovation had introduced, not only into the newspapers but into literature in general, which he called "la littérature industrielle."[18] Serial writers were paid by the line and so padded their material with digressions and long and rare adjectives. One writer boasted of having made a lot of money with the adverb *révolutionnairement*. Publishers, who had to pay to have their books advertised, recouped the cost by publishing in two volumes novels that could be published in one. The ubiquity of advertising made it impossible to tell whether a book review was objective or merely pushing a book in return for a fee, what the French called *faire mousser un livre*. These developments help explain Flaubert's extreme antipathy to newspapers.

The second type of bait used in some newspapers and magazines was the use of illustrations. When created by engraving, illustrations are relatively expensive, and their use would not be financially feasible in low-cost publications. Toward the end of the eighteenth century, Alois Senefelder (1771–1834) invented a process for reproducing drawings known as *lithography*. He noticed that oily fluids will not stick to wetted surfaces but will stick to greasy ones. Using a very fine-grained limestone that he found in a quarry in Bavaria, he drew figures on the polished surface of a stone with a greasy pencil, then wetted the surface. Ink would then stick only to the greasy lines, and he was able to make a reproduction. The stone could be used over and over by regrinding the surface and thus removing the previous drawing. A lithographic printing shop was set up in Paris in 1816. Many artists and editors adopted the process because it allowed them to make and print drawings rapidly and cheaply, and it became especially widespread in the satirical press. Charles Philipon (1800–1862), a pioneer in this field, founded *Le Charivari* (1832), "publiant chaque jour un nouveau dessin," according to its masthead.

Of the many artists who contributed to *Le Charivari*, the best known were Gavarni (Sulpice-Guillame Chevalier, 1804–66), Cham (Amédée de Noé, 1819–79), Grandville (Jean-Isidore-Ignace Gérard, 1803–47), and especially Honoré Daumier (1808–79). Philipon also owned a publishing house with his brother-in-law Aubert, where they published double-format illustrations to help pay the numerous fines levied against the newspaper, as well as illustrated small-format descriptions of social types, known as *physiologies*. The latter were written in a pseudoscientific style designed to amuse the public (*Physiologie de la portière*, *Physiologie de la lorette*, *Physiologie du bas-bleu*, etc.). At the age of fifteen Flaubert himself published a *physiologie* in a small Rouen journal: *Une leçon d'histoire naturelle, genre commis*. It is a satirical description of the copy clerk, a type to be found in all offices before the invention of the typewriter and a frequent target of nineteenth-century writers. Henry Monnier (1799–1877), whom Flaubert knew, founded his career on the creation of a similar type known as Joseph Prudhomme, who first appeared in his *Scènes populaires, dessinées à la plume* (1830). Joseph Prudhomme was meant to be the typical bourgeois— self-satisfied, dogmatic, semieducated, and a bit of a buffoon, whose speech was sprinkled with commonplaces, incoherent metaphors, and clichés. Examples are "Le char de l'état navigue sur un volcan" [The chariot of state is navigating on a volcano] (cf. the sous-préfet in *Madame Bovary:* "qui dirige ... le char de l'É-tat parmi les périls incessants d'une mer orageuse" [who guides ... the chariot of state through the continuing perils of a stormy sea] [*MB*, 208]), "Quand les bornes sont passées, il n'y a plus de limites" [Beyond the boundaries, there are no more limits], and so forth. Prudhomme introduces himself as "professeur d'écriture, élève de Brard et Saint-Omer, expert assermenté près les cours et tri-bunaux" [professor of handwriting, student of Brard and Saint-Omer, sworn expert before the courts and tribunals]; both Bourais in "Un Cœur simple" and Homais are known for their neat handwriting, which for Flaubert is a sign of intellectual mediocrity. Henry Monnier not only sketched the character of Joseph Prudhomme, he played the character on the stage, writing the script himself. Homais is undoubtedly modeled in part (but only in part, see chapter 4) on Joseph Prudhomme, as is Balzac's Poiret in *Le Père Goriot.*

French caricaturists and writers also contributed to many tongue-in-cheek descriptions of French society during the July Monarchy. Some of the better-known ones were *Le Muséum parisien* (1841), *Le Diable à Paris* (1845–46, two volumes), and *Les Français peints par eux-mêmes* (1840–42, eight volumes plus one supplement). Louis Reybaud, who had published numerous studies on social economics, satirized the race for status and riches in his novel *Jérôme Paturot à la recherche d'une position sociale.*[19] The eponymous hero's uncle wants him to take over the family hosiery business, but Jérôme has other ideas. He fancies himself a romantic poet; when he runs out of money he tries saint-simonianism, and so on through a long series of faddish activities, finally resigning himself to being a hosier.

Honoré Daumier's career extended from the first year of the July Monarchy to the early years of the Third Republic. It was Charles Philipon who first recognized Daumier's talent and brought him into the *Charivari*, writing the captions for his lithographs. Daumier is well known for his satirical depictions of lawyers, doctors, and other social types, but the series that best captures the spirit of the July Monarchy (and perhaps to some extent our own epoch) is the *Caricaturana* (*Le Charivari*, August 20, 1836–November 25, 1838), consisting of 100 lithographs depicting a swindler and con man to whom he (or Philipon) gave the name Robert Macaire, probably because the name was already well known. The character originally appeared in a minor melodrama, *L'Auberge des Adrets*, played by the popular actor Frédérick Lemaître. Philipon saw an opportunity to convert him into the epitome of the swindler who flourishes in a period of unrestrained capitalism. The tone is given by the first plate, where Macaire is speaking with his sidekick Bertrand:

—Bertrand, j'adore l'industrie. Si tu veux, nous créons une banque, mais là, une vraie banque! Capital 100 millions de millions, 100 milliards de milliards d'Actions. Nous enfonçons la Banque de France, nous enfonçons les banquiers, les banquistes, nous enfonçons tout le monde!
—Oui, mais les gendarmes?
—Que tu es bête, Bertrand, est-ce qu'on arrête un millionnaire![20]

[—Bertrand, I love industry. If you wish, we'll create a bank, but a real bank, with a capital of 100 million millions, 100 billion billion shares. We'll crush the Bank of France, we'll crush the bankers, the supporters of banks, we'll crush everyone.
—But what about the police?
—Don't be silly, Bertrand. Do millionaires go to jail?]

Other plates depict Macaire as a journalist, a lawyer, a banker, and so on, illustrating the many ways in which con men operated. Flaubert called Robert Macaire "le plus grand symbole de l'époque et comme le mot de notre âge. On ne fait pas de ces types-là tous les jours" [the greatest symbol and icon of our era. We don't create types like that every day] (*CORR* 1:227). The series had a great success, and one can recognize in Lheureux the modern predatory lender and asset stripper, Robert Macaire on a small scale.

Charles Philipon was the driving force behind *Le Charivari*. He seems to have had a vendetta against Louis-Philippe, for the satirical plates against the king were numerous, leading to many lawsuits. The king's full, round face was regularly caricatured as a pear. In the courtroom, Philipon offered as a defense four sketches. The first was of the king, with the caption: "Ce croquis ressemble à Louis-Philippe. Vous condamnerez donc?" [This sketch resembles Louis-Philippe. Will you convict?]. Philipon removed some details to form a second sketch, with the caption: "Alors il faudra condamner celui-ci, qui ressemble au premier" [If so you will have to convict for this one, which resembles the first]. He then removed more details, and produced a third sketch with the caption: "Puis condamner cet autre, qui ressemble au second" [Then convict for this other one, which resembles the second one]. He then removed more details, arriving at the sketch of a pear, with the caption: "Et enfin, si vous êtes conséquens, vous ne sauriez absoudre cette poire, qui ressemble aux croquis précédens" [And finally, if you are consistent, you cannot acquit this pear, which resembles the preceding sketches]. This may be the earliest example of morphing in the media. The judge was not impressed, and for his audacity Philipon was forced to pay a 6,000-franc fine and to publish the judgment on the front page of *Le Charivari*, which he did ... in the form of a pear! After that every caricaturist in Paris used the pear motif, and Philipon even induced schoolboys to draw pears on the city walls as his revenge.[21]

Le Garçon

The vogue for caricature, the satirical representations of the bourgeois, of the king *(le roi-bourgeois)*, of all those in power, serves to explain a strange creation by Flaubert and his friends during their teenage years, a creation known simply as Le Garçon. Reports of this character are fragmentary. Flaubert's niece describes him as "une sorte de Gargantua moderne, aux exploits homériques, dans la peau d'un commis-voyageur. Le Garçon avait un rire particulier et bruyant, qui était une sorte de ralliement entre les intitiés" [a sort of modern Gargantua, of homeric deeds, in the guise of a traveling salesman. The Garçon had a special, noisy laugh, which was a kind of rallying cry among the initiates] (Bruneau, *Les Débuts*, 151). Flaubert was more candid in describing the Garçon to the Goncourt brothers, who note in their diary that the Garçon was

un type tout comme Pantagruel. Il représentait la blague du matérialisme et du romantisme, la caricature de la philosophie d'Holbach. Flaubert et ses amis lui avaient attribué une personnalité complète et tous les caractères d'un homme et d'un caractère réel, compliqué de toutes sortes de bêtises provinciales. Ce fut une plaisanterie lourde, obstinée, patiente, continue, héroïque, éternelle, comme une plaisanterie de petite ville ou d'Allemand.

Le *Garçon* avait des gestes propres, qui étaient des gestes d'automate, un rire saccadé et strident, qui n'était pas du tout un rire, une force corporelle énorme.[22]

[a type just like Pantagruel. He represented the parody of materialism and romanticism, the caricature of d'Holbach's philosophy. Flaubert and his friends attributed to him a complete personality and all the characteristics of a real man and personage, complicated by all sorts of provincial idiocies. It was a heavy, obstinate, patient, continuous, heroic, eternal joke, like a joke about a small town or a German.

The *Garçon* had his particular gestures, the gestures of an automaton, a jerky and strident laugh, which was not really a laugh at all, and tremendous strength.]

The Goncourt diary goes on to say that Flaubert, his sister, and their friends also concocted dramatic performances based on the Garçon in the hospital's billiard room. They imagined zany defenses of defendants and funeral orations for living people. Whenever Flaubert and his friends walked in front of Rouen Cathedral, one of them would remark: "C'est beau, cette architecture gothique, ça élève l'âme" [That Gothic architecture is beautiful, it elevates the soul]. Immediately another one, playing the role of the Garçon, would reply: "Oui, c'est beau ... et la saint-Barthélemy aussi! Et l'Edit de Nantes [i.e., la révocation de l'Edit de Nantes] et les dragonnades, c'est beau aussi" [Yes it's beautiful, and so is the Saint Bartholomew's Day massacre, and the revocation of the Edict of Nantes, and the dragnets; all that is beautiful, too].[23] In such remarks one can see a precursor of Alfred Jarry's Ubu Roi and, to some extent, of Homais. The Garçon, although bourgeois, is at the same time an antibourgeois. Like Flaubert and his friends, as well as many romantics, he is a member of the bourgeoisie who opposes the values of the bourgeoisie (see Bruneau, *Les Débuts*, 150–60).

The Garçon, to whom Flaubert refers occasionally in his correspondence, represents Flaubert's, as well as many other contemporary writers', strong opposition to the social changes taking place during the July Monarchy, changes that later in the century, and up to the current day, will be grouped under the general term of *américanisme*.[24]

Le Garçon has a number of possible sources: Rabelais's Gargantua or Pantagruel, Daumier's and Philipon's Robert Macaire, and Mayeux, the grotesque, leering, malicious caricature made famous by the caricaturist Charles-Joseph Traviès de Villers (1804–59).

LITERARY INFLUENCES

As early as adolescence, Flaubert read widely. Besides the authors that were part of the curriculum, he avidly read the popular romantic authors: Byron, Hugo, Goethe, and Dumas.[25] The author that Flaubert referred to most often is Goethe, whose *Werther* and *Faust* he read as a teenager; his admiration knew no bounds: "Je ne vise pas à être un Gœthe, parce que les chandelles pâlissent devant le soleil" [I don't aim to be a Goethe, because candles pale in the sunlight] (*CORR* 1:421). To George Sand he wrote: "Voilà un homme, ce Gœthe! Mais il avait tout, celui-là, tout pour lui" [There's a man for you, that Goethe! He had everything, and everything going for him] (*CORR* 4:203). In literary discussions, Flaubert would brook no disagreements regarding the eminence of his favorite authors. After a conversation with Victor Hugo, Flaubert wrote to a correspondent: "Vous n'imaginez pas les inepties dites par ce grand homme sur le compte de Gœthe, dans l'avant-dernière visite que je lui ai faite. Je suis sorti de chez lui scandalisé, malade!" [You can't imagine the stupidities uttered by that great man concerning Goethe, during the next-to-last visit that I paid him. I was scandalized when I left him, ill even] (*CORR* 4:920). As he grew older, Flaubert continued to read Goethe and to appreciate his other works. During the composition of *Madame Bovary*, Flaubert was strongly influenced by Goethe's novel *Die Wahlverwandschaften* (Elective Affinities), which treats seriously (albeit tragically) the same theme Rodolphe exploits cynically to seduce Emma: fate destined us for each other, our love obeys a cosmic law higher than conventional morality, and so forth. Of Goethe's precepts, Flaubert especially valued: "[In a work of art] *Tout dépend de la conception*" [In a work of art everything depends on its conception]. For Flaubert, "cet axiome du grand Gœthe est le plus simple et le plus merveilleux résumé et précepte de toutes les œuvres d'art possibles" [this axiom from the great Goethe is the simplest and most marvelous summary and precept of all possible works of art] (*CORR* 2:157). It was a precept that he strove to follow in his own writing.

Flaubert's reading ranged across many centuries: Latin and Greek classical writers, Montaigne, La Bruyère, Shakespeare (whom he read in the original), Spinoza, Voltaire, and many others. He also read social satirists frequently while planning and drafting *Madame Bovary:* Rabelais (who emphasized the democracy of the body), Cervantes (who mocked romantic ideas two hundred years before there *was* a romanticism), and the Ancients. He studied Latin, Greek, and English for most of his life. One reason for his slowness in composition could be the vast amount of reading that he did every year.

Some authors, such as Montaigne, he returned to repeatedly. His first mention of Montaigne was in 1836, in two short stories that he wrote as a schoolboy. In 1838 he contemplated writing a study of Rabelais and Montaigne. Later references indicate how strongly he was attracted to Montaigne, calling him his "père nourricier" (*CORR* 2:529), and often recommending the *Essays* to his correspondents: "Mais je me récrée à lire le sieur de Montaigne dont je suis plein; c'est là mon homme" [I am enjoying myself reading Montaigne; I am full of him; he's my man] (*CORR* 1:52); "Il y a un homme dont vous devriez vous nourrir, et qui vous calmerait, c'est Montaigne" [There is a man who should give you sustenance, and who would calm you, and that is Montaigne] (*CORR* 2:719). Reading Montaigne before retiring was like having a little chat (*CORR* 2:250).

Several factors account for this attraction. There is, of course, a superficial similarity in their situations: both spent much of their lives separated from the world, the better to concentrate on their writing, although they both traveled as well. Both suffered from physical disabilities: Montaigne from renal calculus, Flaubert from epilepsy. More important, however, is the similarity of ideas:

Je relis du Montaigne. C'est singulier comme je suis plein de ce bonhomme-là! Est-ce une coïncidence, ou bien est-ce parce que je m'en suis bourré toute une année à dix-huit ans, où je ne lisais que lui? Mais je suis ébahi souvent de trouver l'analyse très déliée de mes moindres sentiments! Nous avons mêmes goûts, mêmes opinions, même manière de vivre, mêmes manies. (*CORR* 2:460)

[I am rereading Montaigne. It's strange how I am full of that guy! Is it a coincidence, or is it just because I stuffed myself with his writings when I was eighteen, when I only read him? But I am often astounded to find the subtlest analysis of even my slightest feelings. We have the same tastes, the same opinions, the same style of life, the same manias.]

Flaubert early in life (1839) admired Montaigne's famous "Que sais-je?" and the latter's skepticism was an attitude that Flaubert shared from childhood on. Many of Montaigne's ideas echo throughout Flaubert's correspondence: "L'obstination et ardeur d'opinion est la plus sûre preuve de bêtise" [The stubbornness and heat of opinion is the surest proof of stupidity]; "Je n'enseigne poinct je raconte" [I do not teach, I narrate]; and, especially, "La pluspart des occasions des troubles de ce monde sont Grammairiennes" [Most of the problems of this world are grammatical].[26]

As a result, Flaubert was able to turn to Montaigne to clarify or reinforce his ideas and, as seen previously, to find calm. Montaigne's direct style also appealed to Flaubert. Because of this strong attraction dating from a young age, it is difficult if not impossible to determine with certainty whether Montaigne had a definite influence on Flaubert's thought or whether Flaubert was attracted to Montaigne by a preexisting attitude of skepticism about the world.

Flaubert's attraction to Rabelais stems from the earlier writer's creation of what Flaubert called "le lyrisme dans la blague" [lyricism in jest]; he himself aspired to it, but felt unable to reach it (*CORR* 2:85). Laughter represented for Flaubert the most eminent way of looking at life, and, agreeing with Rabelais, he considered it to be "le propre de l'homme" [the essence of humanity] (*CORR* 2:529). Contemporaries recount that Flaubert had a taste for all types of tasteless and exaggerated gags and facetiae. Maxime du Camp recounts that as they were returning across the desert from their visit to the Red Sea, their dromedary fell and broke all their water skins. They spent two and one-half days without water. In the meantime Flaubert began one of his exasperating teases, asking Maxime whether he remembered the lemon ice cream that Tortoni served and expatiating on how wonderful lemon ice cream is, its taste, its freshness, and so on, until Maxime wanted to kill him.[27] This type of humor can be seen especially in Le Garçon (see previous discussion).

It is difficult for modern readers to realize the impact that romantic writers had on young people at the beginning of the nineteenth century, when the models of prose style were classical and neoclassical, characterized by an oratorical tone, traditional (and therefore mainly dead) images, logical construction. Then came Chateaubriand, "le premier des maîtres modernes" (the first of the modern masters), in Gustave Lanson's words.[28] In *Les Natchez*, Chateaubriand attempted to transmit to his readers visual impressions of the exotic landscape of the New World, eschewing for the most part the neoclassical rhetoric of the time and making use of visual imagery, exotic vocabulary, and a rhythmic prose. As a teenager, Flaubert followed the fashion of his generation and adopted the world-weariness of René and Werther, but he soon rejected Chateaubriand's ideas; after reading *Les Mémoires d'Outre-Tombe* he wrote: "Quel homme c'eût été, sans sa poétique! Comme elle l'a rétréci! Que de mensonges, de petitesses! Dans Gœthe il ne voit que Werther, qui n'est qu'une des mansardes de cet immense génie" [What a man he would have been without his poetics! How that constricted him! How many lies and how much pettiness! In Goethe he can only see Werther, which is only one aspect of that immense genius] (*CORR* 2:86). What Flaubert retained from Chateaubriand was the painterly and musical, rather than rhetorical, aspect of style. With Chateaubriand, "l'art n'est plus décoration, draperie ou placage; il n'est plus un accessoire ou un outil: il est le but, et la matière même du travail littéraire est tout artistique" [art is no longer mere decoration, drapery or superposition; it is no longer an accessory or a tool; it is the end, and the very material of literary work is artistic] (Lanson, 215). Flaubert could not agree more (see chapter 4).[29]

Honoré de Balzac, too, had an influence on Flaubert, who mentioned *La Physiologie du mariage* in 1839. Balzac points out the dangers of sending girls to boarding schools, where they pick up noxious ideas from the older girls (a common criticism during the late eighteenth and early nineteenth centuries). He also points out the dangers of novels, which give women a skewed view of life. The woman who reads "se crée une existence idéale auprès de laquelle tout pâlit; elle ne tarde pas à tenter de réaliser cette vie voluptueuse" [creates for herself an ideal existence in comparison with which all else pales; she soon tries to live this sensual life] (Balzac, *La Comédie humaine* 11:1020). These and numerous other elements of Balzac's book appear in Flaubert's novel.[30]

OTHER INFLUENCES

It should not be surprising that Flaubert's friends and surroundings influenced him. His earliest friends were Ernest Chevalier, who betrayed the ideals of the young romantics to enter bureaucratic life (see previous discussion) and Alfred Le Poittevin. The latter, five years older than Flaubert, was a member of an old Norman family. His mother had attended the same convent school as Flaubert's mother, and his sister was the mother of Guy de Maupassant, for whom Flaubert had a special affection and helped with his early attempts at writing. Alfred Le Poittevin was a young writer with a pessimistic turn of mind similar to Flaubert's and was much interested in philosophy, in particular Spinoza and Hegel. It was through his influence that Flaubert began to read philosophy and familiarize himself with the ideas of Victor Cousin and Hegel, especially the relationship between form and content, an idea that would remain the cornerstone of his aesthetic views all his life (see Bruneau, *Les Débuts*, 461–64, and chapter 4 of this volume). Le Poittevin's death in 1848 had a great effect on Flaubert.

Louis Bouilhet (1821–69) became Flaubert's friend about 1846. He had studied medicine with Flaubert's father but was attracted to literature, writing poetry and plays, with little success. He was an excellent classical scholar and supported himself for many years tutoring students in Latin. Each submitted to the other whatever he wrote and received frank criticism in return. It was Bouilhet who suggested to Flaubert that he use the Delamare story for *Madame Bovary* and also provided the source for the Goncourt brothers' novel *Sœur Philomène*.[31]

In March 1843 Flaubert met Maxime Du Camp, the ambitious son of a surgeon and destined to become a prominent man of letters in France. It was he (and Louis Bouilhet) who advised Flaubert to forget about writing lyrical works like the *Tentation de saint Antoine* and to attempt a more down-to-earth subject. Flaubert followed their advice and wrote *Madame Bovary*. Flaubert and Du Camp made a long tour of the Middle East (1849–51), where Du Camp took the first photographs of the region. When Du Camp became editor of the *Revue de Paris*, he promised Flaubert that he would publish his novel, *Madame Bovary*. Their close friendship cooled somewhat when Du Camp kept hounding Flaubert to go to Paris and make a career for himself and, later, when the editors of the *Revue de Paris* made cuts in the novel, but they continued to correspond. When

Flaubert heard about the February (1848) Revolution, he joined Du Camp in Paris, and they observed the mobs together, details that Flaubert used in *L'Education sentimentale* of 1869. After Mérimée's correspondence was published in 1874, they decided to burn their letters to each other. As a result, relatively few remain.[32]

NOTES

1. The "infernal machine" consisted of a row of twenty-four musket barrels arranged so that one person could fire them all. Passing Fieschi's lair during the royal procession commemorating the July Revolution, the king was slightly injured, but eighteen people near him lost their lives. Fieschi was captured and executed.

2. Conflicts between church and state and between conservatives and liberals continued in France well into the twentieth century. In 1864 Pope Pius IX issued his *Syllabus of Errors,* condemning such modern errors as pantheism, rationalism, indifferentism, socialism, communism, and so forth. The dissolution of the worker-priests in the mid-twentieth century, because too many of them were being converted to socialism or communism, reflects the continuing difficulty of reconciling the teachings of the pope with the teachings of Jesus.

3. Alban de Villeneuve-Bargemont published his *Economie politique chrétienne ou Recherche sur la nature et les causes du paupérisme en France et en Europe et sur les moyens de le soulager et de le prévenir* in 1834. One of the most prolific investigators in this area was Dr. Louis-René Villermé, whose most important work, reedited in the twentieth century, was undoubtedly his *Tableau de l'état physique et moral des ouvriers employés dans les manufactures de coton, de laine et de soie* (1840). The index to the *Revue des Deux Mondes* for 1831–74, under the rubrics "Economie Sociale" (368–71) and "Industrie et Populations ouvrières" (376–80), lists many articles on this topic during the 1830s and 1840s.

4. "Sur une chronologie de *Madame Bovary.*" *Les Amis de Flaubert,* 42 (May 1973): 4–9.

5. Madame Rollet and her spinning wheel thus represent the past. Berthe's being sent to work in a cotton mill represents the future and points the way to Zola's novels.

6. In 1845 he and Du Camp considered doing a philological study, but nothing came of it. See Maxime Du Camp, *Souvenirs littéraires* (Paris: Hachette, 1906), 1:170–71.

7. Edmond and Jules de Goncourt, *Journal,* 4 vols., Robert Ricatte, ed. (Paris: Flammarion, 1959), 2:964; also in *CORR* 4:1023.

8. See Leleu, Gabrielle, Madame Bovary: *Ebauches et fragments inédits.* 2 vols. (Paris: Conard, 1936), 2:69–70.

9. See Charles B. Clayman, ed., *Encyclopedia of Medicine* (New York: Random House, 1989), 963.

10. Pierre-Charles-Alexandre Louis, *Recherches sur les effets de la saignée dans quelques maladies inflammatoires* (Paris: Baillière, 1835). Pierre Louis advocated quantitative methods in medicine.

11. Oliver Wendell Holmes, "Some of my Early Teachers." *Medical Essays 1842–1882. The Writings of Oliver Wendell Holmes,* 14 vols. (Boston & New York: Houghton Mifflin, 1891–1906), 9:428.

12. Germaine de Staël-Holstein, *De la littérature,* 2 vols., Paul van Tieghem, ed. (Geneva: Droz, 1959), part 1, chapter 2.

13. Du Camp, *Souvenirs littéraires,* 1:173.

14. Flaubert saw her in Rouen in June 1840. He wrote an enthusiastic review that was never published (see Bruneau, *Les Débuts littéraires de Gustave Flaubert* [Paris: Colin, 1962], 269–70).

15. Honoré de Balzac, *La Comédie humaine,* 12 vols. Pierre-Georges Castex, ed. (Paris: Gallimard, 1979), 10:1186.

16. For a history of the press in France, see Charles Ledré, *Histoire de la presse* (Paris: Fayard, 1958); Claude Bellanger et al., *Histoire générale de la presse française,* 3 vols. (Paris: Presses Universitaires de France, 1969).

17. See Alfred Nettement, *Etudes critiques sur le feuilleton-roman.* Première Série. (Paris: Lagny Frères, 1847), 2–3.

18. See Charles-Augustin Sainte-Beuve, "De la littérature industrielle," *Revue des Deux-Mondes* Series 4, vol. 19 (Sept. 1, 1839): 675–91.

19. Louis Reybaud, *Jérôme Paturot à la recherche d'une position sociale* (Paris: Paulin, 1846).

20. See, for example, Honoré Daumier, *Les cent Robert Macaire* (Paris: Les Arts et le Livre, 1926).

21. Champfleury, *Histoire de la caricature moderne* (Paris: Dentu, n.d.), 99.

22. *Journal* (Paris: Flammarion, 1959), entry for April 10, 1860, 1:729; also in *CORR* 3:873.

23. The Saint Bartholomew's Day massacre occurred August 23–24, 1572. Many Huguenots in Paris and the provinces were ambushed on the occasion of the marriage of the protestant king of Navarre (Henri de Bourbon) and the sister of the king of France (Marguerite de Valois). The Edict of Nantes (April 15, 1598) gave the Huguenots equal political rights with the Catholics and brought an end to the Wars of Religion. Louis XIV revoked the Edict in 1685, making the practice of the reformed religion illegal. Even before the revocation, Huguenots were rounded up and forced to convert *(les dragonnades).*

24. Huysmans furnishes a good example in 1891: "[le Naturalisme] n' est pas qu'in-expert et obtus, il est fétide, car il a prôné cette vie moderne atroce, vanté l'américanisme nouveau des mœurs" [[Naturalism] is not only unskillful and obtuse, it is fetid, for it has preached this atrocious modern life, boasted the new Americanism of morals]. *Là-bas* in *Œuvres Complètes,* 23 vols., Lucien Descaves, ed. (Paris: Crès, 1939), 12:6.

25. See Bruneau, *Les Débuts,* 26–33, for details of Flaubert's reading.

26. Michel de Montaigne, "De l'art de conférer" *Œuvres complètes,* Maurice Rat, ed. (Paris: Gallimard, 1962), 917; "Du Repentir," 784; "Apologie de Raymond Sebond," 508.

27. *Souvenirs littéraires,* 1:358–60. Flaubert does not mention this incident in his correspondence or his *Notes de Voyages.* Edouard Maynial is skeptical of this and others of Du Camp's accounts of the trip to the Orient; see his *Jeunesse de Flaubert* (Paris: Mercure de France, 1913), 178–252.

28. Gustave Lanson, *L'Art de la prose* (Paris: Fayard, 1908), 208.

29. For an excellent study of Flaubert's style, see Albert Thibaudet, *Gustave Flaubert* (Paris: Gallimard, 1935), 221–85.

30. Claudine Gothot-Mersch gives an overview of Balzac's possible influences on *Madame Bovary* in her *Genèse de Madame Bovary* (Paris: Corti, 1966), 51–54.

31. On Louis Bouilhet, see Léon Letellier, *Louis Bouilhet (1821–1869), sa vie et ses œuvres d'après des documents inédits* (Paris: Hachette, 1919), and Alan Raitt's edition of

Flaubert's short monographs on Bouilhet's career, *Pour Bouilhet* (University of Exeter, 1994).

32. One hundred letters to Flaubert have been located and published; see Maxime Du Camp, , *Lettres inédites à Gustave Flaubert,* Giovanni Bonaccorso and Maria di Stefano, eds. (Messina: EDAS, 1978).

Chapter 4

Ideas

FLAUBERT'S AESTHETICS

Any mention of Gustave Flaubert invariably conjures up images of the recluse at Croisset, anguishing over the "affres du style" (the torments of style), over the choice of a word or the harmony of a sentence, putting his paragraphs to the test of the "gueuloir" and devoting his life exclusively to art. Albert Thibaudet coined for him the label "Flaubert ou le style, ou la religion du style" [Flaubert or style, or the religion of style],[1] an especially apt phrase, not only because of Flaubert's unusually strong dedication to art, but because it is primarily through his stylistic innovations that he occupies such an important rank in the history of French, indeed of world, literature. Recognized as a master of description,[2] admired for his painter's touch[3] and for the use of comparisons that, more than mere ornamentation, were in fact an "instrument d'analyse ou d'expérimentation psychologique" [an instrument of analysis or psychological experiment] (Brunetière 158). Flaubert's contributions to the art of prose were indeed many.

Gustave Flaubert never wrote a treatise on aesthetics, although he intended to.[4] The documentation that we have consists of remarks by Guy de Maupassant and the Goncourt brothers, Flaubert's preface to Louis Bouilhet's *Dernières Chansons*,[5] ideas attributed to the character Jules in chapter 27 of the first *Education sentimentale*, and, most important, his correspondence, which is a treasure trove of ideas, reactions to current events and publications, critiques of books and articles on all sorts of subjects, and the like.[6] Given the disparate nature of his remarks on aesthetics, one tends to receive expositions of his ideas with some skepticism. Nevertheless certain key ideas reappear often in his letters and form the basis of a consistent aesthetic and even what one might term a worldview.

In examining Flaubert's ideas two problems arise from the outset: to what extent can one receive seriously views expressed during his adolescence, and when can one say that he has reached a mature view of art and the world? As shown in chapter 3, the young Flaubert shared the enthusiasms of the romantic generation: Byron, the Chateaubriand of *René*, the Goethe of *Die Leiden des jungen Werthers*, the excessive emotions found in the cheap romantic literature of the 1820s and 1830s. This enthusiasm finds an outlet in many of the stories that Flaubert wrote during his teenage years—for example, "Rage et impuissance," "Quidquid volueris," "Le Chant de la mort," and "Mémoires d'un fou"—in which we find the gloominess, even the rebellious cynicism adopted by so many members of Flaubert's age cohort. He also absorbed the visions of the legendary Orient described by Byron, "l'Orient turc, l'Orient du sabre recourbé, du costume albanais et de la fenêtre grillée donnant sur des flots bleus" [the Turkish Orient, the Orient of the curved scimitar, of the Albanian costume and the barred window looking out over blue waves] (*CORR* 1:709).

Flaubert's ideas on aesthetics derive in part from his attitude toward life and the world. Highly sensitive, he exhibited a strong contempt for the society of his day, the foibles, the self-centeredness, the *bêtise* of his compatriots, and especially the mercantilism of the July Monarchy and the Second Empire. Flaubert, like the romantics, was disillusioned with life, which never matched his expectations. Rather than retreat into the addiction of alcohol or drugs, enter the frenzy of commercial or political life, or join a monastery, Flaubert chose to spend most of his time at home in Croisset, outside Rouen, to dedicate himself to art.

Foremost in Flaubert's views on art was a notion that he shared with the late romantics: the autonomy of art, a key idea among the German idealists that he undoubtedly first encountered in school. His philosophy teacher was Charles Mallet, whose *Manuel de Philosophie*, the textbook used in the class, contains an exposition of the philosophy of Victor Cousin (1792–1867), the French disciple of Schlegel and Hegel (see Bruneau, *Les Débuts*, 32). Flaubert stated his adherence to Cousin's formulations on art in a letter to Louise Colet in 1846: "Tu diras au Philosophe [Cousin's nickname] de t'expliquer l'idée du Beau pur telle qu'il l'a émise dans son cours de 1819 et telle que je la conçois" [Tell the Philosopher to explain to you the idea of Pure Beauty that he developed in his course of 1819—that's how I conceive of it] (*CORR* 1:339). The theory of the autonomy of art would come to be known by the term *L'art pour l'art* and was promoted by authors such as Baudelaire, Banville, Renan, Gautier, and the Goncourt brothers, as well as Flaubert.

Flaubert was a vociferous advocate of the autonomy of art in his correspondence, in the salon of Madame Sabatier and at the Magny dinners.[7] The Goncourt brothers' journal contains many references to Flaubert's impassioned disquisitions on literature; they called him "un torrent qui se precipite" [a rushing torrent] and a "canal qui marche" [canal in motion].[8] Flaubert's views, as well as those of other proponents of *l'art pour l'art*, put him in direct opposition to the utilitarian movements that were becoming more prevalent during the July

Monarchy and the Second Empire. The latter regime was especially anxious to control artists, and, in addition to instituting a strict system of censorship, promoted the notion that the arts should serve a moral purpose. For Flaubert, "Il faut aimer l'art pour l'art lui-même; autrement, le moindre métier vaut mieux" [You must love art for itself; otherwise, the lowest trade is better] (*CORR* 3:585–86). As he wrote to Maupassant, the artist should follow only one principle: "tout sacrifier à l'art" [sacrifice everything to art] (Flaubert, *Œuvres*, ed. Nadeau, 18:208).[9] In this respect Flaubert followed Cousin's main precept: "Il faut de la religion pour la religion, de la morale pour la morale, comme de l'art pour l'art" [Religion must be for religion, morality for morality, and art for art]. The goal of the artist must be the creation of Beauty, which lies in the spiritual realm of the eternal and the absolute: "La morale de l'art consiste dans sa beauté même" [The morality of art consists in its beauty] (*CORR* 2:652). So the artist must strip the work of art of the dross that naturally tends to corrupt it—personal harangues, special pleading, sentimentality, moralism: "franchement, l'art ne doit servir de chaire à aucune doctrine sous peine de déchoir! On fausse toujours la réalité quand on veut l'amener à une conclusion qui n'appartient qu'à Dieu seul" [Frankly, art must not serve as a pulpit for any doctrine, else it will degenerate! You always falsify reality when you want to bend it to a conclusion that belongs to God alone] (*CORR* 3:352–53). Is it a touch of self-parody that Binet, who is unable to sell any of his useless creations, seems the only character to fit Flaubert's definition of the artist?

Some members of the romantic generation of 1830 express similar ideas. As early as 1835, Flaubert too had absorbed this attitude: in a letter to his friend Ernest Chevalier, he urges: "Occupons-nous toujours de l'Art qui plus grand que les peuples, les couronnes et les rois, est toujours là, suspendu dans l'enthousiasme, avec son diadème de Dieu" [Let's always occupy ourselves with Art, which, greater than peoples, crowns and kings, is always there, suspended in enthusiasm, with its holy diadem] (*CORR* 1:21). But to Flaubert's disgust, many turned to adopting humanitarian or political goals: Lamartine went into politics; Hugo took an interest in the fate of John Brown, presided over the sessions of the international peace movement in Paris in 1849 (the American delegate was the "learned blacksmith" Elihu Burritt), and wrote *Les Misérables*, which Flaubert criticizes harshly, concluding "les dieux vieillissent" [The gods are aging] (*CORR* 3:237). Even Maxime Du Camp, with whom Flaubert had hiked through Normandy and Brittany and had taken the momentous trip to the Near East, his closest confidant along with Alfred Le Poittevin and with whom he had shared dreams of a literary career, even he had defected. The defection may in fact have occurred as early as 1850 in Egypt, where Flaubert and Du Camp had met Charles Lambert-Bey, a graduate of the Ecole Polytechnique working in Egypt, whom Du Camp called "l'homme le plus intelligent que j'aie jamais connu" [the most intelligent man I have ever met] (*Souvenirs littéraires*, 1:343). Lambert was an ardent saint-simonian, a doctrine that was beginning to interest Du Camp, who later frequented the remaining saint-simonians in Paris. Flaubert, as was his wont, defended the doctrine of *l'art pour l'art* against this "utilitaire" (*CORR* 1:645). Evidence that their points of view had diverged became clear in 1855, when Du Camp was editor of the *Revue de Paris*. He published a mediocre collection of poetry, *Les Chants modernes,* in the preface of which he declares (shades of Homais!): "Les poètes antiques, tourmentés déjà par les regrets du passé, ont placé l'âge d'or derrière nous, aux premiers temps de la terre. Ils se sont trompés; j'en jure par l'éternel progrès, l'âge d'or est devant nous!" [The ancient poets, already tormented by nostalgia for the past, situated the golden age behind us, in the earliest times. They were wrong; I swear by eternal progress, the golden age is before us!] (Quoted by Jean Bruneau in *CORR* 2:1283). In the same year he wrote an article to which Flaubert took strong exception: "Maxime tonnait l'autre jour contre H. Heine, et surtout les Schlégel, ces pères du romantisme qu'il appelait des réactionnaires" [Maxime was fulminating the other day against Heine and especially the Schlegels, those fathers of romanticism that he calls reactionaries] (*CORR* 2:599). These developments increased Flaubert's sense of isolation and his contempt for contemporary society, while increasing his fervor for *l'art pur*.

For Victor Cousin and Gustave Flaubert, the essence of Beauty in a work of art lies in its Form; ideas and emotions are of secondary importance: "La beauté transsude de la forme" [Beauty oozes from the form] was how Flaubert expressed the concept (*CORR* 1:350). Or rather, idea and form are indissolubly linked; one cannot exist without the other. The artist, having with great effort found the appropriate form, will have expressed the idea in its full purity. "Où la Forme en effet manque, l'Idée n'est plus. Chercher l'un, c'est chercher l'autre.... l'Art est la Vérité même" [Where the Form is lacking, the Idea does not exist. Looking for one is the same as looking for the other.... Art is Truth itself] (*CORR* 2:91). "Il n'y a pas de belles pensées sans belles formes, et réciproquement" [There are no beautiful thoughts without beautiful forms, and vice versa] (*CORR* 1:350). These concepts explain why Flaubert spent so much time composing his mature works, four and one-half years for *Madame Bovary,* for example. Flaubert believed that a novel is not something you express, but something you make. Finding the appropriate form that expresses the precise idea requires intense labor, even suffering. For the writer, form means style, and Flaubert's struggles with style are legendary. "On n'arrive au style qu'avec un labeur atroce, avec une opiniâtreté fanatique et dévouée" [One arrives at style only by means of terrible labor, and a stubborn, dedicated fanaticism] (*CORR* 1:303). His correspondence resounds with complaints such as the following: "Si vous saviez combien je m'y torture, vous auriez pitié de moi" [If only you knew how much I am torturing myself, you would have pity on me] (*CORR* 2:16).

It is difficult to grasp what Flaubert considered good style; his terminology is sometimes highly imaged, sometimes vague, sometimes mystical. One conception is a style "qui serait rythmé comme le vers, précis comme le langage des sciences, et avec des ondulations, des ronflements de violoncelle, des aigrettes de feu; un style qui vous entrerait dans l'idée comme un coup de stylet, et où votre pensée enfin voguerait sur des surfaces lisses, comme lorsqu'on file dans un canot avec bon vent arrière" [that would be rhythmical like verse, precise like scientific language, and with undulations, cello-like thrumming, tongues of flame; a style that would penetrate the idea like a stiletto, and where your thought would sail over smooth surfaces, as when one moves in a rowboat with the wind behind] (CORR 2:79). Style is felt rather than defined logically; the key to it is rhythm. Flaubert read aloud, in stentorian tones, everything that he wrote, a process known as his *gueuloir*. There is an essential relationship between the right word and the musical word (Nadeau, 16:158), or, in general terms: "Plus une idée est belle, plus la phrase est sonore; soyez-en sûre" [The more beautiful an idea, the more harmonious the sentence; you can be sure of it] (CORR 2:785). This is why Flaubert devoted many hours to ridding his sentences of cacophony and attending to their cadences.

Although art should not have as its goal anything other than the search for Beauty, it nevertheless can prove useful, for in the realm of the Absolute, Beauty and Truth fuse; the work of art allows one to assimilate the True by means of the Beautiful (CORR 2:698). Thus, although Truth is not the primary goal of art, it will naturally be found if the artist has attained the Beautiful. Flaubert cites two amusing examples of how this occurred in his case. After having written the official's speech in the *Comices agricoles* scene, Flaubert found in the local newspaper the same words attributed to a speech given by the war minister the day before: "Non seulement c'était la même idée, les mêmes mots, mais les mêmes *assonances* de style" [Not only was it the same idea, the same words, but the same stylistic *sonorities*] (CORR 2:387). Flaubert draws a general conclusion from this coincidence, namely that literature can attain the precision of the sciences. The second example concerns the composition of *Bouvard et Pécuchet*, just a few days before his death. Flaubert, as was his practice, consulted a number of botanists about a puzzling observation he had found in Rousseau. Frédéric Baudry, an old friend, rather than answer his questions, told him not to meddle in questions of botany.[10] Finally, Flaubert consulted a professor of botany at the Jardin des Plantes, who confirmed his hypothesis. Once again he arrived at a similar conclusion about the relationship between Art and Truth: "J'avais raison, parce que l'esthétique est le Vrai ... , La réalité ne se plie point à l'idéal, mais le confirme" [I was right, because the aesthetic is the True ... , Reality does not bend to the ideal, but confirms it (*Œuvres*, ed. Nadeau, 18:650).

The relationship between reality and the work of art was crucial for Flaubert, because he found himself in a dilemma: how to reconcile the notion of pure art with the necessity (as he saw it in the middle of the nineteenth century) of writing about contemporary life. Balzac had blazed the trail, but his style was defective: "Quel homme eût été Balzac, s'il eût su écrire! Mais il ne lui a manqué que cela" [What a man Balzac would have been, if only he had known how to write. But that was all he lacked] (CORR 2:209). The subject matter of classical writers and the early romantics was artificial. Already in the first *Education sentimentale*, Jules (echoing Flaubert's own evolution) decides to eschew the hackneyed subjects of his generation, the ones that so attracted Emma Bovary: Louis XIII boots, storms, romantic boat rides on the lake, ruins, and so forth (Nadeau, 3:263–64). However, because reality is dull and sordid, the work of art must not merely copy it, but use it as a springboard in order to rise to the level of Beauty. The task of the artist is to ennoble the subject matter, to strive for generality in a process that inevitably involves terrible drudgery, similar to the work of the alchemist who carries out a thousand distillations to arrive at final purity. Because of the ennobling quality of art, subject matter is indifferent: "C'est pour cela qu'il n'y a ni beaux ni vilains sujets et qu'on pourrait presque établir comme axiome, en se posant au point de vue de l'Art pur, qu'il n'y en a aucun, le style étant à lui tout seul une manière absolue de voir les choses" [That's why there are no beautiful or ugly subjects and why one could almost pose as an axiom, taking the point of view of pure Art, that there are no subjects, since style is by itself an absolute way of looking at things] (CORR 2:31) or, more succinctly: "Yvetot donc vaut Constantinople" [Yvetot is just as good as Constantinople] (CORR 2:362). In one of his more imaginative passages, Flaubert compares the artist to a pump: "Il a en lui un grand tuyau qui descend aux entrailles des choses, dans les couches profondes. Il aspire et fait jaillir au soleil en gerbes géantes ce qui était plat sous terre et ce qu'on ne voyait pas" [He has in him a huge pipe that descends into the bowels of things, into the deepest layers. He aspirates and sprays out in giant showers, sparking in the sun, what was flat and invisible under the ground] (CORR 2:362).

Few writers were willing or able to devote the time and energy to their art that Flaubert did, and he does not hesitate to criticize them for putting other considerations first. Balzac's ambition was "Glory, not Beauty" (Nadeau 16:75). In Les Misérables, Hugo uses a style that is "intentionally incorrect and trivial" (CORR 3:235). And in like vein Flaubert criticizes Zola, Huysmans, and Daudet, as well as his bêtes noires, contemporary journalists.

Such then are Flaubert's main aesthetic ideas. Although one cannot say that they form a tight logical system, they are related and recur as a constant refrain throughout his correspondence. One can find the same ideas in writers such as Charles Baudelaire and Théophile Gautier and in artists such as Paul Gauguin. Gautier, whom Flaubert met often at the Magny dinners and at the house of Aglaé Sabatier, wrote in 1856: "Nous croyons à l'autonomie de l'art; l'art pour nous n'est pas le moyen, mais le but; tout artiste qui se propose autre chose que le beau n'est pas un artiste à nos yeux; nous n'avons jamais pu comprendre la séparation de l'idée et de la forme.... Une belle forme est une belle idée, car que serait-ce qu'une forme qui n'exprimerait rien?" [We believe in the autonomy of art; art for us is not a means, but the goal; any artist who pursues anything but beauty is not an artist in our eyes; we have never been able to understand the separation of idea and form.... A beautiful form is a beautiful idea, for what kind of form would it be that expressed nothing?][11] Thirty years later the idea was still alive in a letter from Gauguin to a friend: "Un conseil, ne peignez pas trop d'après nature. L'art est une abstraction[,] tirez-la de la nature en rêvant devant et pensez plus à la création qui résultera, c'est le seul moyen de monter vers Dieu en faisant comme notre Divin Maître, créer" [Here is a bit of advice: do not copy nature too closely. Art is an abstraction, draw it out from nature while dreaming before it, and think more about the creation that will result; that is the only way to rise toward God and create as does our Divine Master].12

One must ask: does Flaubert's practice correspond to his theory? The artful rhythms and the absence of dissonance in his prose illustrate his aesthetics well. Flaubert exhibits a veritable mania for avoiding the use of *qui* and *que* in his writing, for those two words quite literally produce cacophony. Unfortunately for Flaubert, they play a major role in French, in constructing dependent clauses. Avoiding them has far-ranging repercussions, because the entire sentence where they occur must be recast. French classical writers took as a model Latin sentence structure, which is highly periodic. The result was, as Flaubert noted, that "jusqu'à nous, jusqu'aux très modernes, on n'avait pas l'idée de l'harmonie soutenue du style. Les *qui*, les *que* enchevêtrés les uns dans les autres reviennent incessamment dans ces grands écrivains-là. Ils ne faisaient nulle attention aux assonances." [Before us, before the moderns, writers had no idea of the sustained harmony of style. The words *qui* and *que* occur constantly in those great writers. They paid no attention to sonorities](*CORR* 2:350). For an example of what Flaubert is talking about, it suffices to read aloud a number of sentences from Descartes's *Discours de la méthode*, or Voiture's letters, considered a model of style in the seventeenth century.

The first radical structural change produced by avoiding the word *que* involves reported speech and thoughts. Because the monotony of long passages of direct discourse led Flaubert to reduce their number considerably (in contrast to Balzac, for example), he was led quite naturally to the structure known as *free indirect style*, which arises when one suppresses the coordinating conjunction *que* and the introductory verb in indirect discourse while maintaining the same pronouns and verb tenses, as in the following example: "[Emma] souhaitait un fils: il serait fort et brun.... Un homme, au moins, est libre: il peut parcourir les passions et les pays" [Emma wished for a son: he would be strong and dark-haired.... A man, at least, is free: he can experience the passions and travel to different countries] (*MB*, 153). Using this device risks ambiguity—the reader is likely to attribute the expression of an idea to the author rather than to a character, as the public prosecutor did in the following passage: "Sans cesse les yeux d'Emma revenaient d'eux-mêmes sur ce vieil homme à lèvres pendantes, comme sur quelque chose d'extraordinaire et d'auguste. Il avait vécu à la Cour et couché dans le lit des reines!" [Emma's eyes constantly, automatically turned toward this old man with protruding lips, as if toward something extraordinary and august. He had lived at Court and slept in the beds of queens!] (*MB*, 109). An advantage of free indirect style, in addition to avoiding cacophony, is that it allowed Flaubert to maintain an ironic distance from the thoughts and dreams of his characters, as he does in *Madame Bovary*. His highly ironic stance reflects his attitude toward life in general; "Irony seems to dominate my life," he wrote in 1852 (*CORR* 2:84). Free indirect style became a standard device among the generation of naturalist writers and persists to this day among French writers as a valued narrative figure.

The second result of avoiding the subordinating words *qui* and *que* is a sharp reduction in dependent clauses. In French many adverbial clauses can be replaced by a preposition followed by a noun; for example, *avant qu'il n'arrive* can be replaced by *avant son arrivée*. A more elegant transformation would be to replace the sentence *Parce que vos affaires vont bien, vous devenez dédaigneux* by the sentence *La prospérité vous rend dédaigneux* (cf. "La hardiesse de son désir protesta contre la servilité de sa conduite") [The boldness of his desire protested against the pusillanimity of his conduct] (*MB*, 78).

Such substitutions, known as *nominal expressions,* can suggest fine nuances of meaning.[13] The grammarians Georges and Robert LeBidois offered the following definition of nominal expressions: "On appelle 'tours nominaux' ceux dans lesquels une idée verbale (action) ou une caractérisation (attribut ou épithète) se trouve exprimée par un nom ou substantif" [We call "nominal expressions" those in which a verbal idea (action) or a characterization (attribute or epithet) is expressed by a noun].[14] Classical French authors freely used the second type, that is, an abstract noun representing a quality. Classical theater abounds in examples like: "Ma passion s'oppose à mon ressentiment" [My passion opposes my resentment].[15] Salon society, attempting to be elegant, turned this device into a fad, humorously caricatured by Molière in *Les Précieuses ridicules* with remarks such as this: "la brutalité de la saison a furieusement outragé la délicatesse de ma voix" [The rigors of the season have furiously outraged the delicateness of my voice].[16] Flaubert used such expressions rather circumspectly in *Madame Bovary;* they became more frequent in his later works, and after Flaubert, certain authors such as the Goncourt brothers and Alphonse Daudet became so enamored of the structure, constructing bizarre sentences, that Maupassant played the role of Molière in satirizing them in the preface to *Pierre et Jean:* "Ceux qui font tomber la grêle ou la pluie sur la *propreté* des vitres, peuvent aussi jeter des pierres à la simplicité de leurs confrères. Elles frapperont peut-être les confrères qui ont un corps, mais n'atteindront jamais la simplicité qui n'en a pas" [Those who cause hail or rain to drop onto the cleanness of the window panes, can just as well throw stones at the simplicity of their colleagues. The stones will perhaps strike their colleagues, who have a body, but will never reach their simplicity, which has none].[17]

The principle of the autonomy of art, shared by all advocates of *l'art pour l'art,* also has consequences for Flaubert's style. Victor Cousin asserts that "l'art ne doit avoir pour but que d'exciter le sentiment du beau, il ne doit servir à aucune autre fin" [Art must have no other purpose than to generate the feeling of beauty; it must serve no other end] (p. 226). Flaubert expanded on this idea, declaring that the artist must be "impassible" [impassive], "impersonnel," and "impartial."[18] By *impassible* Flaubert means that the artist refuses to state his opinions and conclusions in a work of art: "Il faut avant tout, dans une narration, être dramatique, toujours peindre ou émouvoir, et *jamais déclamer*" [In a narration, it is always necessary to be dramatic, always paint or move, and *never lecture*]. By the word *peindre* he means that the pure work of art is a *representation*, an idea that he stressed again and again: "L'art est une représentation, nous ne devons penser qu'à représenter" [Art is a representation, we must think only of representing things] (*CORR* 2:157). Because art is a representation, the artist keeps his personal opinions to himself: "un romancier *n'a pas le droit d'exprimer son opinion* sur quoi que ce soit" [An artist does *not have the right to express his opinion on anything*] (*CORR* 3:575).

The impersonal artist refuses to include lyrical, autobiographical passages in the work of art. Concerning *Madame Bovary* Flaubert pointed to the novel's impersonality: "Je n'y ai rien mis ni de mes sentiments ni de mon existence.... C'est un de mes principes qu'il ne faut pas *s'écrire*. L'artiste doit être dans son œuvre comme Dieu dans la création, invisible et tout-puissant; qu'on le sente partout, mais qu'on ne le voie pas" [I have included nothing about my feelings or my life.... It is one of my principles that the artist must not describe himself. He must be in his work like God in His creation, invisible and all powerful; let him be felt everywhere, but remain invisible] (*CORR* 2:691).

Impartialité implies the author's refusal to derive a work of art from a priori principles or preconceived notions. The procedure must be analogous to that used in the sciences: "Il faut pourtant que les sciences morales prennent une autre route, et qu'elles procèdent comme les sciences physiques, par l'impartialité" [It is necessary that the moral sciences take another path, and that they proceed like the physical sciences, by impartiality] (*CORR* 2:786).

The belief that art must be a representation made Flaubert avoid the lyrical, highly emotive passages, as well as the long digressions, that often occur in the works of earlier authors. This principle led him to a number of characteristic devices, such as the use of elaborately developed scenes, that Flaubert termed *tableaux*, in which the speech and gestures of characters are minutely noted and in which the narrative tempo of the action slows down. The concept is somewhat subjective, but critics traditionally identify four of these scenes in *Madame Bovary*: Emma's wedding reception, the ball at the Vaubyessard chateau, the *Comices agricoles* (agricultural fair), and the visit to the opera. In these tableaux, events are presented from the point of view of an anonymous witness or sometimes from the point of view of one of the characters. In the wedding scene, for example, the arrival of the guests is described from a definite vantage point, as if the reader were standing just inside the entrance to the farm: "De temps à autre, on entendait des coups de fouet derrière la haie; bientôt la barrière s'ouvrait: c'était une carriole qui entrait" [From time to time, cracks of a whip were heard on the other side of the hedge; soon the gate opened: it was a carriage coming through] (*MB*, 85). The location of a fictional observer is suggested by the word *derrière*, which we have translated here as "on the other side of." Both visual and aural sensations are reported. The sentence could be termed *iconic*, because the order of presentation of details reflects the trajectory of the carriage that approaches the presumed observer.[19] Earlier in the novel, details of Emma's presentation parallel the temporal order and the increasing acuity of Charles's perceptions. His first impressions, fleeting and incomplete, are: "Une jeune femme, en robe de mérinos bleu garnie de trois volants, vint sur le seuil de la maison" [A young woman dressed in a blue merino dress with three flounces came to the door of the house] (*MB*, 73). Shortly thereafter, the reader learns more about Emma as Charles observes additional details, for example, her fingernails: "Ils étaient brillants, fins du bout, plus nettoyés que les ivoires de Dieppe, et taillés en amande" [They were shiny, narrow at the ends, more polished than Dieppe ivory, and trimmed in an almond shape] (*MB*, 74). Rather than tell us directly that Emma does little work on the farm, Flaubert, following his principle that the author must proceed by representation, suggests the idea by the description of her nails. The scene is localized by the comparison "ivoires de Dieppe," Dieppe being a seaport in Normandy through which ivory was imported.

Flaubert occasionally increases the distance between observer and scene to such an extent that the observer (and the reader) can observe very little, a most unusual technique. One example occurs just after Charles has asked Monsieur Rouault for Emma's hand. The old man says that he will have to ask Emma, and if the answer is yes, then he will open a shutter so that Charles can see. Charles waits forty-nine minutes before the shutter opens. The reader might well wonder what could have been discussed in all that time and probably feels frustrated in not being able to overhear the conversation. A second example occurs when Emma, desperately trying to raise funds to pay her debts, pays a visit to the tax collector Binet. Madame Caron and Madame Tuvache watch from the latter's attic, but they cannot hear the conversation, only observe the gestures. The reader is left to reconstruct reality.

The techniques of scene and tableau allow Flaubert to stop the action (or very nearly so) and examine the thoughts and reactions of one of the characters, as one can see, for example, in the scene at the opera. As Emma observes the beginning of the opera, she is transported back to her youthful reading of Walter Scott, and the reader observes the action on the stage through Emma's eyes. As the action develops, Emma sees in it a reproduction of her own loves and travails but then realizes the difference between life and art: "Elle connaissait à présent la petitesse des passions que l'art exagérait. S'efforçant donc d'en détourner sa pensée, Emma voulait ne plus voir dans cette reproduction de ses douleurs qu'une fantaisie plastique bonne à amuser les yeux, et même elle souriait intérieurement d'une pitié dédaigneuse" [She now recognized the pettiness of passion that art exaggerated. Forcing herself to take her mind off her troubles, Emma attempted to see in this reproduction of them a visual fantasy good only for amusement, and she even smiled inwardly with disdainful pity] (*MB*, 294).

The reader might well think that Emma is cured; she has made the same discovery that Flaubert made years earlier, but her romanesque illusions are soon transferred to the singer Lagardy. Flaubert reports her thoughts by means of free indirect style: "Ils se seraient connus, ils se seraient aimés!" [They would have known each other, they would have loved each other!] (*MB*, 295). However, the lowering of the curtain interrupts Emma's fantasies, plunging her into the real world again.[20]

A consequence of treating art as a representation is that Flaubert concentrates on presenting the impressions experienced by his characters, often using abstract nouns, as in the example quoted previously ("petitesse des passions"). These impressions frequently represent a psychological reaction to a scene or event; as Emma dreams about Léon, Flaubert tells us that "la flamme de la cheminée faisait trembler au plafond une clarté joyeuse" [The flames from the fireplace caused a joyous light to flicker on the ceiling] (*MB*, 167), or later, after her first amorous meeting with Rodolphe, she experiences a quasi-mystical reaction, rendered by a series of abstract nouns: "Elle entrait dans quelque chose de merveilleux où tout serait passion, extase, délire; une immensité bleuâtre l'entourait" [She entered something marvelous where everything would be passion, ecstasy, delirium; a bluish immensity surrounded her] (*MB*, 229). The words *passion, extase, délire* recall an earlier triad of abstract nouns, "Et Emma cherchait à savoir ce que l'on entendait au juste dans la vie par les mots de *félicité*, de *passion* et d'*ivresse*, qui lui avaient paru si beaux dans les livres" [And Emma tried to figure out what exactly was meant in life by the words *felicity, passion, intoxication*, which had seemed so beautiful in books] (*MB*, 94). The qualification of the abstract noun *immensité* by means of an adjective is a typical Flaubertian trait. The use of abstract nouns to depict Emma's fantasies points to a serious defect in her thinking, that is, a fundamental misunderstanding of the role that abstract words play in language. They often evoke, but seldom denote. Because they appear in similar grammatical structures, Emma mistakenly believes that abstract and concrete words have similar semantic content, leading her to search for the fundamental meaning of the former in much the same way as she would for the latter. Part of Emma's tragedy lies in being unable to see that such words, at least as used in romantic novels, were merely empty sounds.

His refusal to comment on his characters led Flaubert to rely on description to communicate meaning, a procedure that caught the attention of most early reviewers of *Madame Bovary*. Barbey d'Aurevilly characterized him as a "*descripteur* jusqu'à la plus minutieuse subtilité" [A descriptor of the most minute subtlety].[21] Sainte-Beuve was more nuanced, praising Flaubert for his tableaux and his style.[22] But in answering criticisms of *Salammbô* Flaubert wrote: "Il n'y a point dans mon livre une description isolée, gratuite; toutes servent à mes personnages et ont une influence lointaine ou immédiate sur l'action" [In my book there is not a single isolated, gratuitous description; they all help present my characters and have either a distant or immediate influence on the action] (*CORR* 3:278). Not all readers agree; Roland Barthes wrote that Flaubert's descriptions serve no purpose other than to signify reality, to say in effect "we are the real,"[23] while Jonathan Culler has maintained that the meanings of

Flaubert's descriptions are basically irrecoverable.[24] Flaubert's technique burdens the reader, who must decipher passages that seem opaque and who therefore may be lured into overly elaborate interpretations. Yet certain set pieces in the novel—Charles's cap, the wedding cake, the description of Rouen as Emma begins her Thursday rendezvous,[25] the blind beggar—seem to beg for interpretation. Albert Thibaudet wrote that the cap "already contains all Yonville" and as such communicates Flaubert's ironic vision of his region.[26] The wedding cake is another ironically presented object, for it is a model of poor taste, reproducing the clichés of early romantic literature (the kind that appeals to Emma) and appears well-nigh inedible because of the excessive number of sweets. Yet the pastry chef from Yvetot, just starting out in that area, has outdone himself, and the presentation of the cake evokes exclamations of wonderment from the guests (as will happen again during the fireworks at the *Comices agricoles*).

Ambiguity can be found, too, in some of Flaubert's descriptions, for example that of the blind beggar, whom critics have variously seen as the "ugly truth of life in Rouen,"[27] or Emma's moral and spiritual blindness,[28] or Emma's conscience.[29] Seen in the context of the current discussion, the text of the blind beggar's song represents a good example of how Flaubert inserts commentary into the novel without intervening directly, in accord with his precept that "l'auteur dans son œuvre, doit être comme Dieu dans l'univers, présent partout, et visible nulle part" [the author must be in his book like God in the universe, everywhere present and nowhere visible] (*CORR* 2:204). In commenting on *Uncle Tom's Cabin*, Flaubert criticizes Stowe's commentaries on slavery (among other things) and asks the question: "Est-ce qu'on a besoin de faire des réflexions sur l'esclavage? Montrez-le, voilà tout" [Is it necessary to utter one's ideas about slavery? Show it, that's enough] (*CORR* 2:204). Flaubert believed that the alert reader should be able to infer the message contained in a book, if the book is well written (Nadeau 16:142). This attitude led to a conundrum, however, for Flaubert's books, except for *Madame Bovary* (whose success was a result of the notoriety of Flaubert's trial), were not popular. How then could he account for this lack of success without losing self-esteem? One of his reactions continues an idea already found in the romantics, namely that the true artist is a member of an elite corps and writes for an elite group of readers (or for himself or herself alone). The masses will never, or at least not in the foreseeable future, learn to appreciate pure art: "Ce qu'il y a de considérable dans l'histoire, c'est un petit troupeau d'hommes (trois ou quatre cents par siècle, peut-être) et qui depuis Platon jusqu'à nos jours n'a pas varié; ce sont ceux-là qui ont tout fait et qui sont la conscience du monde. Quant aux parties basses du corps social, vous ne les élèverez jamais. Quand le peuple ne croira plus à l'Immaculée Conception, il croira aux tables tournantes" [Of great importance in history is a small group of men (three or four hundred each century, perhaps) and which from Plato to our days has not changed; they are the ones who have done everything and who are the conscience of the world. As for the lower parts of the social corpus, you will never elevate them. Even if the people stop believing in the immaculate conception, they will believe in seances] (*CORR* 3:479).

It is thus a betrayal of the artist's vocation to seek popularity: "Donc, chercher ce qui peut plaire me paraît la plus chimérique des entreprises. Car je défie qui que ce soit de me dire par quels moyens on plaît. Le succès est une conséquence et ne doit pas être un but" [So, looking for what may please [the public] is the most chimerical of enterprises. Success is a result and must not be a goal] (Nadeau 16:143). The true artist has no better choice than to retreat into his ivory tower, an image Flaubert used often: "Il faut, abstraction faite des choses et indépendamment de l'humanité qui nous renie, vivre pour sa vocation, monter dans sa tour d'ivoire et là, comme une bayadère dans ses parfums, rester seuls dans nos rêves" [Given the state of things and independently of humanity that rejects us, we must live to fulfill our vocation, ascend into our ivory tower and there, like a dancing girl shrouded in her perfumes, remain alone in our dreams] (*CORR* 2:77). Or, in more succinct terms: "Je monte dans ma tour d'ivoire et ferme ma fenêtre" [I am going up into my ivory tower and shutting my window] (*CORR* 3:403).

Flaubert's pessimism increased as he approached old age. He lived through the stupidities of the Franco-Prussian war and the Paris Commune. He impoverished himself trying to save his beloved niece's husband from bankruptcy, finally in desperation accepting the humiliation of a stipend from the state. Paradoxically the painful process of writing was also the one activity that brought him joy; living the illusion of his characters was a "delicious" activity. When composing the seduction scene, he was both Emma and Rodolphe, riding through the forest on an autumn afternoon (*CORR* 2:483). For the reader of great literature, the effect comes from an appreciation of the form: a feeling of calm and serenity (*CORR* 2:317, 417).

Flaubert's aesthetic ideas belong to another age: neoplatonism is no longer fashionable. Moreover there is an odd asynchrony between his neoplatonic affirmations about art and truth, mainly derived from Victor Cousin, and Flaubert's ingrained skepticism, which was one of the reasons he gave for banning authorial interventions in the work of art. The human mind is incapable of arriving at definitive truths, "nous sommes un fil et nous voulons savoir la trame" [We are a thread and we want to know the weft] (*CORR* 1:680). And yet the work of art for Flaubert constitutes an exception, able to "assimilate the True by the intermediary of the Beautiful" (*CORR* 2:698). Later in life he modified his views somewhat, claiming: "faire vrai ne me paraît pas être la première condition de l'Art. Viser au beau est le principal" [Seeking the truth doesn't seem to me to be the primary condition of Art. Aiming at the beautiful is the principal thing] (Nadeau 16:241). Flaubert lived through too many revolutions and wars, all of them fought out of principle, to believe humanity capable of attaining absolute truth: "How can we, with our limited senses and our finite intelligence, arrive at the absolute knowledge of the true and the good? Will we ever grasp the absolute? If we want to live, we must give up on having a clear idea of anything" (*CORR* 2:88). Flaubert hated all fanaticisms, for the primary trait of the fanatic is an insistence upon conclusions. Yet the lasting contribution of Gustave Flaubert was not so much his ideas but his art. He influenced the naturalist generation of writers profoundly, of course, but his compositional techniques continued to influence writers well into the twentieth century.

THE SIGNIFICANCE OF HOMAIS

Although many of the attitudes adopted by Flaubert as a teenager were an exaggerated pose, some seem part of his nature, persisting throughout his life, albeit in a mitigated form, as the source of some of his ideas. One of these attitudes was his fundamental pessimism. From an early age, he tended to look on the negative side of things. "I am one of those who are always disgusted from day to day" (*CORR* 1:37). As he matured, he began to observe the world analytically, with what he called "le coup d'œil médical de la vie" [the clinical view of life] (*CORR* 2:78): "The deplorable mania of analysis is wearing me out. I doubt everything, and even my own doubt," he wrote in 1846 (*CORR* 1:282). This "mania," undoubtedly reinforced by the lugubrious atmosphere of the hospital in which he was raised, engendered in the young man astounding visions: "Je n'ai jamais vu un enfant sans penser qu'il deviendrait vieillard, ni un berceau sans songer à une tombe. La contemplation d'une femme nue me fait rêver à son squelette" [I have never seen a child without thinking about what he would become as an old man, nor a cradle without thinking of a grave. Seeing a nude woman makes me think of her skeleton] (*CORR* 1:275). Dr. Larivière, most probably modeled after Flaubert's father, also possesses the *coup d'œil médical de la vie:* his gaze is "more penetrating than his scalpels" (*MB,* 395).

Flaubert's piercing gaze often produces an *Entfremdungseffekt* (alienation effect): objects and people become separated from any rational context, and their actions and words seem devoid of meaning.[30] The most striking of Flaubert's characters created on this model is Félicité of "Un cœur simple," who "seemed like a woman made of wood, functioning in an automatic manner" ("Un cœur simple," Nadeau 16:24). The *Entfremdungseffekt* can be seen in *Madame Bovary,* for example, in the creation of the character Binet, the local tax collector, who spends much of his spare time making napkin rings on his lathe. Observed from outside, Binet too resembles an automaton: "Il était seul, dans sa mansarde, en train d'imiter, avec du bois, une de ces ivoireries indescriptibles, composées de croissants, de sphères creusées les unes dans les autres, le tout droit comme un obélisque et ne servant à rien, et il entamait la dernière pièce, il touchait au but! Dans le clair-obscur de l'atelier, la poussière blonde s'envolait de son outil, comme une aigrette d'étincelles sous les fers d'un cheval au galop; les deux roues tournaient, ronflaient; Binet souriait, le menton baissé, les narines ouvertes, et semblait enfin perdu dans un de ces bonheurs complets, n'appartenant sans doute qu'aux occupations médiocres, qui amusent l'intelligence par des difficultés faciles, et l'assouvissent en une réalisation au-delà de laquelle il n'y a pas à rêver" [He was alone in his attic, imitating in wood one of those indescribable ivory objects, crescents and spheres carved within one another, the whole thing as straight as an obelisk, and completely useless. He was starting the very last portion, he was approaching his goal! In the half-light of the shop, the blond dust flew out from his implement, like a shower of sparks from the hooves of a horse; the two wheels turned and hummed; Binet smiled, with lowered chin and flaring nostrils, and seemed lost in one of the those moments of complete happiness that are doubtless part of mediocre tasks and that amuse one's intelligence with easy difficulties, and satisfy it with a completed task that is the limit of one's dream] (*MB*, 379–80). Adding to this effect is the frequently encountered structure *(A voit B agir)* [A sees B acting], especially when metonymy is involved, for example, "On voyait alternativement passer et repasser les épaulettes rouges et les plastrons noirs" [One could see passing by, each in its turn, the red epaulettes and the black dickeys] (*MB*, 198).

Flaubert's gaze uncovers the absurdity of life, and, as a consequence, the absurdity of language. At age nine he precociously describes one of his father's visitors from that point of view: "comme il y a une dame qui vient chez papa et qui nous contes (sic) toujours de bêtises je les écrirait [*sic*]" [since there is a lady who visits papa and who always says stupid things, I'll write them down] (*CORR* 1:4). The project of recording people's *bêtises* became a life long project, usually referred to as the *Dictionnaire des idées reçues*. Traces can be found in the first *Education sentimentale* of 1845, where Henri Gosselin prefigures Homais (Bruneau, *Débuts*, 415), but Flaubert first mentioned the project in 1850: "Tu fais bien de songer au *Dictionnaire des Idées reçues*. Ce livre *complètement fait* et précédé d'une bonne préface où l'on indiquerait comme quoi l'ouvrage a été fait dans le but de rattacher le public à la tradition, à l'ordre, à la convention générale, et arrangée de telle manière que le lecteur ne sache pas si on se fout de lui, oui ou non, ce serait peut-être une œuvre étrange et capable de réussir, car elle serait toute d'actualité" [You are right to think about the Dictionary of Received Ideas. This book, completely done and preceded by a good preface in which one would show how the book had been written with the goal of enamoring the public with tradition, order, and general conventionality, and organized in such a way that the reader doesn't know whether he is being made fun of or not, would perhaps be a strange work, and one capable of success, for it would be completely relevant] (*CORR* 1:678–79).

Flaubert rarely mentioned his project, but it is clear from his correspondence that he was continually collecting materials and reflecting on what form the project would take. In 1852 he was more specific; at this time he planned a true dictionary, but tongue-in-cheek, with such entries as (*CORR* 2:208):

ARTISTES: sont tous désintéressés [Artists: are all disinterested].

LANGOUSTE: femelle du homard [The crayfish: a female *lobster*].

FRANCE: veut un bras de fer pour être régie [France: needs an iron hand].

BOSSUET: est l'aigle de Meaux [Bishop Bossuet: the eagle of Meaux].

FENELON: est le cygne de Cambrai [Archbishop Fénelon: is the swan of Cambrai].

It would be an alphabetical listing of everything that one must say in society *"pour être un homme convenable et aimable"* [to be a proper and sociable man]. As such, it is a valuable resource for researching the social conversation of the nineteenth century.

Flaubert also planned a preface to his dictionary; it would expand to occupy an entire volume: "Ce serait la glorification historique de tout ce qu'on approuve. J'y démontrerais que les majorités ont toujours raison, les minorités toujours tort. J'immolerais les grands hommes à tous les imbéciles, les martyrs à tous les bourreaux, et cela dans un style poussé à outrances, à fusées. Ainsi pour la littérature, j'établirais, ce qui serait facile, que le médiocre, étant à la portée de tous, est le seul légitime et qu'il faut donc bannir toute espèce d'originalité comme dangereuse, sotte, etc." [It would be the historical glorification of everything that the public approves. I would show that majorities are always right, that minorities are always wrong. I would sacrifice great men to all the imbeciles, martyrs to all the executioners, and I would do it in an exaggerated style. Thus for literature, I would demonstrate (this would be easy) that the mediocre work, being available to everyone, is the only legitimate one, and that any kind of originality must therefore be banned as dangerous, stupid, etc.] (*CORR* 2:208).

The preface evolved into the first volume of *Bouvard et Pécuchet;* the *Dictionnaire* grew to encompass other formats: *L'Album de la marquise,* and the *Catalogue des idées chic,* into which Flaubert poured innumerable ridiculous quotations that he had collected over many years. But he did not wait until his last, unfinished, volume to draw on the *Dictionnaire;* many extracts occur already in *Madame Bovary.* In some cases it is difficult to evaluate details of the novel without consulting the *Dictionnaire.* Of course the romantic clichés used by Léon and Emma are readily recognizable. In the *Dictionnaire* we find: "MER. Image de l'infini. Donne de grandes pensées" [Sea: image of the infinite. Stimulates great thoughts].[31] In *Madame Bovary* this becomes: "Oh! j'adore la mer, dit M. Léon" [Oh, I adore the sea], and "Et puis, ne vous semble-t-il pas, répliqua Madame Bovary, que l'esprit vogue plus librement sur cette étendue sans limites, dont la contemplation nous élève l'âme et donne des idées d'infini, d'idéal?" ["And then, doesn't it seem to you," replied Madame Bovary, "that the mind sails more freely over this infinite space, whose contemplation exalts your soul and stimulates ideas of the infinite, the ideal?"] (*MB,* 146).

Homais represents provincial prejudices about the big city: "Et puis, l'eau de Paris, voyez-vous! les mets de restaurateurs, toutes ces nourritures épicées finissent par vous échauffer le sang et ne valent pas, quoi qu'on en dise, un bon pot-au-feu. J'ai toujours, quant à moi, préféré la cuisine bourgeoise: c'est plus sain!" [And then, the water in Paris, you see! Restaurant meals, all those spicy foods will heat up your blood and are not worth, no matter what people say, a good stew. I have always preferred middle class food: it's healthier!](*MB,* 187–88). But how should one react to the following sentence? "Homais demanda la permission de garder son bonnet grec, de peur des coryzas" [Homais asked permission to keep his felt cap on, for fear of catching cold] (*MB*, 144). If one consults the *Dictionnaire*, the significance of Homais's headgear becomes clear: "BONNET GREC. Indispensable à l'homme de cabinet—donne de la majesté au visage" [Bonnet grec: indispensable for the intellectual—lends a look of majesty to one's face] (Bollème 241). Homais pretentiously wants to ensure that his audience notices his hat, which advertises his status as an intellectual.

Flaubert's *coup d'œil médical de la vie* skewers the pretensions of those around him, as did the authors of *physiologies* and caricaturists of the day. But Flaubert's thrusts are more than just casual jests; the stupidity of many of his contemporaries genuinely pained him, as did their indifference to or unawareness of what he considered their stupidity. It becomes a metaphysical entity, impossible to eradicate: "La bêtise est quelque chose d'inébranlable; rien ne l'attaque sans se briser contre elle. Elle est de la nature du granit, dure et résistante" [Stupidity is something unshakeable; nothing can attack it without shattering against it. It is like granite, hard and resistant] (*CORR* 1:689). As an example, he cites a certain Thompson who wrote his name on Pompey's column in Alexandria in letters six feet high: "Cela se lit à un quart de lieue de distance. Il n'y a pas moyen de voir la colonne sans voir le nom de Thompson, et par conséquent sans penser à Thompson. Ce crétin s'est incorporé au monument et se perpétue avec lui. Que dis-je? Il l'écrase par la splendeur de ses lettres gigantesques. N'est-ce pas très fort de forcer les voyageurs futurs à penser à soi et à se souvenir de vous?" [You can read that from half a mile away. There is no way to see the column without seeing Thompson's name, and consequently, without thinking about Thompson. That idiot has riveted himself into the monument and will live for all time with it. Or rather, he overwhelms it by the splendor of his huge letters. Isn't it a bit much to force future travelers to think of you and to remember you?] (*CORR* 1:689). Flaubert goes on to say that all idiots are like Thompson. He is thankful that while traveling, his encounters with them are brief; but in everyday life idiots are everywhere, and they are so healthy!

The desire to see one's name writ large, similar to the modern desire to be famous, to be on television, is an example of *bêtise*, and it announces from the beginning of part two of *Madame Bovary* how the reader is meant to react to the character Homais: "Sa maison, du haut en bas, est placardée d'inscriptions écrites en anglaise, en ronde, en moulée. Et l'enseigne, qui tient toute la largeur de la boutique, porte en lettres d'or: *Homais, pharmacien*" [His house, from top to bottom, is plastered with inscriptions written in Italics, in script, in block letters. And on the sign, which stretches across the whole width of the shop, is written *Homais, Pharmacist*, in gilt letters] (*MB*, 136).[32]

Homais's presence poses a problem for the reader: why does a secondary character occupy so much space and have such an influence on events? Zola remarked that the character that stands out the most is Homais, but he did not pursue the point, choosing rather to place Homais within a well-known tradition, dubbing him "the incarnation of our Joseph Prudhomme."[33] Although Homais is better educated than Prudhomme, parallels between them abound.[34] Both are long-winded, sententious, and concerned with self-image. Both affect an elevated style of speech, but express themselves with skewed logic, non sequiturs, truisms, and clichés that render them ridiculous. Prudhomme pronounces tautologies as if they were great discoveries: "Otez l'homme de la société, vous l'isolez" [Remove man from society and you isolate him],he opines.[35] Homais sometimes repeats the same idea in a different form: "Je l'ignore, docteur, et même je ne sais pas trop" (*MB*, 396). Both men consider their profession an exalted calling. Homais distinguishes himself from Binet: "il y a bien de la différence, voyez-vous, entre quelqu'un qui a reçu de l'éducation et un ancien carabinier qui est percepteur" [There is a great difference, you see, between someone who has an education and a former soldier who is a tax collector] (*MB*, 139). Both characters tend to get carried away in the flood of their own rhetoric. In a scene where intonation and gesture play a comic role, Homais berates Justin, who, having been sent to fetch a pan from the Capharnaüm, takes the first one to hand, which happens to be next to a jar of arsenic (*MB*, 319–20). In similar fashion Joseph Prudhomme, called to testify in court, launches into a tirade in praise of the king and authority, in spite of the judge's objections, and must be forcibly removed by the bailiffs.[36] And finally, both characters make liberal use of clichés and *idées reçues*.

Homais, however, is more than a mere buffoon: he is a remarkable storehouse of information—agronomy, chemistry, medicine, pharmacy, philosophy, history, music, food—nothing seems unfamiliar to him: "La tête d'ailleurs plus remplie de recettes que sa pharmacie ne l'était de bocaux, Homais excellait à faire quantité de confitures, vinaigres et liqueurs douces, et il connaissait aussi toutes les inventions nouvelles de caléfacteurs économiques, avec l'art de conserver les fromages et de soigner les vins malades" [Homais's head was more stuffed with recipes than his pharmacy was with bottles. He excelled in making many kinds of jams, vinegars and cordials; he was familiar also with all the recently invented inexpensive cooking stoves, along with the art of conserving cheeses and treating bacterial spoilage in wine] (*MB*, 162).

Homais takes great pride in his practical skills, such as making jam. During the jam-making season, "on admirait devant la boutique du pharmacien, un tas beaucoup plus large, et qui dépassait les autres de la supériorité qu'une officine doit avoir sur les fourneaux bourgeois" [In front of the pharmacist's shop, people admired a much larger pile (of pans of jam set out to cool) that exceeded the others with that superiority that a pharmacist's laboratory should have over a housewife's stove] (*MB*, 319).

As Tony Tanner points out, Homais is "he who writes labels, or the very spirit of labeling, spreading his platitudes over every aspect of human activity, forcing the world into the bottles and boxes of his shop, which are the external analogue of the accumulating rows and shelves of packets and blocks of decontextualized 'information' in his mind."[37] We might not like to think of him in this way, but Homais is engaged in a typically *human* activity, the attempt to make sense of a seemingly chaotic world. In the scene already mentioned, when Homais berates Justin for taking a pan from the Capharnaüm, Flaubert writes "He was undergoing one of those crises where one's entire soul shows confusedly everything that it contains" (*MB*, 321). Quoting Tanner again: "It is a crisis in which M. Homais sees the seething indistinct, unclassifiable, undifferentiated confusion that is within him." Homais's obsession with labeling and making distinctions ("il faut faire des distinctions," he says in this scene) is his (all-too-human) attempt to tame the terrifying chaos of existence. Homais's problem is that he (like Bouvard and Pécuchet after him) remains at the level of taxonomy, unable to integrate the disparate pieces of information that come flooding in upon him. Yet by causing Homais to succeed, Flaubert precociously suggests that the packaging of information imparts power in the modern world (cf. computerized data banks of financial or personal information).

Nonetheless, he occasionally errs. For example, he attempts to provide Charles with meteorological data about Yonville: "The thermometer (I have made the observations) descends in winter as far as four degrees, and in the hot season, reaches twenty-five, thirty degrees centigrade at the most, which would give a maximum of twenty-four Réaumur, or, in other words, fifty-four Fahrenheit (English measure), and no more!" (*MB*, 145). Twenty-five degrees centigrade equals seventy-seven degrees Fahrenheit, and thirty degrees centigrade equals eighty-six degrees Fahrenheit (Homais has forgotten to add the required thirty-two degrees above the freezing point in converting from centigrade to Fahrenheit). More significantly, every piece of medical advice that he gives is wrong.

But Homais is not always entirely wrong. Homais's advice to Emma as she sets out on her first horseback ride with Rodolphe is not out of place: "An accident can happen so quickly! Be careful!" (*MB*, 224). But he misreads the situation: "Your horses may be skittish." This example typifies Flaubert's ironic ambiguity—the alert reader catches the symbolism of the horse as desire, extended by the word *fougueux* and signaling what will transpire in the ensuing scene—while Homais reads signs superficially and obscurely. He realizes, for example, that Justin spends a lot of time at the Bovarys' house but thinks that he is interested in the maid (*MB*, 162).

Homais is an evangelist for progress, a word that figures in Flaubert's *Dictionnaire des idées reçues*: "PROGRES: Toujours mal entendu et trop hâtif" [Progress: always poorly understood and too rapid] (Bollème, 302). As an evangelist, he will not rest till everyone has been converted to his notion ("mal entendu") of progress. Thus Madame Lefrançois should replace her billiard table with a pool table: "Il faut marcher avec son siècle!" [You have to keep up with the times!]"(*MB*, 138). However, his most telling exhortation to progress concerns the clubfoot operation: "Il conçut cette idée patriotique que Yonville, pour se mettre au niveau, devait avoir des opérations de stréphopodie" [He got the patriotic idea that Yonville, in order to keep pace, should have operations of strephopodia] (*MB*, 241). There is no consideration here of Hippolyte's welfare; the stable boy seems to get along quite well despite his deformity. Homais believes the operation should take place for reasons of civic pride, to put Yonville on the map. And the first person that the perspicacious (in this case) Homais tries to win over to the idea is Emma, with the irresistible argument of "célébrité vite acquise à l'opérateur" [rapid fame for the surgeon]. Emma easily lets herself be deluded and convinces Charles to consent to performing the operation—Charles, who had only with difficulty passed his examinations for *officier de santé* (Flaubert omits any mention of the illegality of such an operation for an *officier de santé*). The entire town becomes infected with the *bêtise,* and Hippolyte finally consents also, "car ce fut comme une conjuration. Binet, qui ne se mêlait jamais des affaires d'autrui, madame Lefrançois, Artémise, les voisins, et jusqu'au maire, M. Tuvache, tout le monde l'engagea, le sermonna, lui faisait honte" [It was like a conspiracy. Binet, who never interfered in other people's affairs, Mrs. Lefrançois, Artémise, the neighbors, even the mayor, Mr. Tuvache, everyone urged him, preached to him, made him feel ashamed] (*MB,* 243). Homais (from the Latin word for *man*)[38] is everyman, and as such his *bêtise* is part of all of us: "Il y a un fond de bêtise dans l'humanité qui est aussi éternel que l'humanité elle-même" [There is a bedrock of stupidity in humanity that is as eternal as humanity itself] (*CORR* 3:479). Flaubert did not exempt even himself from *bêtise:* "Ma propre bêtise me dégoûte moi-même" [My own stupidity disgusts me myself] he wrote in 1846 (*CORR* 1:276).

Flaubert's contempt for journalists is well known; newspapers were for him a rich source of *bêtises,* a "gribouillage imbécile" (idiotic scribbling), and "funestes établissements" (deadly establishments), and they were one of the causes of "l'abrutissement moderne" (modern debasement).[39] Journalism was responsible for Théophile Gautier's failure ever to reach his potential (*CORR* 2:78–79). Homais's greatest influence, inherently ignoble in Flaubert's view, comes from his role as journalist. Because it was not economically feasible for every small town to publish a newspaper, urban newspapers carried news of the surrounding villages and farms in columns written by local correspondents. As the correspondent for *Le Fanal de Rouen* for Buchy, Forges, Neufchâtel, Yonville, and surrounding areas, Homais, albeit on a small scale, shapes the public's view of happenings in those villages and does not hesitate to use this forum to disseminate his own prejudices. We have already seen how his zeal to enhance the reputation of his hometown (some might now call this *civic spirit*) leads him to urge the operation on Hippolyte. But when the operation proves a disaster, Homais never writes the article, for a disaster would not reflect well on Yonville. The patriotic motif does, however, appear in Homais's article on the *Comices agricoles* in part 2, chapter 8, where the earlier presentation of events in the narrator's (somewhat more objective) voice guides the reader's interpretation of Homais's text. A close reading brings out some of Flaubert's key ideas.

Homais begins his article with a rhetorical flourish: "Pourquoi ces festons, ces fleurs, ces guirlandes? Où courait cette foule, comme les flots d'une mer en furie, sous les torrents d'un soleil tropical qui répandait sa chaleur sur nos guérets?" [Why all these festoons, these flowers, these wreaths? Where was this crowd running, like the waves of a furious sea, under the torrential tropical sun that shed its heat onto our fields?] (*MB*, 220). The modern reader might not recognize the traditional rhetorical devices that Homais uses here, taught in the schools of nineteenth-century France, where the students were required to elaborate on familiar topics using well-worn set phrases, a practice Flaubert roundly condemned.[40] Among the authors whom he criticized for this defect were Casimir Delavigne and Jacques-Arsène Ancelot. Emile Gérard-Gailly points out that on August 9, 1852, while Flaubert was writing the *Comices Agricoles* scene, Ancelot read a poem to inaugurate statues of Bernardin de Saint-Pierre and Casimir Delavigne at Le Havre. The poem begins with the same device of the rhetorical question that Flaubert parodies, with the same tired reference to the rushing crowd:

> Où va cette foule empressée
>
> Désertant son foyer, ses comptoirs, ses sillons?
>
> Pourquoi, sur cette mer par les vents caressée,
>
> A la cime des mâts ces mille pavillons?[41]

> [Where is this hurried crowd going
>
> Deserting its hearth, its shop counters, its plowed furrows?
>
> Why, over this sea caressed by the winds,
>
> These thousand flags at the tops of the masts?]

Ancelot writes in the tradition of Delavigne, for in one of the latter's *Mésséni-ennes*, one finds:

> D'où vient ce bruit lugubre? Où courent ces guerriers
>
> Dont la foule à longs flots roule et se précipite?[42]

> [Whence this ominous noise? Where do these warriors run
>
> As their crowd unfurls in long waves and rushes on?]

Delavigne was one of Flaubert's *bêtes noires*, "un Louis-Philippe en littérature" [a Louis-Philippe of literature] (*CORR* 2:96). Thus when Louise Colet, in her poem "Pradier," used the same rhetorical flourish ("Pourquoi ce funèbre cortège / De chars de deuil, d'amis en pleurs?" [*CORR* 2:927]), Flaubert's remark: "c'est un peu Delavigne de tournure" [that's a bit like Delavigne] (*CORR* 2:106) amounts to rather sharp criticism.

Homais's tired rhetoric continues with well-worn phrases, such as "l'air martial de notre milice" [the martial air of our militia], "débris de nos immortelles phalanges" [the remains of our immortal phalanxes], and "au son mâle des tambours" [at the virile sound of the drums]. Comparing the crowds to a furious sea and the Normandy sun to a tropical one is hyperbole, while the word *torrents* is simply inappropriate when referring to the sun. Homais takes the opportunity to remind his readers that he is the author of a pamphlet on cider, and he cites his toast, the longest of all, to industry and the arts. His description of the fireworks display is deliberately misleading. Instead of an operatic decor or a scene from the *Thousand and One Nights*, the narrator has shown the reader a different milieu, one in which the women are molested in the darkness and where the fireworks display is a complete failure. Homais's article is designed to give the impression that the official events have been a great success, thus enhancing the reputation of Yonville but at the same time underscoring Homais's fawning attitude before authority. The article ends with his anticlerical jibe: "On y a seulement remarqué l'absence du clergé. Sans doute les sacristes entendent le progrès d'une autre manière. Libre à vous, messieurs de Loyola!" [The only absence we were struck by was that of the clergy. Doubtless the sacristes understand progress in another way. As you wish, gentlemen of Loyola!] (*MB*, 221).

Homais's significance lies in more than just supplying comic relief—his words have disastrous effects, as we see in the clubfoot episode. It was also Homais who suggested that Charles take Emma to the opera in Rouen, a decision that will lead to Emma's affair with Léon and her personal destruction. Although the reader might attribute his suggestions to a misguided altruism, he also has a dark side, which led Albert Camus to remark, perspicaciously: "Mais que l'on donne une police à M. Homais, il ne sera plus ridicule" [If Homais had a police force, he would no longer be ridiculous] (*L'Homme révolté*, Paris: Gallimard, 1951, 274). The significance of Camus's remark becomes clear when we examine Homais's role in the episode of the blind beggar. Flaubert had originally planned on having a legless man sitting beside the road between Yonville and Rouen but changed his mind—indeed, the blindness of the beggar could well suggest the blindness of the characters. In any event, in order to motivate the beggar's presence in Yonville at the time of Emma's death, Flaubert has Homais invite the blind man to his pharmacy for his "pommade antiphlogistique" [antiinflammatory ointment] (*MB*, 374). But Homais's ointment has no effect, and the blind beggar, from his post along the Yonville-Rouen road, so informs all the passersby. Flaubert does not hesitate to clarify Homais's motivations: "Dans l'intérêt de sa propre réputation, voulant s'en débarrasser à toute force, il dressa contre lui une batterie cachée, qui décelait la profondeur de son intelligence et la scélératesse de sa vanité" [In the interest of his reputation, and wanting to get rid of him in any way possible, he (Homais) mounted a hidden attack against him, which betrayed his profound intelligence and the wickedness of his vanity] (*MB*, 419). For six months straight, Homais uses his position as journalist to publish articles against the blind beggar, even inventing incidents to strengthen his campaign; in other words, he manufactures the news. Thanks to Homais's efforts the blind beggar is incarcerated, not for the reasons given in the newspaper articles, but rather because the blind beggar is a constant reminder to everyone that Homais was unable to cure the beggar's scrofulous condition. Homais's success leads him to expand his zealous efforts to reform society: "Dès lors il n'y eut plus dans l'arrondissement un chien écrasé, une grange incendiée, une femme battue, dont aussitôt il ne fît part au public, toujours guidé par l'amour du progrès et la haine des prêtres" [From then on, there was not a dog run over, a barn burned, a woman beaten, about which he did not promptly inform the public, always guided by the love of progress and hatred for the priests] (*MB*, 419).

Homais's ambition inspires him to yet greater heights; his love of taxonomy leads him to publish a book, *Statistique générale du canton d'Yonville, suivie d'observations climatologiques.* And in a sentence reminiscent of *Bouvard et Pécuchet,* one that Flaubert must have intended to be ironic, we read: "la statistique le poussa vers la philosophie" [statistics impelled him toward philosophy] (*MB*, 420). At this point Homais's ambition knows no bounds. He becomes involved in politics and covets the cross of the Legion of Honor. There will be no stopping him, for "l'autorité le ménage et l'opinion publique le protège" [the authorities treat him with kid gloves and public opinion protects him] (*MB*, 425).

Critics have long been puzzled by the ending of *Madame Bovary,* a sort of epilogue that continues long after the heroine's death, depicting Homais's triumph and reception of the *Croix d'honneur.* In the introduction to her edition of *Madame Bovary,* Claudine Gothot-Mersch wrote: "Quant à la conclusion du roman, ce n'est pas la moindre ironie de l'auteur que de faire triompher à la fin le personnage dont il s'est moqué le plus" [As for the conclusion of the novel, the triumph of the character of whom the author has made the most fun is not the least of his ironies] (Paris: Garnier, 1971, lxii).

We must not be misled by the apparent irony of Homais's triumph. Homais has designated himself the heir of Enlightenment thought, a *philosophe.* The notion of Progress is the guiding myth of the modern world, but in Homais's mouth (in everyone's mouth?), it becomes a cliché like all the others. Instead of a beacon, Homais is in the same situation as the semaphore operator whom Flaubert observed in 1847 during his hiking trip with Maxime du Camp: "Quelle drôle de vie que celle de l'homme qui reste là, dans cette petite cabane à faire mouvoir ces deux perches et à tirer sur ces ficelles; rouage inintelligent d'une machine muette pour lui, il peut mourir sans connaître un seul des événements qu'il a appris, un seul mot de tous ceux qu'il aura dits. Le but? Le but? Le sens? Qui le sait? ... Un peu plus, un peu moins, ne sommes-nous pas tous comme ce brave homme, parlant des mots qu'on nous a appris et que nous apprenons sans les comprendre" [What a strange life that man leads, in his little cabin moving those two vanes and pulling on the wires. As far as he is concerned, he's the unintelligent mechanism of a mute machine. He could die without understanding a single event that he has received, or a single word of all those he has transmitted. The goal? The purpose? The meaning? Who knows? ... More or less, aren't we all like that poor guy, uttering words that have been taught us and that we learn without understanding them?][43]

As Dr. Larivière said of Homais: "Ce n'est pas le *sens* [sang] qui le gêne" [It's not an excess of blood/common sense that is bothering him] (Paris: Garnier, 1971, lxii).[44] Homais nevertheless draws conclusions, and for Flaubert "La bêtise consiste à vouloir conclure" [Stupidity consists in wanting a conclusion] (*CORR* 1:680). According to Rémy de Gourmont, Flaubert "ne séparait pas la stupidité de la méchanceté" [did not distinguish stupidity and evil],[45] and indeed Homais's *bêtise* is in reality an insidious and destructive force, against which the naive Emma and Charles are helpless.

Just as there are Emmas suffering in twenty villages of France, so too are there Homaises triumphant in every city, town, and village. Flaubert bequeaths to the reader a dark vision of the future: the inevitable rise to power of the Homaises of the world, the triumph of *bêtise*, and the rise of the totalitarian state. As Banville wrote,

> Homais ne mourra jamais! / Il revient en Croquemitaine.[46]
>
> [Homais will never die! / He will return as the bogeyman.]

NOTES

1. Albert Thibaudet, *Gustave Flaubert* (Paris: Gallimard, 1935), 221.

2. Emile Zola, "De la description," in Zola, *Œuvres complètes*, 15 vols. Henri Mitterand, ed. (Paris: Cercle du Livre Précieux, 1966), 1299–1302 (10:1301).

3. Ferdinand Brunetière, *Le Roman naturaliste* (Paris: Calmann-Lévy, n.d.), 155.

4. He seems to have mulled over this idea quite a bit in 1853: "Il y a des jours où la main me démange d'écrire cette préface des *Idées reçues* et mon *Essai sur le génie poétique français*,"*CORR* 2:310–11. See also 411, 427, 450.

5. See Nadeau 14:489–509 and Gustave Flaubert, *Pour Bouilhet*, Alan Raitt, ed. (Exeter, UK: University of Exeter, 1994).

6. See Maupassant's preface to *Pierre et Jean;* Jean Bruneau has published pertinent extracts from the Goncourts' *Journal* in *CORR* 3:867–85 and 4:1017–27.

7. Aglaé Sabatier, known as *La Présidente*. See André Billy, *La Présidente et ses amis* (Paris: Flammarion, 1945).

   At the Magny restaurant, every other Monday, founded by Sainte-Beuve and Gavarni. Regular attendees were Flaubert (when he was in Paris), Gautier, Taine, the Goncourt brothers, Sainte-Beuve, Berthelot.

8. *Journal*, 4 vols., Robert Ricatte, ed. (Paris: Flammarion, 1959), 2:46.

9. Victor Cousin, *Cours de philosophie sur le fondement des idées absolues du vrai, du beau et du bien*, Adolphe Garnier, ed. (Paris: Hachette, 1836), 224. We use this edition because it purports to reproduce the notes from Cousin's course in 1818, published with his authorization. This may well have been the edition consulted by Flaubert himself, as suggested in his remark to Louise Colet mentioned previously.

10. Born in Rouen, he married the daughter of Antoine Sénard, the lawyer who defended Flaubert in the trial of *Madame Bovary* (see *CORR* 1:959–60).

11. Quoted by Albert Cassagne in Cassagne, *La Théorie de l'art pour l'art en France* (Paris: Dorbon, 1959), 137.

12. Maurice Malingue, ed., *Lettres de Gauguin à sa femme et à ses amis* (Paris: Grasset, 1949), 134.

13. For an excellent study of this device, see Alf Lombard, *Les Expressions nominales dans le français moderne* (Uppsala: Almquist, 1930.)

14. Georges and Robert Le Bidois, *Syntaxe du français moderne,* 2 vols. (Paris: Picard, 2nd ed., 1968), 2:77.

15. Pierre Corneille, *Le Cid* IV.4, v. 811.

16. Molière, *Les Précieuses ridicules,* Scene 10.

17. Guy de Maupassant, "Le roman," in Maupassant, *Romans* (Paris: Gallimard, 1987), 703–15 (715).

18. For a full discussion of these terms, see Marianne Bonwit, "Gustave Flaubert et le principe d'impassibilité," *University of California Publications in Modern Philology* 33 (1950): 263–420.

19. The term *iconic sign* in logic refers to a sign that resembles the object to which it refers.

20. A similar event occurs when Charles calls Emma to come downstairs to dinner as she is reading Rodolphe's farewell letter in the attic. The everyday expression "Soup's on!" underscores the mundane reality that is Yonville. (*MB,* 274)

21. Jules Barbey d'Aurevilly, *Le XIXe Siècle. Des Œuvres et des hommes* (Paris: Mercure de France, 1964), 206.

22. Charles-Augustin Sainte-Beuve, "Madame Bovary, par M. Gustave Flaubert," in Sainte-Beuve, *Causeries du Lundi,* Vol. 13. (Paris: Garnier, 1850), 351.

23. Roland Barthes, "L'effet de reel," *Communications* 11 (March 1968): 84–89.

24. Jonathan Culler, "Description and Meaning," in *Flaubert: The Uses of Uncertainty* (Ithaca, NY: Cornell University Press), 91–109.

25. For a discussion of this scene, see Mieke Bal, "Descriptions: pour une théorie de la description narrative: à propos de *Madame Bovary* de Flaubert," in her *Narratologie; les instances du récit: essai sur la signification narrative dans quatre romans modernes* (Paris: Klincksieck, 1977): 87–111.

26. Albert Thibaudet, *Gustave Flaubert* (Paris: Gallimard, 1935), 96.

27. Murray Sachs, "The Role of the Blind Beggar in *Madame Bovary,*" *Symposium* 22 (1968): 72–80.

28. Eugene F. Gray, "Emma by Twilight: Flawed Perception in *Madame Bovary,*" *Nineteenth-Century French Studies* 6 (1978): 231–40.

29. Max Aprile, "L'aveugle et sa signification dans *Madame Bovary,*" *Revue d'Histoire Littéraire de la France* 76 (1976): 385–92.

30. Compare Roquentin's reactions in Sartre's *La Nausée.*

31. Geneviève Bollème, *Le second volume de Bouvard et Pécuchet* (Paris: Denoël, 1966), 292.

32. Compare "sorel" in large letters on the sawmill that mars the landscape in Stendhal's *Le Rouge et le Noir.*

33. *Les Romanciers naturalistes,* in *Œuvres complètes,* 15 vols. Henri Mitterand, ed. (Paris: Cercle du Livre Précieux, 1966), 11:108.

34. For parallels between Homais and Prudhomme, see Roger Bismut, "Henri Monnier, modèle de Flaubert," *Les Amis de Flaubert* 27 (December 1965): 15–17; Jean Pom-

mier, "Flaubert et la naissance de l'acteur," *Journal de Psychologie Normale et Pathologique* (April–June 1947): 187–88. For references to Prudhomme in Flaubert's correspondence, see Jacques Douchin, "La Satire 'Prud'hommesque' dans la correspondance de Flaubert," *Les Amis de Flaubert* 25 (December 1964): 13–23.

35. Quoted by Catherine Cœuré in her introduction to Monnier's *Scènes populaires*. (Paris: Flammarion, 1973), 23.

36. Henry Monnier, *Scènes populaires* (Paris: Flammarion, 1973), 94.

37. Tony Tanner, *Adultery in the Novel: Contract and Transgression* (Baltimore: Johns Hopkins University Press, 1979), 273.

38. On one of his scenarios for the novel, Flaubert wrote: "Homais vient de Homo = l'homme." *Madame Bovary, nouvelle version*, Jean Pommier and Gabrielle Leleu, eds. (Paris: Corti, 1949), 118.

39. Such remarks abound in Flaubert's correspondence; see, e.g., Nadeau, 18:292; *CORR* 4:704, 3:606.

40. There were many criticisms of this form of education during the nineteenth century. Jules Vallès's character Jacques Vintras confesses that, in order to complete his assignments, "Je vole à droite, à gauche, je ramasse des *rejets* au coin des livres. Je suis même malhonnête quelquefois. J'ai besoin d'une épithète; peu m'importe de sacrifier la vérité! Je prends dans le dictionnaire le mot qui fait l'affaire, quand même il dirait le contraire de ce que je voulais dire. Je perds la notion juste! Il me faut mon spondée ou mon dactyle, tant pis!—la *qualité* n'est rien, c'est la *quantité* qui est tout" [I steal material left and right; I grab parts of lines from books. I am even sometimes dishonest. If I need an adjective, sacrificing the truth is of little concern! I take the word that I need from the dictionary, even if it says the opposite of what I mean. I'm losing any concept of what's right! I need my spondee or dactyl, too bad!—*quality* is nothing, *quantity* is everything]. *L'Enfant* (Paris: Garnier-Flammarion, 1968), 242.

41. Emile Gérard-Gailly, *Le grand amour de Flaubert* (Paris: Aubier, 1944), 277.

42. Casimir Delavigne, "La Mort de Jeanne d'Arc," in *Œuvres complètes de Casimir Delavigne* (Paris: Didier, 1855), 492.

43. *Par les champs et par les grèves*, in *Les œuvres de Gustave Flaubert*, ed. Maurice Nadeau (Lausanne: Editions Rencontre, 1964), 2:211.

44. In the nineteenth century, the words *sens* and *sang* were homonyms, thus the double meaning here.

45. Rémy de Gourmont, "Flaubert et la bêtise humaine," in *Promenades littéraires*, 3 vols. (Paris: Mercure de France, 1963), 2:164.

46. Théodore de Banville, *Odes funambulesques* (Paris: Calmann-Lévy, 1859), 226.

Chapter 5

Narrative Art

A STRUCTURAL OVERVIEW OF THE NOVEL

Madame Bovary is built up with an intricate interweaving of many three-part structures (A-B-C). Three is a favorite number for story tellers ("the third time is the charm") because readers, like most of the larger animals, are constructed according to the rules of binary symmetry: left and right; two eyes, ears, arms, legs, lungs, kidneys. Our sets of fingers and toes, and the two sides of our face, mirror each other. Two-ness is natural to us; three-ness suggests an external world whose complexity often exceeds the limitations of our bodies and our understanding. We experience a third part of something (for instance, a baby in a family, a rival in a love triangle, a moral ambiguity somewhere between good and evil) as an interesting, exciting, or alarming novelty that compels our attention. Flaubert keeps our attention alive by concealing meaningful three-part structures inside the ostensible and least important one: the three numbered divisions of the novel. The more we reread him, the more we discover of these hidden treasures.

The largest of these structures is a frame (A, C) and a story (B), composed of (A) Charles's childhood and first marriage (part 1, chapters 1–5); (B) Charles's marriage to Emma (part 1, chapters 6–9, part 2, part 3, chapters 1–8; (C) Charles as a widower; the death or anticipated death of every member of his and Emma's family (part 3, chapters 9–11).

Like a comet across the sky, Emma appears as an extraordinary but transient event in Charles's very ordinary life. This pattern pervades literature, from Jenny in Erich Segal's *Love Story* or Joy in C. S. Lewis's *Surprised by Joy* back to Helen of Troy in Goethe's *Faust* or the heroines of Novalis, Petrarch, Dante, and so on.

But these other authors are, in the broadest sense, optimistic romantics: their invented women reorient the male protagonists toward superior values, whereas Emma reorients Charles toward false values, toward the foolish, self-absorbed delusions of a debased romanticism that Flaubert seeks to satirize.

Because Flaubert is deeply pessimistic, in his novels the third time is not the charm, but the curse. His bitter irony, associated with three-ness, already appears in the title. Selfish Emma wants to be special. By marrying Charles, she escapes the farm; but not only does she symbolically lose her own identity in taking Charles's name, she becomes merely the third in a series of Madame Bovarys—the earlier two being Charles's mother and his first wife.

Emma's three attempts to find happiness in relationships with men—marriage to Charles, platonic devotion to Léon (part 2, chapters 2–6), adultery with Rodolphe (part 2, chapters 9–13) and with Léon (part 3, chapters 1–7)—all fail. Flaubert mocks the illusion that a passionate, all-absorbing love can ensure happiness by showing at one time or another that all the participants in adultery become bored with it or resentful of their partner's domination or indifference. He further underlines his irony with situational echoes: they insinuate that what the exciting novelty of a new sexual partner conceals an unvarying monotony. In the adulterous relationship with Rodolphe, Emma rediscovers "all the platitudes of marriage"; Léon 2 (the sexual lover) finally proves no more satisfying than Léon 1 (the platonic lover); and the role reversal that occurs between her liaison with Rodolphe (where Emma is dominated) and Léon 2 (where she dominates) does not make her any more happy. In a sense, Emma and Charles are star-crossed lovers—not because they cannot get together, but because Emma cannot understand or appreciate Charles's devotion, and Rodolphe cannot understand or appreciate Emma's. But Flaubert dramatizes her extraordinary allure twice, when Rodolphe almost yields to the invitation to flee abroad with her and later when she visits him for the last time and he briefly regrets having left her, although, as a cynical womanizer, he obviously will never wish to be bound by any lasting commitment. At the end, Flaubert starkly reduces the false variety of three-ness to a dead end when he describes the three expensive nesting coffins in which Charles insists Emma be buried. Flaubert's pessimistic belief that we humans can hope for no improvement in our lot echoes throughout the second and third parts of the novel in the noise of the tax collector Binet's lathe, on which he tirelessly produces useless napkin rings—closed circles like the life in which we are trapped. No wonder Flaubert cherished the religion of art as a way of escaping that trap through the act of describing it.

Throughout the second half of the novel of deluded passion, a second novel of social satire starts to grow, like a large fungus on a tree. Emma's narcissistic sense of entitlement—because she feels herself superior to others, she thinks she deserves to ignore their rules—leads first to the recklessness of adultery, but next to prodigal expenditures and growing indebtedness that leads her to steal from her husband. The financial tangles that ensnare her allow Flaubert opportunities to develop the character of the venal, unscrupulous merchant Lheureux, the emblem of bourgeois materialism. At the same time, the pretentious, ignorant pharmacist Homais and a series of failed, often disastrous medical treatments (of the clubfooted man Hippolyte; the blind man; Emma poisoned by arsenic) serve to satirize positivism, the myth that scientific progress will improve society. There may be no such progress, Flaubert implies—and if there were, we would remain just as immoral.

Flaubert reinforces the pessimistic tone of his ending by dwelling on the triumphs of the mean and unworthy. Lheureux prospers spectacularly; Homais wins renown by receiving the medal of the Legion of Honor, in return for his having helped rig an election; nor can any doctor succeed in establishing a practice in Yonville after Charles's death, because Homais's theatrical but illegal and ill-founded medical consultations overawe the townspeople with respect for his displays of knowledge.

TRADITIONAL ANALYSES OF THE ART OF FICTION

Analyses of stories conventionally distinguish between *event* (in a technical sense) and *act*. An event in this sense is an act of God, a natural disaster, an illness, a political or economic transformation, or any circumstances "independent of the will" of the characters, as the French expression has it. Event-driven stories such as adventure stories (danger sought) or stories of courage in the face of crisis (danger imposed) contrast with psychological stories, act-driven narratives where the initiatives taken by the characters are paramount. The major difference is that between reaction and action. Those stories Flaubert set in recent times have few events—or, if they do depict major events (such as the Revolution of 1848 in *L'Education sentimentale*), they are peripheral to the characters' central concerns. Flaubert's emplotment is character-driven.

Nevertheless, his pessimistic world emphasizes temptation rather than duty—not what one should do, but what one wants to do, regardless of the consequences. The tragic hero usually sacrifices desire for duty; the weak Flaubertian character sacrifices duty for desire. The richness of his characters depends on their ineffectual struggles against temptation and on the intricacy of their self-justifications. Typically, they become aware of something forbidden, feel its attraction but hesitate to pursue it, then yield to impulse that leads to a disastrous outcome. This process corresponds to the three stages of sin in Catholic theology: the surprise of the senses, morbid delectation (thinking how virtuous you are for resisting temptation serves as an excuse for you to dwell on it by way of compensation), and the consent of the will in attempting to sin.

A *story* refers to the actions and events an author chooses to tell about. *Narrative art* refers to how these basic elements of the story are filtered—who knows about them, and how?—and to how they are arranged. Some may be presented out of chronological sequence, with flashbacks or flash-forwards. Some may be repeated, or told more than once from different points of view. Some may be understood by the characters, or by some characters, and others understood only by the narrator and reader. Some may be deliberately omitted or merely suggested. More than one story may be woven together, and parallel stories may at times echo or contrast with others.

Flaubert's *Madame Bovary* presents a fairly straightforward chronological sequence of events in a disastrous marriage, concluding with Emma's suicide and Charles's pathological melancholy and death after she dies. Flaubert makes two major exceptions to this linear construction: he frames Emma's story with accounts of Charles's childhood and of his decline; and he interrupts his story often but briefly to report his characters' fragmentary memories, daydreams, and schemes. He also links his detailed reports of moments of crisis with briefer patches of iterative narration, with summaries of events that occur regularly during periods of calm. Narrative structure depends on the interplay between progress and delay, the latter being effected by background information; character portraits and analyses; descriptions of landscapes, towns, interiors, and objects; repetitions and variations on a theme for the sake of virtuosity; and pithy maxims about the human condition.[1] Flaubert's style, like Balzac's, is to set his scenes and his backgrounds in great detail. Balzac, however, gathers his long descriptions at the beginning of his novels: often the story remains static for some time as background information accumulates. In contrast, Flaubert practices the art of *détails différés* (postponing the presentation of certain details), often introducing them eventually from a character's point of view instead of from the omniscient narrator's.

Flaubert, like all other novelists, wants to suggest that his novel is more than just a story he is telling; it is a little world with its own laws and structures that go far beyond what we can perceive at first glance. So he fills the work with advance mentions, allusions, foreshadowing, symbols, and situational echoes whose meanings become clear only on a second reading. Emma reveals her narcissism and hedonism by touching herself and by contemplating her face in the mirror. To symbolize her moral restraint, Flaubert mentions the plaster statue of a priest reading his breviary in the Bovarys' garden. He makes it more susceptible to bear allegorical meanings by not saying where it came from. In time, the surface of the statue starts flaking off, it loses a foot, and finally it shatters in a fall from the wagon during the Bovarys' move from Tostes to Yonville (part 1, chapter 9, 125; part 2, chapter 3, 152). Emma's whippet, Djali (named after the beautiful gypsy La Esmeralda's performing goat in Hugo's *Notre-Dame de Paris*), a representation of her fancy, runs away and is lost during that same move (part 2, chapter 1, 143). She blames Charles. When Homais informs Emma about her new residence in Yonville, he mentions that a gate in the back wall, leading to the alley, allows one to come and go without being seen from the street—an important aid to Emma and Rodolphe's adultery later (part 2, chapter 2, 146). The comparison between her mind and an empty attic, where the spider of boredom spins, foreshadows her despair and near-suicide in her real attic, where she reads Rodolphe's insincere farewell letter (part 1, chapter 7, 105).

PLOT CONSTRUCTION

A default narrative plot consists of a single-stranded chain that produces a domino effect. One thing leads to another, while the consequences become increasingly serious. In *Madame Bovary*, the heroine has apparently been spoiled during childhood and adolescence, so that she feels entitled to more than her share of admiration, money, and love. Her superior intelligence makes her the center of attention in the convent school she attends, and the romantic literature that she surreptitiously reads there provides pernicious models of a world centered on the emotional needs of a female protagonist to whom all others are subservient. That she reads such fictional models literally transforms Emma into a profoundly asocial being with no awareness or consideration of the needs of others. Dissatisfied with her mediocre, boring husband, she slides down a slope of flirtation, adultery, embezzlement, and death.[2]

At each step within his plot, Flaubert had the choices of making Emma succeed, fail, or return to some starting point, enlightened by experience. Each time, she succeeds only in doing something self-destructive. Compared to Flaubert's *L'Education sentimentale*, *Madame Bovary* illustrates the contrast between a dramatic plot and an anticlimactic plot. In *Madame Bovary*, tension builds steadily as the protagonist's frustration intensifies. Emotionally isolated in a boring small town, she takes increasingly serious risks, until at last her fragile construction of sex, lies, and buying on credit collapses, leading her to a brief psychotic break and a gruesome suicide. In contrast, the antihero of *L'Education sentimentale*, Frédéric Moreau, strolls just outside the edge of momentous historical events, without ever becoming implicated in them, without ever committing himself to anything, and without ever rising above mediocrity. That his accidentally inherited money gives him instant access to and credibility with many people merely underscores the irony of his ordinariness, and at the conclusion the novel trails off into futile memories. The impulsive Emma leaps before she looks; Frédéric never leaps at all. As a pair, they illustrate the gender-based clichés: that women commit too readily, whereas men fear commitment to others.

NARRATIVE UNITS: THE RHYTHMS OF A STORY

As poems may be built up from stanzas, and plays from acts and scenes, prose fiction is constructed with *narrative units*, or basic segments of the action. Short units create a rapidly moving story, where the landscape of action is emphasized. Long units emphasize the landscape of thought. Narrative units usually range from about four to twenty pages, creating the rapid tempo of a Voltaire or the leisurely meandering of a Proust, a Lawrence Sterne, or a Charles Dickens. Flaubert's narrative units, usually corresponding to his chapters, are of moderate, average length—about ten pages each. In this respect he resembles most other realist and naturalist novelists.

The author may leave narrative units strictly implicit, by presenting a continuous text divided only into paragraphs, with no distinct chapters, or parts, or titles. At this extreme, marked for impersonality, the controlling presence of the narrator has been entirely concealed by eliminating obvious cues to how fast the story moves and how we might interpret it. Closer to the mid-range of possibilities, the unmarked or default choice introduces *typographical self-consciousness:* the division of the text into numbered but untitled chapters. Such is Flaubert's procedure. At the other, interventionist extreme, an author can interject his or her personality by adding signs of *interpretive self-consciousness,* dividing the text into parts as well as chapters, with titles for the parts or the chapters, or both; epigraphs and footnotes (such as those intended to present homosexuality as natural in Manuel Puig's *Kiss of the Spider Woman*). Taken together, titles, epigraphs, or footnotes can even form a mininarrative.

To his typographical self-consciousness, Flaubert adds a nuance of interpretive self-consciousness by dividing his text into three parts containing nine, fifteen, and ten chapters, respectively. The lack of symmetry among these numbers shows that the author is not imposing an overarching, transcendent symbolism on his text (unlike Dante in *The Divine Comedy,* for example, where all the stanzaic and narrative units consist of three parts, or multiples of three, corresponding to the Holy Trinity: thus the overall structure reveals the triune God). However, given the outcome, suicide, Flaubert's three parts implicitly correlate adultery with a Fall: Emma, the dissatisfied wife, passes from platonic love (part 1) to a first adultery (part 2: thus she becomes what French Classical literature called *une femme sensible*) to a second adultery (part 3: thus Emma becomes what Classicism called *une femme galante,* a recidivist, and therefore, by suggestion, irredeemable). In contrast, romantic novelists, less concerned with verisimilitude, often title their parts (e.g., Balzac in *Le Père Goriot*) or chapters (e.g., Stendhal in *Le Rouge et le Noir*).[3]

SITUATIONAL ECHOES

Many echoing situations pervade the novel with a two-edged irony that simultaneously undermines the effusions of the characters, who believe their feelings are unique to themselves, with the ironic reality of sameness in human behavior, while often also contrasting one instance of behavior with another. Charles must marry one wife to whom he is not attracted and who is overly dependent on him—reduplicating in a less callous mode his own father's attitude toward his mother—and then can marry Emma, to whom he is blindly devoted, reduplicating his mother's initial attitude toward his father. His mother loses (103) and at last regains (415) his exclusive devotion, only to lose it again in a quarrel over his daughter Berthe, who becomes a symbolic surrogate for Emma. After having been excessively criticized by his first wife in concert with his mother, Charles is indulged by Emma in concert with her father (70–71, 76–78). To Charles after the wedding night, the universe does not extend past the silky circle of Emma's skirt, and then Léon in turn is fascinated by that garment—both men displaying an infantile dependent attitude (94, 338). Charles initially wins Emma's respect by successfully mending one patient's leg (her father's) and then loses it by ruining another (Hippolyte's, part 1, chapter 2, and part 2, chapter 11). Emma at first plays the piano to show off and then, later, to create an excuse to meet Léon each week in Rouen (101, 332–34). Her impulsive attempts to express some affection for her daughter are thwarted, first when Berthe throws up on her mother's lace collar and later when she sees that Berthe is dirty. Emma reveals her willingness eventually to surrender to Rodolphe by leaving her hand in his, as she does later with Léon (215, 308). Charles's, and then Léon's, relationship with Emma progresses from a timid, platonic phase to a separation of several months or more, and then resumes as a frankly sexual relationship. Both Rodolphe and Léon meet Emma in the alley behind her garden wall, and both arrange a discreet, secret mail drop (330, 332). With both men, she eventually seeks a morbidly codependent relationship that drives them away (266, 356). When Emma takes a romantic boat ride with Léon, she learns that Rodolphe probably took the same trip with a joyous group shortly before (328–30). Her near-suicide after Rodolphe leaves her foretells her actual suicide after she learns that she cannot count on Léon or Rodolphe for financial help (274;). At the beginning of her liaison with Léon, a walking tour of the cathedral used by her to delay her decision is followed by a coach tour of Rouen during which the liaison is consummated (312–16, 317–18). The inept interruption of their courtship by the sexton who wants to show Léon the cathedral, infuriating him, will be echoed by the inept interruption by Homais, who wants Léon to show him Rouen, infuriating Emma (312–16, 351–55). Flaubert mentions that Emma has drawn a veil over her face when she first leaves Léon after their lovemaking and later, habitually, when she returns to him (318, 336). Both Emma's father and she must sell some land when they encounter financial difficulty (79, 345). By chance, Emma hears precisely where the pharmacist Homais keeps his arsenic, long before she decides to kill herself with it; his elaborate warning against the dangers of the arsenic aggravates those dangers later (320–21, 389–90). Dr. Canivet must intervene first successfully, to save Hippolyte from dying of gangrene, and then unsuccessfully to save Emma from arsenic poisoning. In the second of these episodes, Dr. Larivière, who unlike Canivet might have been able to save Emma had he been notified in time, reduplicates Canivet's intervention. During Emma's wake, Homais and Bournisien have two doctrinal quarrels before achieving a quasi-reconciliation (404, 407–9). Charles first discovers the farewell letter from Rodolphe, which he can imagine is platonic, and, later the frankly sexual letters from both Rodolphe and Léon, which leave no possibility for doubt (417, 422). Many of these paired events or situations are not extraordinary; but by choosing to mention the repetitions, Flaubert emphasizes how ordinary and predictable our life often is, although we who live it may feel intensely joyous, adventurous, or despairing.

When Flaubert wishes to convey that a repeated motif forms part of a dramatic progression, he uses triplication—a three-part movement—rather than reduplication. So the bench under the arbor in the Bovarys' garden first witnesses Léon's and Emma's chaste conversations, then her exciting sexual encounters with Rodolphe, and, finally, Charles's depression, despair, and death (236, 424). As Emma desperately seeks money to pay her debts after leaving Léon in Rouen, she first approaches the lawyer Guillaumin but refuses to have sex with him, then apparently tries to seduce Binet, who recoils, and finally, Rodolphe, who does not have the money that she needs. After Emma and Charles are dead, little Berthe has three potential caregivers, but her paternal grandmother dies soon, her maternal grandfather is paralyzed, and her aunt cannot afford to keep her. At the same time, in Yonville, three doctors in succession fail to establish a practice there, because Homais's illegal competition is too strong. The blind man, who vis-à-vis Emma represents unreasoning sexuality through his condition and his song (he may have become blind from syphilis), appears three times, ever more intimately associated with her: first, begging for alms near the coach that takes her to her assignations with Léon; then, clinging to the side of the coach and sticking his head in the window (a habitual act, but presented separately from and after the first scene involving him); and finally, outside Emma's window as she dies, while she hallucinates his hideous face appearing among the shadows of death as an emblem of eternal punishment. In contrast to Emma, Homais, who sins with impunity, manages after her death to have the blind man committed to an asylum, so that he cannot continue to denounce the failure of Homais's medicinal salves to everyone he meets.

Aside from the blind man, motifs that occur more than thrice in the text generally reflect mediocrity, transience, inauthenticity, and self-deception. To evade personal responsibility, characters blame fate rather than themselves (213, 252, 271, 424). Emma's common sense does not prevent her from being overcome by dangerous desires (205, 209, 211, 283, 294, 304). Pride impels her to rash decisions (172, 253, 311, etc.). She and Léon model most of their feelings and expectations on books (94, 171, 230, 292, 330). And over everything that seems desirable, as Stirling Haig pointed out, hangs a bluish haze that suggests vague, infinite vistas suddenly opening before the characters (71, 73, 81, 110, 149, 225, 226, 229, 307 twice, 309, 310, 364).[4]

CHARACTERIZATION

Traditional novels often present characters with a two-paragraph description by an omniscient narrator, first describing their physical appearance and, next, their personality and moral essence. Flaubert, instead, tends to present fragmentary images of characters' physical appearance progressively as it strikes other characters in the story and then makes omniscient but limited appraisals of his characters' personality and motives only after they have acted. Thus he sometimes creates the illusion that his characters can act independently of the narrator. In *Madame Bovary* he uses three basic character types, of which two modes may combine in one person: the prey, deluded or weak people deceived and exploited by others (Charles, Emma, Catherine Leroux, little Berthe); the predators, lucid, unscrupulous dramatic movers, highly effective in realizing their desires (Emma, Rodolphe, Lheureux, Homais, Lestiboudois); and those who, whether embittered or self-satisfied, seem destined forever to repeat the same words and actions without ever rising above the repetitious routines of their daily lives (Binet, Madame Lefrançois, Madame Rollet, Madame Homais, Bournisien, Hivert, l'Aveugle, and many others). After his fling with Emma, Léon, weak and irresolute as either predator or prey, will give up music, renounce the imagination, and foreswear anything out of the ordinary.

SOCIAL DENSITY

A major dimension of characterization is the choice of how many different people and types to include. Nobles, bourgeois, peasants? Children, adults, the elderly? Women, men? Animals portrayed as thinking or feeling beings? How many characters appear and in how broad a range? *Madame Bovary* has considerable *social density* (contains many fictional people), but little *ecological density* (no representations of animal consciousness). And the novel's social range is limited. Except for episodic appearances such as the ball at La Vaubyessard, in *Madame Bovary* Flaubert does not treat the nobility or the peasantry in detail (unlike, say, Balzac or Zola), but limits himself mainly to the middle class and their servants.[5] In age range, Madame *Bovary* offers sensitive sketches of two relatively old men (Emma's and Charles's fathers), of Berthe as an infant and as a small child, and of the infatuated adolescent Justin, but focuses on young adults and adults. Emma may be only about eighteen when she first meets Charles.

As the leading realist novelist of France, Flaubert places limited, mainly middle-class characters in a setting that was recent and recognizable for his original intended audience, French people from 1856 to 1880. Such stories are the opposite of exotic or escapist. Their main point is that one cannot escape fatigue, boredom, mutilation, death, financial difficulties, sordid political intrigues, and—except for the servant Félicité in "Un cœur simple"—despair. It is foolish to hope for salvation from any quarter—friends, lovers, lawyers, leaders, or the gods. But such stories are *not* realistic insofar as the main characters can help determine a range of outcomes—there's only failure.

From the beginning, Flaubert's characters are burdened with insurmountable handicaps in the race of life. Thinly disguised tag-names *(noms étiquettes)* foreshadow this condition by predefining a character's essence or by reflecting hopes that contrast ironically with the characters' fates.

1. *Fantasies of romantic love and adventure will lead only to bitter disappointment.* "Héloïse," the name of the twelfth-century lady passionately loved by Peter Abelard, a philosopher twenty years older than she, ironically labels Charles's unwanted, unattractive, older first wife. "Emma" suggests a heroine from the British romanticism that seduced Emma Bovary in the convent school and depraved her taste. "Hippolyte," the dashing young hero of Jean Racine's classical tragedy *Phèdre* and so named because of his gift for taming and riding horses, will become a crippled stable boy in *Madame Bovary*.

2. *The most unworthy and unscrupulous characters will triumph.* "Lheureux," the predatory, fawning merchant and usurer, means "the fortunate one." "Vinçart," one of his accomplices, suggests *vaincre*, "to triumph." "Homais," the pharmacist who illegally practices medicine and who abets election fraud to be awarded the Legion of Honor medal by the government, seems a disparaging diminutive for "man" *(homme)*.[6]

3. *Proper names, standing for the social presentation of the self in everyday life, often form ludicrous antitheses to the true character of the persons in question, hinting at the pretentiousness of rural attitudes.* "Léon" (lion), Emma's second lover, is timid and pusillanimous. "Félicité" (happiness), Emma's young maid, is destined to a life of servitude. "Mademoiselle Lempereur" (the emperor) is the piano teacher in Rouen who, after Emma's death, charges Charles for lessons Emma didn't take from her. *L'Hirondelle* (the swallow) is a muddy, low-slung vehicle with windows you can hardly see out of (unlike a so-called bird's-eye view and unlike the romantic image of the swallow).

4. *The inescapable mediocrity of other characters is stamped on them like a badge of infamy that they can't recognize.* "Bournisien," the priest, is implicitly *borné* (limited) by his religious fanaticism. "Binet" (from *biner*, a word meaning "to do something twice") endlessly turns out useless napkin rings on his lathe. Dr. "Canivet" (suggesting *canif*, or "pen-knife") can only cut off Hippolyte's leg; he chooses exactly the wrong treatment for Emma's arsenic poisoning (an emetic, given instead of a vomitive, spreads the poison more widely through her system). "Lieuvain," the municipal counselor who gives the closing address at the county fair *(Comices agricoles)*, means "an empty place"; in French, *vain* can describe something unreal, insignificant, or ineffectual.

Many characters have names associated with farm animals—especially with calves—so many that Jonathan Culler whimsically claimed *Madame Bovary* illustrated "vealism" more than "realism": Charles's first wife was Héloïse Dubuc (as in *bouc*, "ram," with apophany); his own last name, Bovary, suggests "bovine." Léon will marry a Mademoiselle Léocadie Lebœuf (the steer). In short, Flaubert's realistic style is actually more essentialist than existentialist; he has prejudged his characters. What Charles cries out to introduce himself to his class—"Charbovary"—suggests *char à bœufs* (a cart drawn by cattle) and prepares the ironic motif of Emma Bovary's futile desires to escape from the country. Emma will want to name her first child Georges, which, unknown to her, comes from the ancient Greek word for "farmer" (compare the Roman poet Vergil's *The Georgics*). Thus she would symbolically return her child to the boring condition she had wanted to escape by marrying Charles.

Flaubert understands that much of our mental life is not task oriented: he richly presents the mingling of past, present, and future, and our preoccupation with chance impressions. The motif of clothing frequently suggests Emma's superficiality: she is taken in by appearances. The soft leather boots Rodolphe wears when he escorts her to the county fair, and which he has chosen in the knowledge that she had probably not ever seen such footwear before, impress her. When she hesitates to go for a horseback ride with him, knowing the dangers of being seduced, Charles generously offers to buy her a riding habit, and the prospect of wearing it is decisive for Emma.

A warning symbolic subtext in Flaubert often clashes with his characters' superficial impressions. On the way to his fateful meeting with Emma, for example, Charles has hallucinations in which the unpleasantness of his medical training and his marriage merge. Consciously, he registers the relative wealth and comfort of the Rouault farm. Unconsciously, because Flaubert associates the color blue with the ideal throughout *Madame Bovary*, the blue wax Emma has used to seal her letter, the blue wool upholstery in her father's carriages, and her blue dress attract him.[7] But Flaubert also warns us of impending danger: Charles's horse unaccountably shies at the entrance of the farm; Emma's shell-rimmed spectacles and her thin hands have something masculine about them; and her polished, almond-shaped nails are an ominous sign for the thoughtful reader that this country girl is a narcissist who does not do much hard work on her father's farm. Later, Léon's carefully groomed nails suggest that he shares her shallow self-absorption.

STYLE

Style means both the distinctive character of a particular set of words and the activity that selects them from among the expressive resources of language: sounds, rhythms, emotional coloration, figures of speech, and typography—to say nothing of grammar, syntax, and lexicon. Telling a story always includes creating an illusion, a semblance of reality.[8] Most characteristic of Flaubert's style is a subtle, complex interplay of identification and distancing between the viewpoint of the storyteller and of the characters. This interplay inspired Faulkner and many great contemporary novelists, so much so that Flaubert has been called the father of the modern novel.

Whereas romanticism adopted an inflationary style, making characters and events larger than life, realism is a deflationary, demystifying style. Romantics sought exotic and therefore imposing subjects in earlier times, distant lands, the supernatural, and altered states of consciousness (any mental condition other than rational waking reality). Realists focused on the *hic et nunc,* the here and now. You feel you could still easily go see where the story took place. The first chapter of part 2 in *Madame Bovary* brings out these two tendencies most clearly. Flaubert narrates in the present tense as he takes us on a tour of Yonville, "in a hybrid region ... without any particular distinction. There the worst Neufchâtel cheese of the whole area is made, but it's expensive to raise crops [which otherwise would be a wiser choice than dairy farming], because you need a lot of fertilizer for the crumbly soil full of sand and pebbles" (134). "Since the events we are about to relate nothing new, actually, has happened in Yonville" (137).

Flaubert achieves distancing of point of view through a combination of realism and irony. Realism in literature acknowledges that the material world exists independently of our hopes and desires. Nor can we always control our bodies and our minds. We become hungry, weak, tired, and ill. The realistic character may be disfigured or crippled and undergo medical treatment. Emma Bovary suffers from anorexia (see Lilian Furst) and "brain fever" (a staple of the Victorian novel, when the author wants to give the heroine a time-out). Flaubert's characters undergo a bloodletting treatment, a broken leg, an amputation, and a lurid death by poison. Sex is not idealized either. Constrained by harsh censorship, Flaubert nevertheless makes delicate allusions to what in many of the United States is still the felony of "sodomy" (meaning, primarily, oral or anal intercourse) in the later stages of Emma's affairs with Rodolphe and Léon.

The minds and feelings of realistic characters are imperfect too. They feel petty, intolerant, jealous, envious, or afraid. Often they are confused, mistaken, or ignorant. They have only an inkling of the world and the people around them. In realism there are no heroes, although we can usually sympathize with or at least pity some of the characters. In contrast, the idealized physical hero never needs to rest, sleep, or eat. The idealized intellectual hero, a detective such as Sherlock Holmes, for example, can read a person's life story from their body, face, and clothes. Physical and intellectual heroes alike are always supremely self-confident and unfailingly resourceful. Perhaps the greatest difference between high art (in the favorable sense) and popular culture (in the unfavorable sense) in critics' minds is that in the latter, the main characters tend to be purely good or evil, saved or damned. Moral ambiguity is lacking.

Money, of which the idealized hero has a limitless supply, becomes a major limitation for the realistic character, who needs to work or steal to make a living. (The romantic hero was once defined as "a person without a job"; referring to his obscure early years, the great abstract expressionist painter Willem De Kooning said "the trouble with being poor is that it takes all your time.") The dowry is an important issue in both of Charles's marriages. Flaubert provides much technical detail concerning Emma's borrowing, the power of attorney she obtains to administer her family's financial affairs, and bankruptcy procedures. When she has spent all her and Charles's money and can borrow no more, she can no longer be free, and she commits suicide.

Flaubert's "de-euphemizing" metaphors and similes reflect the inevitable, fateful progression from good or neutral to bad or worse that forms the tightly constructed, pessimistic realist plot.[9] Traditionally, a metaphor—an arbitrary verbal transformation of one thing into another—improves a situation. Military combat is glory; death is sleep, or release, or a journey; a young woman is a rose (from a feminist viewpoint, of course, this comparison forces her to be decorative, frail, passive, and immobile). But Flaubert, in this respect a modernist, often invents metaphors that debase the experience they convey. So when Charles remarries Emma and is besotted with her, his mother feels desolate at no longer being preferred. She is compared to an impoverished person looking through the window of her former house at the new owners obliviously enjoying a meal (part 1, chapter 7, 103). Motherly love has been demoted to a purely material affair, like food. Likewise, shortly after marrying Emma, Charles ruminates on his happiness (chewing it as a steer would chew a cud) like a person still enjoying the taste of truffles after a fine meal: "le cœur plein des félicités de la nuit, l'esprit tranquille, la chair contente, il s'en allait ruminant son bonheur, comme ceux qui mâchent encore, après dîner, le goût des truffes qu'ils digèrent" (part 1, chapter 5, 93). After she has returned home from the weekend and ball at the chateau of La Vaubyessard, Emma's heart still bears the indelible traces of her contact with wealth, as her dancing slippers preserved the indelible yellow stains of the floor wax from the ballroom ("Elle serra pieusement dans la commode sa belle toilette et jusqu'à ses souliers de satin, dont la semelle s'était jaunie à la cire glissante du parquet. Son cœur était comme eux: au frottement de la richesse, il s'était placé dessus quelque chose qui ne s'effacerait pas") (part 1, chapter 8, 116). Sometimes Flaubert contrasts our exalted hopes and depressing realities in the same complex metaphor. Speaking of the impossibility for Emma to communicate the depths of her devotion to Rodolphe with the few trite phrases she has at her disposal, Flaubert remarks that human language is like a cracked cauldron on which we beat out tunes fit only to set bears dancing, when we had hoped to make the stars weep in sympathy: "La parole humaine est comme un chaudron fêlé où nous battons des mélodies à faire danser les ours, quand on voudrait attendrir les étoiles" (part 2, chapter 12, 259). Flaubert stresses this motif of incommunicability, the realization that we can't share our feelings, by introducing it into nearly all the obligatory scenes—long-expected, crucial confrontations between characters. When Charles first comes to school; when he tries to ask Emma's father for her hand in marriage; when Emma and Léon are finally alone together, on a walk; when Léon takes leave of her to go to Paris; when she seeks spiritual help from the priest Bournisien; when Emma and Rodolphe have their last rendezvous—all the characters can do is stammer incoherently or utter clichés. To their inarticulateness contrasts the grotesque, inexhaustible written and spoken verbiage of Homais, even emptier than the stammering because it reflects no true feeling.

When a Flaubertian metaphor or simile seems highly positive, it ordinarily refers to a bygone, now inaccessible possibility for happiness, and it is often couched in flat, sarcastic, contemptuous language. Before she married Charles, Flaubert observes, Emma had convinced herself that she finally possessed that grand passion that had been hovering in the skies above her head like a great pink bird ("cette passion merveilleuse qui jusqu'alors s'était tenu comme un grand oiseau au plumage rose planant dans la splendeur des ciels poétiques") (part 1, chapter 6, 99–100). But soon she experiences Charles as the sharp goad, digging into her flesh, of the complex harness (of conventional restraints on women in nineteenth-century France, where a wife had to obey in all matters and where divorce was outlawed between 1814 and 1886) that confined her on every side.

FLAUBERT'S DESCRIPTIONS AS IMPLIED SATIRIC JUDGMENTS

In his *Writing Degree Zero*, Roland Barthes spoke of "the reality effect" created by detailed descriptions such as the list of unused objects heaped up in Madame Aubain's parlor in the tale "Un cœur simple." By simply "being there" without moving the plot or symbolizing hidden meanings, Barthes claims, objects in such descriptions simply convey the message "we real objects are here: this is a realistic novel." Flaubert creates a reality effect not only with descriptive details but also by the junk pile of his characters' language. Italics call attention to inelegant, trite moments when the characters use schoolboy and classroom slang, as in part 1, chapter 1, or express clichéd views, or misuse French. Such slangy or colloquial phrases signal us that "I (the character) am here," as a distinct individual who does not use the elevated literary language of the author. At times, characters' speech serves a satiric function by unmasking their ignorance.

Flaubert's critics often emphasize the inarticulateness of his creatures, related to *Madame Bovary*'s pessimistic motif of incommunicability in general—but the true situation is not so simple. Some of them indulge in effusions but report their strong feelings in ordinary language. Old Rouault, a demonstrative, affectionate person, expresses himself in a burlesque style when he comes to pay Charles for setting his leg and to comfort him after the loss of his first wife. He speaks of his own despair after Emma's mother died years ago. With excessive detail, he lists six symptoms of his own despair, then four expressions of his rage at the unfairness of his loss, and finally, four signs of his recovery from grieving. He concludes with four pieces of advice for Charles, concerning how it would do him good to get out once again. An added irony is that Charles is secretly pleased to be free of his unattractive, nagging first wife (79–80).

Flaubert's satiric thrust appears even more frequently and more characteristically in a mode of understatement, which is reserved for the narrator. To deride both his characters' ludicrous aspirations and mediocre accomplishments, the author sarcastically deploys adverbs (the linguistic mode par excellence of passing judgment), particularly *même* and *presque* ("even" and "nearly"). In addition to teaching him to read, Charles's mother *even* teaches him to sing two or three old romances; later, by dint of hard study at school he once *even* receives an honorable mention in one class. When he goes away from home to pursue his studies in Rouen, he loses weight, and, with his hollow cheeks, comes to look *nearly* interesting. Later, to please Emma he buys her a second-hand *boc* (two-wheeled, horse-drawn carriage) that *"nearly* resembles" a "tilbury" (a fashionable English version of the same). The third main vehicle of Flaubert's sarcasm is the family of verbs meaning "to try or attempt." Inspired with a sensuous religious fervor in her convent school, Emma *tried* to fast for an entire day (95). After moving to Yonville and having few patients at first, Charles does chores around the house and *even tries* to paint the attic with some leftover paint (152).

POINT OF VIEW: RENDERING THE CHARACTERS' INNER LIVES

Despite the peremptory dismissiveness of such casual notations of his characters' failed intentions, however, Flaubert succeeds at other times in endowing them—Emma in particular—with a rich inner life. One can apprehend this life most readily in the if-then sentences. There are at least three types of them, referring (1) to things that *will* happen if one acts; (2) to things that *might* happen under the right conditions; or (3) to things that *should* happen but won't because circumstances don't allow it or (from a character's perspective) because life is unfair. The first is the working hypothesis, a plan that can be carried out in the real world of the characters: if I do X, the result will be Y. The practical-minded Rodolphe reasons: If I say I love Emma, I can easily seduce her because she is unhappy, sexually frustrated, and bored. The grasping merchant Lheureux believes that if he establishes a mail and passenger service to compete with Madame Lefrançois's *L'Hirondelle,* he will be able to gather all the commerce of Yonville in his hands. The second type of hypothesis, in *Madame Bovary,* often appears as an opportunity that one character suggests to another. Flaubert uses such hypotheses ironically. Charles mistakenly thinks that if Emma were to move away from Tostes, or start riding horseback, or enjoy the distraction of the opera in Rouen, her health would improve. Homais and Emma argue that if Charles operated on Hippolyte's clubfoot, the stable boy would be able to walk normally, and Charles would become famous. Emma tries to persuade Rodolphe that if he ran off with her to Italy, they both would be happy forever. Rodolphe knows the last suggestion is impractical and only pretends to go along with it. Most of the other suggestions are proposed by the meddling Homais, and the outcomes of them are disastrous: Emma's two affairs, Charles's disgrace, and Hippolyte's loss of one leg. All the medical treatments in the novel actually fall into this category: Flaubert quietly satirizes medicine, and his father and older brother, who were doctors, by showing that none of the proposed cures work. Emma needed to be made to vomit up the arsenic she had swallowed; in other cases, patients recover only by resting and being left alone. Charles has a reputation for being successful with chest colds because he prescribes only mild medications. In the third type of hypothesis, either the characters or the narrator himself may imagine *counterfactuals:* conceivable but impossible circumstances other than those in which they find themselves. Benjamin Bart calls these hypotheses "parastories" when they are proposed by the narrator and none of the characters are aware of them. For example, if Emma had grown up in town rather than on a farm, the narrator speculates, she might have been able to appreciate the calm of the country (95–96), but as it was, she needed strong sensations. Daydreaming about impossible alternative lives frequently preoccupies Emma: she longs to be a heroine in a sentimental novel and, also, to live in Paris. Her thwarted sense of entitlement leads her to speculate bitterly about what her life would have been had she been born an aristocrat or had she found a better, more intelligent, romantic, and competent husband. Unlike the other characters, she tries to act out many of her fantasies, playing at being devoutly religious, an ideal mother, or a loving wife—but she quickly tires of the routine and the lack of glamour in these roles. Money, again, becomes part of the problem. If she had been able to afford a fancy layette for her baby, Flaubert observes, she might have felt more affection for her (part 2, chapter 3, 153).

TRANSPARENT MINDS: THE OMNISCIENT NARRATOR AND THE CHARACTERS' INNER LIVES

Flaubert suggests a system of laws governing human emotional life. Sometimes he does so simply by stating a generalization. When Léon misses an assignation with Emma because Homais drags him off to look at a trained dog, Flaubert explains Léon's motivation as cowardice and stupidity, but also "that indefinable feeling that compels *us* [emphasis added] to perform the most distasteful acts" (part 3, chapter 6, 355). Sometimes a parallel between two people's feelings makes a general insight obvious, for instance, when Emma's dissatisfaction is compared to that of the wigmaker in Yonville who self-deceptively broods that his talents have been unappreciated, and his life blighted, only because he couldn't live in Paris (part 1, chapter 9, 125). At other times, more subtly, Flaubert only implicitly echoes one part of the text with another. For instance, our spouse's achievements enhance our own sense of worth: Charles feels vicarious pride when his neighbors admire his wife, her artistic and musical talents, and her imaginative housekeeping (part 1, chapter 7, 102). Later, she hopes to be able to enjoy the reflected glory of her husband if he successfully performs an operation to straighten Hippolyte's clubfoot (part 2, chapter 11, 242). We discover such parallels as if by chance or feel them subliminally; in either case, the device works powerfully to carry the conviction of psychological realism: "Oh yes, that's what people and the world are like. Here's another example." Such insights allow us readers to feel vaguely that we may transcend our mundane condition by coming to comprehend it.

But Flaubert's pessimistic work always contests our momentary exhilaration at achieving superior understanding. He deflates us with ironic quotations of his characters' banal, unreflective expressions to convey his conviction that attempts at communication always prove futile. Literary critics have lamented the absence of an "irony mark"—a typographical convention to show the reader when the author is not taking the discourse seriously. But such ironic punctuation already exists in several forms, for example, in the hyphenated strings of words that report racist stereotypes in Francophone literature or in the italics with which Flaubert reports vividly realistic and characteristic but stereotyped discourse typical of a particular milieu.

Flaubert can't write effective dialogue in his realistic novels because he believes either that ordinary people are inarticulate, or else that any possible verbal expression of their imagination is limited to clichés. Most of his characters speak banalities unwittingly, believing themselves profound; a few unscrupulous scoundrels use conversational clichés cunningly, to manipulate and deceive others. When two characters seem in perfect harmony, as do Léon and Emma on their first meeting, Flaubert is secretly mocking them. He wrote to Louise Colet that he had composed their conversation "dans une grande intention du grotesque" (*CORR* 2:172; October 9, 1852)—in a serious effort to make them seem grotesque. When two characters disagree articulately, as do Bournisien the priest and Homais the pharmacist in their conversations, they also speak in clichés and are equally ridiculous. Too scornful to bother even reproducing the first intimate conversation of Emma and Charles at the beginning of their courtship, Flaubert simply notes curtly that "les phrases leur vinrent" [the things people ordinarily say came to them] (part 1, chapter 3, 82). He reserves eloquent, penetrating verbal exchanges for his fantasy literature, notably, the three versions of *La Tentation de saint Antoine*, which depicts an idealized life of the mind. But his more pessimistic final work, *Bouvard et Pécuchet*, portrays even the search for knowledge as just another hopeless struggle with clichés.

In addition to explicit indeterminacy, when Flaubert retreats from omniscience, he also creates implicit indeterminacy.[10] The reasons why Emma was sent to the convent school remain unclear: was it because her mother had just died, and her father did not know what to do with her? Or did one or both of her parents see Emma's convent education, which included music and drawing and which was prima facie inappropriate preparation for helping to manage a farm, as compensation for their own frustrated sense of entitlement and superiority to their condition? Or did they want to use their relative wealth to ascend socially by training their one surviving child to "marry up"? All we can conclude is that Emma's upbringing made her adjustment to her realistic prospects impossible.

Flaubert often feigns a retreat from omniscience about his own creation by expressing uncertainty about his characters' motives. For example, when Emma could not spend as much as she wanted on her daughter's layette, she lost interest in it, and "son affection, dès l'origine, en fut *peut-être* [emphasis added] atténuée de quelque chose" [from the outset, her affection for her child was *perhaps* somewhat diminished as a result] (part 2, chapter 3, 153). Many such examples can be found.

Flaubert frequently uses an impressionistic style to report the characters' blurred perceptions and their gradual apprehension of images at first dimly perceived. Such literary impressionism may have both a realistic and an ironic effect. As realism, it veils the narrator's omniscience by limiting the scope and the acuity of sense impressions to the immediate scene. Often, in *Madame Bovary*, awareness is impaired by dim or hazy light. Feelings, too, swim into focus only gradually in the protagonists' minds. Irony emerges from the contrast between the narrator's omniscient lucidity and the characters' vague understanding—a contrast heightened by the motif of incommunicability, the assumption that human language often proves inadequate, misleading, or totally ineffectual. Charles Bovary's stammering of his name in class, when first being introduced, and his stammering of his prospective father-in-law's name, which is all he can muster as a request for permission to marry Emma, exemplifies such difficulties.

Flaubert's desire to combine two perspectives simultaneously—the impressionistic and the omniscient—betrays itself two glaring contradictions in the initial scene introducing Charles as the new boy who has just arrived at his school. The passage that begins "Resté dans l'ombre, derrière la porte, si bien qu'on l'apercevait à peine.... " [We could hardly see him in the shadow of the doorway....] (part 1, chapter 1, 61) lists nineteen physical details. After this minute description, and an account of Charles's parents and childhood, the narrator sums up "Il serait maintenant impossible à aucun de nous de se rien rappeler de lui" [it would be difficult for any of us to recall anything about him today] (part 1, chapter 1, 67).

Flaubert balances the impressionistic and omniscient modes better in his tableaux. At Emma and Charles's wedding, the first such ensemble scene, he begins with impressionistic narration, describing how an observer would gradually discern more and more detail as the forty guests arrive. One hears the sound of a vehicle approaching, then sees it (any one of six varieties of carriage) stop to disgorge a mass of people, who become differentiated into men, women, and children, and then, into five distinct social levels marked by their clothes (85–89). These descriptive inventories (six types of carriage, five levels of social rank) betray the intrusion of the encyclopedic authorial consciousness amid the loose, imprecise perceptions of the undifferentiated characters.

THE IMPORTANCE OF GESTURES IN FLAUBERT

Flaubert's novels are rich in gestures, involuntary responses that reveal characters' inner lives. Through gestures, he can disguise omniscience as realism. His characters seem to exist not merely as sets of words but also as physical presences assuming various postures and moving through space. Flaubert enhances this twofold impression by noting postures and gestures that the characters *think of* assuming or making without actually doing so. References to gestures are shown in italics in the following quotations. Charles Bovary in his first class was as attentive as at a sermon, *"n'osant même croiser les cuisses, ni s'appuyer sur le coude"* ([not even daring to cross his legs, nor to lean on his elbow] (part 1, chapter 1, 62). A little later, as he awkwardly holds his visored cap on his knees: *"Levez-vous,* dit le professeur. *Il se leva:* sa casquette tomba. Toute la classe se mit à rire. *Il se baissa* pour la reprendre. Un voisin *la fit tomber d'un coup de coude; il la ramassa* encore une fois"* ["Stand up," said the teacher. He stood up: his cap fell to the floor. The whole class broke into laughter. He bent down to pick it up. A boy sitting next to him knocked it off with his elbow; Charles picked it up again.] (part 1, chapter 1, 62).

Much later, musing over his bungled operation on Hippolyte as the stable boy howls with pain next door during his amputation, Charles suddenly thinks out loud. "Mais c'était peut-être un valgus? … Emma *tressaillant leva la tête* pour deviner ce qu'il voulait dire.… Emma *mordait ses lèvres blêmes, et roulant entre ses doigts* un des brins du polypier qu'elle avait cassé, *elle fixait sur Charles la pointe ardente de ses prunelles"* [But maybe it was a valgus? … Emma, shuddering, raised her head in order to discover what he was talking about.… Emma bit her pale lips, as she rolled one of the branches of coral she had broken off between her fingers, and glared at Charles with fiery eyes] (part 2, chapter 11, 253).

Near the conclusion, when Emma's father leaves after her funeral, he says to Charles, "Et puis, jamais je n'oublierai ça, dit-il *en se frappant la cuisse,* n'ayez peur! vous recevrez toujours votre dinde. Mais, quand il fut au haut de la côte, *il se détourna … Il mit sa main devant ses yeux …"* [And then, I'll never forget this, he said, slapping his thigh, don't worry! You'll always get your turkey. But when he had reached the crest of the rise, he turned back … He put his hand in front of his eyes … "] (part 3, chapter 10, 415).

HALFWAY BETWEEN NARRATOR AND CHARACTER: *STYLE INDIRECT LIBRE*

Flaubert's representation of his characters' consciousness is rightly celebrated for its skillful ambiguity and its artfulness. (1) As the omniscient narrator, he can report directly what they said or thought, as *direct discourse.* (2) Or he can report the characters' words and thoughts as *indirect discourse* in the third person, with tags (*incises* in French)—she said, she thought—that show who was thinking or speaking and how. (3) Using summaries of their words or actions, the narrator can range from the uncertainty of a naive observer to a godlike insight into the characters' secret mental and emotional lives. (4) Finally, in *style indirect libre* ("free indirect style" or "represented discourse" in English, *erlebte Rede* in German), he can hover halfway between the characters' and the narrator's consciousness.

Generalizations in Flaubert often cannot be unequivocally attributed to either the character or the omniscient narrator. For instance, "a woman's will trembles in every breeze, but is always held back like a veil" ("Sa volonté [celle d'une femme], comme le voile de son chapeau retenu par un cordon, palpite à tous les vents, il y a toujours quelque désir qui entraîne, quelque convenance qui retient") (part 2, chapter 3, 153). Is this Emma or the narrator reflecting on the constraints of being a woman? Rhetorical questions can function likewise. When Léon accompanies Emma to the wet nurse to visit her daughter, their conversation languishes. They love each other but don't dare say so. "Didn't they have anything else to say to each other?" (part 2, chapter 3, 160). Is one or both of them thinking or feeling this, or only the narrator?

A fine example of the use of represented discourse, often quoted, appears at the end of part 1, chapter 1: Flaubert is speaking of Charles's relations with his first wife. Having never known anything better, he does not realize that he is unhappy with her; she, having hoped for a more affectionate husband in exchange for her dowry, is openly discontented with him but remains powerless to awaken his feelings. When Charles unwittingly falls in love with Emma, his wife soon becomes aware of his unconscious disloyalty but only reinforces it by further complaints:

Il lui fallait son chocolat tous les matins, des égards à non plus finir. Elle se plaignait sans cesse de ses nerfs, de sa poitrine, de ses humeurs. *Le bruit des pas lui faisait mal;* on s'en allait; la solitude lui devenait odieuse; revenait-on près d'elle, *c'était pour la voir mourir, sans doute.* Le soir, quand Charles rentrait, elle sortait de dessous ses draps ses longs bras maigres, les lui passait autour du cou, et, l'ayant fait asseoir au bord du lit, se mettait à lui parler de ses chagrins: *il l'oubliait, il en aimait une autre! On lui avait bien dit qu'elle serait malheureuse;* et elle finissait en lui demandant quelque sirop pour sa santé et un peu plus d'amour.

[(1) She had to have her hot chocolate every morning, and no end of special treatment. (2) She complained unceasingly of her nerves, her chest, her humors [according to old-fashioned medical theory, four "humors," or basic bodily fluids governed one's health and moods]. (3) The sound of footsteps bothered her; (4) [so] you [Charles] went away; solitude became hateful to her; [but if] you [Charles] came back to her side, (5) it was probably to see her die. (6) In the evening, when Charles returned from his rounds, she stuck her long, skinny arms out from under the covers, passed them around his neck, and, having made him sit down on the edge of the bed, started telling him about her causes for unhappiness: (7) he was forgetting her, he loved someone else! They'd *told* her she'd be unhappy; (8) and she concluded [her complaints] by asking him for some syrup for her health, and a little more love.]

In this passage, iterative omniscient narration, summarizing daily occurrences in Charles's relations with his first wife, yields to explosions of discontent, themselves iterative, but reported in *style indirect libre* in units 4, 5, and 7, which use the language of Charles's wife.

CONCLUSION

The control over his characters that Flaubert apparently relinquishes with represented discourse, he recaptures not only with the denouement but also with a dense accumulation of implicit ironies. The only lasting convert to Emma's ideal of romantic passion is her despised husband, Charles, who languishes and dies for love of her. But the only memorial to her that remains in Yonville obliterates any traces of her revolt against the ordinary. After her funeral, Homais helps Charles plan a grandiose monument to her. For an inscription, the pharmacist can come up with only the most conventional statement: "Sta viator" (Pause, traveler, to pay respects, for you are treading on the ashes of a hero), but at length imagines the conclusion "amabilem conjugem calcas!" [You are treading on a loveable wife!]. The monument inflicts multiple, supreme ironies on Emma. Instead of escaping the town she loathed, her body and her memory, with her tombstone, remain rooted in the earth of Yonville like a column. Her pride is cruelly humbled: as Homais's inscription suggests, anyone now can tread on that prideful woman, who will be remembered only as a wife, the condition that painfully imprisoned her. After Emma's extraordinary adventures, sham drives out truth, and convention triumphs.

NOTES

1. Stirling Haig, "theolocutives." These are maxims and similar aphoristic statements with which a narrator claims privileged, universally valid insights and wisdom. See Haig, *Flaubert and the Gift of Speech: Dialogue and Discourse in Four Modern Novels* (Cambridge, UK: Cambridge University Press, 1986), 14–18.

2. See Michael Riffaterre, "Flaubert's Presuppositions." 76–86 in Laurence M. Porter, ed. *Critical Essays on Gustave Flaubert* (Boston: Hall, 1986).

3. Balzac abandoned this practice in the later editions of his works.

4. Homais, however reprehensible and self-serving, often intoxicates himself with his own words, a condition that makes him only more active and pernicious. Others, such as Lheureux or Rodolphe, have no illusions and follow the shortest path to the money or sex they desire, so that their entire existence becomes inauthentic as they flatter and lie without scruples. If we condemn Emma more severely than them, for being a bad mother, our attitude may derive from dim childhood memories. Once we all helplessly depended on a caregiver, whereas some of us may manage to navigate life without having to rely on a Lheureux, Rodolphe, or Homais.

5. In contrast, *L'Education sentimentale*, twelve years later, portrays a wide variety of social types from many classes and occupations.

6. Flaubert is said to have written a marginal note "Homais = homo [man]."

7. See Stirling Haig, "The Madame Bovary Blues," in *The Madame Bovary Blues: The Pursuit of Illusion in Nineteenth-Century French Fiction* (Baton Rouge, LA: Louisiana State University Press, 1987), 79–93.

8. For an extended discussion of "semblance," see Suzanne Langer, *Feeling and Form: A Theory of Art* (New York: Scribner's, 1953), 46–48, 88–90, 97–99.

9. See Laurence M. Porter, "Modernist Maldoror: The De-Euphemization of Metaphor," *L'Esprit Créateur* 18.3 (Fall 1978): 25–34.

10. The phenomenologist Roman Ingarden has analyzed such moments as "places of indeterminacy" in the reader's perception of the literary work of art.

Chapter 6

Reception

Flaubert has long been considered the dominant novelist of nineteenth-century France—a great age for the novel. His work—*Madame Bovary* twice as often as his second most influential work, *L'Education sentimentale*—has inspired an exceptional variety of critical approaches. It is now widely considered the greatest French novel before Marcel Proust's *A la recherche du temps perdu*, the last volume of which appeared sixty-five years later.

In an age when the government was still the major patron of the arts, official recognition came slowly to Flaubert. As soon as *Madame Bovary* appeared in serialized form, he and his publisher were tried for offenses against public morals, accused of a titillating depiction of adultery and of expressing disrespect for the established Catholic faith. (Not until the revocation of the Falloux Law, in 1905, was the link between church and state severed in France.)[1] Flaubert would never be elected to the Académie Française, comprising "the forty immortals" among living French writers and thinkers, an honor he richly deserved. From the beginning, however, a few kindred spirits, great authors in their own right, appreciated Flaubert greatly—among them Victor Hugo, Charles Baudelaire, George Sand, and Emile Zola. In the twentieth century, Joseph Conrad, Henry James, Marcel Proust, Somerset Maugham, Franz Kafka, Willa Cather, James Joyce, William Faulkner, Vladimir Nabokov, Mavis Gallant, Jean–Paul Sartre, Nathalie Sarraute, Mario Vargas Llosa, Michel Tournier, and Philippe Sollers among many others were strongly influenced by *Madame Bovary*. We shall first discuss the admiration that Flaubert's masterpiece elicited from great writers and its influence on their own works, before treating the more analytical, judgmental, and often adverse reactions to *Madame Bovary* in the critical essays and personal journals of prominent writers. Finally, we shall mention some cinematic versions of the novel.

FLAUBERT'S POSTERITY: *MADAME BOVARY'S* IMPACT ON GREAT WRITERS

When Flaubert's masterpiece first appeared, the majority of reactions were negative. His meticulous observation, analysis, and structuring seemed excessive. Conventional reviewers missed the emotional effusions (some might say the soppy sentimentality) of romanticism. Edmond Duranty was typical: "*Madame Bovary* ... shows obstinacy in description. It makes one think of a line drawing, to such a degree is it made with a compass and meticulous exactitude: calculated, worked over, everything at right angles, and totally dry and arid. ... In this novel there is no emotion, no feeling, no life, only the great force of an arithmetician. ... This book is a literal application of the mathematics of probability. I am speaking here for those who have been able to read through it. The style is uneven, as always happens with a man who writes *artistically* without *feeling:* here imitation, there lyricism, never anything personal."[2] Barbey D'Aurevilly, a prominent writer of fiction, agreed: "M. Flaubert is a moralist, undoubtedly, since he writes novels of manners, but he is a moralist as little as possible, for moralists are affected somewhere—in their hearts or in their minds—by the things they describe, and their judgment dominates their emotions. M. Flaubert, on the other hand, has no emotions at all; he has no judgment, at least any appreciable judgment. He is an incessant and indefatigable narrator, he is an analyst who never loses his composure; he is a 'describer' even to the most minute subtlety. But he is deaf and dumb to the effect of everything he tells."[3] In other words, Flaubert was attacked for having succeeded in creating an invisible, dispassionate narrator who let events and their outcomes speak for themselves. He was ahead of his time, anticipating the insights of Bertolt Brecht in his essays on the alienation effect in theater. Brecht sought to avoid acting styles that "infected" the audience with the characters' emotions, producing an instinctual identification with those characters, followed by the emotionally purgative effects of pity and terror as recommended by Aristotle. Emotionally sated, the audience would then forget the social problems that had produced the characters' behavior and its tragic consequences. "Acceptance or rejection of [the characters'] actions or utterances was meant to take place on a conscious plane," Brecht explained, "instead of, as hitherto, in the audience's subconscious."[4]

Among Flaubert's acquaintances, the minor writer Ernest Feydeau profited from the vogue and notoriety of *Madame Bovary* by promptly composing an imitation, *Fanny* (1858), another tale of adultery. Ironically, Sainte-Beuve considered *Fanny* the finest production of the realist school, praising it more enthusiastically than he had praised *Madame Bovary* itself.[5] Today, *Fanny* and Feydeau's later writings have only a trivial, pornographic interest.

Guy de Maupassant, the son of a beloved childhood friend of Flaubert, Laure Le Poittevin, became his literary disciple. Flaubert inculcated in him the cult of hard work and meticulous craftsmanship and did much to advance the younger man's career. The novel *Une Vie* (1883) often echoes *Madame Bovary*, and *Pierre et Jean* (1888) satirizes the triumph of unfeeling mediocrity in the manner of Flaubert mocking his creation Homais, the pharmacist in *Madame Bovary*. A Homais-like figure lusting after the distinction of the Legion of Honor (a rough French equivalent to knighthood) also appears in the short story "Décoré" as Monsieur Sacrement.[6]

Victor Hugo was among the few who instantly recognized *Madame Bovary* as a masterpiece. The two men had first met fifteen years earlier, in the sculptor James Pradier's studio. Hugo promptly wrote Flaubert to congratulate him on his novel. Charles Baudelaire also responded at once with a keenly perceptive review, emphasizing Emma's virility but attributing her aberrant behavior to hysteria and pitying her for her limited, unrealistic aspirations. He offered a shrewd analysis of the clubfoot episode. He was the first to see the affinities between some of Emma's hallucinatory experiences, both visual and auditory, and the saint's visions in *La Tentation de saint Antoine*, of which some selections had been published in 1856. Answering and anticipating the stock criticisms of minor writers—Flaubert was heartless, boring, and amoral—Baudelaire heralded Flaubert's psychological insight, emphasizing that a work of art need not preach morality: if it is crafted well, its style and structure serve as vehicles for a tacit ethical message that is both more persuasive and more esthetically satisfying than an overt sermon.

Charles-Augustin Sainte-Beuve, first a prominent romantic poet and confessional novelist and later the most influential literary critic of nineteenth-century France, immediately saw in *Madame Bovary* a masterpiece whose appearance inaugurated a new generation of realism in the novel. He praised Flaubert's style, his descriptions of Normandy, and his character portrayals, which he compared to surgical dissections. However, he complained of Flaubert's "cruelty" toward his characters and of the lack of an idealized protagonist who could have interjected a note of hope.

Emile Zola considered that *Madame Bovary* showed Flaubert to be "the pioneer of our age, the portraitist and philosopher of the modern world" (cited in Dubuc, 136). He found in Flaubert a unique combination of impassioned lyricism and cold-eyed observation. He and Flaubert eventually met in 1869. At first overwhelmed by Flaubert's nonstop ranting against bourgeois mediocrity, Zola became a loyal friend to Flaubert in the 1870s. They formed a group of cronies called Les Cinq, united by their taste for realist-naturalist literature and social critique (the other members were Georges Charpentier, Alphonse Daudet, and Edmond de Goncourt). For the naturalists led by Zola, the novel par excellence was Flaubert's *L'Education sentimentale*. Flaubert's style influenced Daudet, the Goncourts, and Guy de Maupassant substantially. His avoidance of the ugly-sounding relative pronouns *qui* and *que* led to a nominal (noun-dominated) style that, when sought indiscriminately, produced the excessively-ornate *style artiste* in the Goncourts and Daudet, a style mocked ferociously by Flaubert's faithful disciple Maupassant, who in the preface to his novel *Pierre et Jean* recalls his seven-year apprenticeship to the Master and Flaubert's admonition to rely on a supple, varied, sentence structure, rather than on that "bizarre, complicated, rhythmical, and Mandarin vocabulary that they're imposing on us these days under the name of 'l'écriture artiste.'"[7] Flaubert also inspired the naturalists through his use of tableaux (descriptions of large gatherings of people that do not move the plot) and his technique in descriptive passages—geometrically ordered details and the use of filtered light.[8]

Leo Tolstoy denied that *Madame Bovary* had influenced *Anna Karenina*, another classic tale of adultery—or even that he had read Flaubert's novel before the twentieth century. But we can vehemently suspect him of lying. Tolstoy arrived in Paris a month after the trial of *Madame Bovary*, when everybody was still talking about it. His library included the 1858 Russian translation, bound with *Othello*, probably in order to document a study of jealousy. In both novels, a ballroom scene and a waltz create a critical transition. The experience makes Emma forever dissatisfied with her modest circumstances, and it is during a seductive waltz that Kitty realizes Vronsky will forsake her for Anna. Both novels also present an opera scene. Tolstoy's Oblonsky, like Flaubert's Homais, serves as an unwitting go-between, and both men receive unmerited rewards at the end. Both deceived husbands have innocent but disagreeable mannerisms. Both novels employ horse and bird motifs and associate green, velvet, and cigars with worldliness. Both introduce ominous alien figures—a French-speaking railway worker in Tolstoy and the blind man in Flaubert—and use a blue haze to suggest blind ecstasy. Anna and Vronsky do elope to Italy, as Emma had planned to do with Rodolphe. Both novels present ominous premonitions. It appears that Anna may be a highly superior, idealized version of Emma, transformed by the influence of Rousseau: at the end of his life, Tolstoy said Rousseau had been "my master since I was fifteen." Fusing Rousseau's *La Nouvelle Héloïse* with Flaubert, Tolstoy seems to say that adultery, even when undertaken by sensitive, admirable people, dooms them to misery.[9]

THE FIRST HALF OF THE TWENTIETH CENTURY

The major influences of *Madame Bovary* on creative writers in the late nineteenth and early twentieth century were its intricate, carefully crafted structures of allusions, causality, and correspondences; its subtle, fluid representation of consciousness; its satire of a stodgy, complacent middle class and of the delusions of romanticism; and the adultery plot. Flaubert's narrative practice, innovative in its subtle, extensive use of free indirect discourse (a mode of reporting thoughts, words, and impressions that hover between the characters' and the narrator's consciousness) prepared the way for Zola's more nearly cinematic writing, in which the intrusive romantic narrator has been replaced by the narrator who listens. Zola further reduced narrative voice in favor of dialogue and interior monologue (see, for example, *Nana* in 1880). This emphasis anticipated the naturalistic novels of the United States early in the twentieth century, such as John Dos Passos's *U.S.A. Trilogy* or Theodore Dreiser's *An American Tragedy*.[10] Flaubert's skillful use of free indirect discourse directly influenced Henry James, Clarín (pseud. for Leopoldo Clarín Alas), and William Faulkner. James's four essays on Flaubert, published between 1874 and 1902, reflect a shifting, ambivalent attitude toward his predecessor's art, but the 1902 essay, the most substantial, celebrates the author of *Madame Bovary* as the "novelist's novelist" (346), from whom "there is endlessly much to be learned" (316). Sheila Teahan explains: "James reinterprets Flaubert's *style indirect libre* for his limited third-person point of view, using the conditional mood much as Flaubert uses the imperfect tense to modulate subtly [among] perspectives. Especially in such late works as *The Sacred Fount* (1901), *The Beast in the Jungle* (1903), and *The Golden Bowl* (1904), James follows Flaubert in attenuating plot in favor of representing complex dramas of consciousness."[11]

SATIRE OF THE MIDDLE CLASS

Satire inspired by Flaubert's novel was prominent in Henry James, Roger Martin du Gard, Anatole France, Sinclair Lewis, Jean-Paul Sartre, and Nathalie Sarraute. Isabel Archer, in James's *The Portrait of a Lady* (1881), who at the beginning dreams of romantic adventures similar to those dreamed by Emma Bovary, unwittingly plagiarizes the latter in describing her "idea of happiness" to her friend Henrietta Stackpole.[12]

The last six major novels of Anatole France (1844–1924) are satires in the spirit of Flaubert. As the latter satirized the myth of continual human progress embodied in the figure of Homais in *Madame Bovary* and Catholic dogma in the figure of the priest Bournisien, France mocked these mental aberrations in the fantasies *L'Ile des pingouins* (1908) and *La Révolte des anges* (1914), respectively. France, who knew Flaubert personally, said that his elder "carried on a dream of life, with heroic pride, which it was easier to make fun of than to equal. I had scarcely been five minutes with Flaubert, than the little drawing-room, hung with oriental rugs, was dripping with the blood of twenty thousand slaughtered bourgeois."[13]

Roger Martin du Gard (1881–1958) considered Flaubert a kindred spirit because of their shared hatred for the middle class.[14] And he greatly admired Flaubert's craft. "I'm feeling intense emotion as I finish reading *Madame Bovary*. I am delighted to have reread this prodigious book for the nth time. At the beginning, I had reservations. The story opens clumsily, but by the middle, perfection is achieved, and from then right to the end it's a splendid dramatic crescendo in a perfectly balanced work of art. You don't die as much as other people do when you leave works like that behind."[15] Flaubert's incisive descriptions of the monotonous Norman towns and countryside inspired Martin du Gard: the hero of his first published novel, *Devenir!*, echoes the illusions and disappointments of both Emma Bovary and Frédéric Moreau. In this depiction, Martin du Gard was strongly influenced by Jules de Gaultier's *Le Bovarysme*, which defined his title term as "the inherent capacity of human beings to imagine themselves otherwise than as they are."[16] So strong were Roger Martin du Gard's affinities with Flaubert that in 1932 the publisher Gaston Gallimard asked him to write the screenplay for a filmed version of *Madame Bovary*, to be directed by Jacques Feyder.[17]

William Faulkner claimed to reread *Madame Bovary* every year.[18] Flaubert's approach to language, Faulkner maintained in a March 11, 1957, interview, "was almost the lapidary's ... he was ... a man who elected to do one book perfectly, in the characters, and in the method, in the style."[19] Faulkner seemed entranced, above all, by Flaubert's "absolute manner of seeing things," by his style in *La Tentation de saint Antoine* and in *Salammbô* as well as in *Madame Bovary* (Gwynn and Blotner, 56). Faulkner owned Flaubert's *Complete Unabridged Novels*. On a trip to France in 1925, he learned to know the Luxembourg Gardens well. In homage to Flaubert, Faulkner set the meditative final scene of *Sanctuary* in the southeast corner, near Flaubert's statue. He also took a leisurely pilgrimage to Flaubert's haunts in Rouen. In *Sanctuary*, again, the clubfooted Eustace Graham recalls *Madame Bovary*'s Hippolyte Tautain; Horace leaves Belle, as Rodolphe leaves Virginie, his music-hall mistress, in part for the tenuous reason that those women eat shellfish. And several critics have mentioned Faulkner's remark that the rapist Popeye smells like the black ichor that flowed from Emma Bovary's mouth when her body was moved after her death.[20]

More recently, in the school of New Novelists, Nathalie Sarraute (1902–99) asserted, "at this moment, Flaubert is the master for all of us [writers]. Our judgment of him has become unanimous: he is the precursor of the modern novel" (61).[21] Alain Robbe-Grillet's autobiography, *Le Miroir qui revient* (Paris: Minuit, 1984), deliberately echoes the opening scene of *Madame Bovary* when he describes himself entering the lycée Buffon as a new student (205–6). In the same work, Robbe-Grillet exclaims, "Flaubert, c'est moi!" (203), admiringly misquoting his precursor's apocryphal "Madame Bovary, c'est moi." Robbe-Grillet's *Pour un nouveau roman* (Paris: Minuit, 1963) also claims Flaubert as a precursor of the French New Novel. Again, he says, "I think I wouldn't have set about writing if I hadn't read the texts of two authors who have struck me strongly: Flaubert and Kafka."[22] "I don't transcribe," Robbe-Grillet declared elsewhere, "I construct. That was already Flaubert's ancient ambition: to build something from nothing, something that can stand alone without needing to be propped up by anything external to the work of art."[23]

An even more direct homage appeared in 1983 with Jean Audureau's well-regarded play *Félicité* (Gallimard), fancifully based on "Un cœur simple." The in-

tensely lyrical tone brings feelings to life, and the maid daydreams of being surrounded by bright angels or that the parrot has turned into a man who could embrace her. The parrot, now named Pierre, is on stage from the beginning, and
Félicité confides in him, inciting the wrath of her employer, Madame Aubain. The
latter has a phantom lover who comes to her bed. The children, Paul and Virginie,
are already gone. Richard, Félicité's nephew, is mature, insightful, imaginative,
and sympathetic; a new character, the *voyante* midwife Maud, is her friend as
well. Premonitions announce the deaths of Richard and of Paul. At the climax,
on Ash Wednesday, as Madame Aubain is dying and Félicité spins, the maid says:
"I am no longer her servant. No, I am her equal" (75). After that death, Félicité
and Maud remain alone in the house for the last five of the sixteen scenes. At last
the maid has an apocalyptic vision and dies. The dreamy magic realism of this
play recalls Jules Supervielle's manner. The dominant themes are that the human
condition is an unending series of losses and that love—which the servant tries
in vain to teach to the master—is the only reality.

EXPATRIATES IN THE U.S.: HEINRICH MANN
AND VLADIMIR NABOKOV

Heinrich Mann (1871–1950), who fled Hitler's Germany to join the French Resistance, and then escaped to Los Angeles for the last decade of his life, greatly
admired Flaubert's antipathy toward the bourgeoisie, his use of the grotesque,
and his impersonal narrative style combined with intense imaginativeness and
sensitivity. His left-wing views contrasted sharply with his brother Thomas
Mann's relative conservatism. Heinrich Mann's major essay on Flaubert appears
in his *Geist und Tat*. There he exalts Flaubert's cult of art until it attains a vi-
sionary, Proustian intensity. He later devoted a book to the idealist, socialist novelist George Sand (pseud. for Aurore Dupin), the French equivalent to George
Eliot. Flaubert greatly influenced Mann's story "Pippo Spano"; Mann's novel
Die kleine Stadt contains many parallels with *Madame Bovary*.[24]

From the beginning of Flaubert's fame, writers have been inspired by his un-
relenting labors and his cult of art: Guy de Maupassant, Gertrude Stein, Heinrich Mann, and Georges Perec among many others mention this ideal specifically. Vladimir Nabokov, the exemplar of sensitivity to language and literary
structure, mentioned only *Madame Bovary* and the *Dictionnaire des idées
reçues* from among Flaubert's works, but responded with particular acuity to
Flaubert's craftsmanship in his most famous novel. In Nabokov's memoirs,
Speak, Memory, he reports that one day his widowed mother received her late
husband's copy of *Madame Bovary* with "the unsurpassed pearl of French literature" written on the flyleaf, "a judgment that still holds true" (174). "Without Flaubert," Nabokov emphasized in *Lectures on Literature*, "there would have
been no Marcel Proust in France, no James Joyce in Ireland" (147)—in other
words, Western literary history would have stopped short before modernism.

Nabokov shared Flaubert's detestation of philistinism, which the French author labeled *la bêtise*. In *Nikolai Gogol*, Nabokov mentions Rodolphe and Homais (64, 70) as particularly common and pretentious. Charles's ludicrous cap appears in Krug's hallucination in *Bend Sinister*, and Nabokov's extensive, keenly appreciative lecture on *Madame Bovary* emphasizes the recurrent motif of layering in Flaubert's novel, which the cap, the wedding cake, the Bovarys' house at Tostes, and Emma's three nesting coffins exemplify. Nabokov, too, liked to structure his novels around a guiding motif, such as the squirrel in *Pnin*.

The Russian author, eventually an expatriate in the United States, frequently reworked *Madame Bovary* in various ways, most thoroughly in *King, Queen, Knave*. In the foreword to the English translation, Nabokov admiringly alerts his readers to "my amiable little imitations of *Madame Bovary*, which good readers will not fail to distinguish, represent a deliberate tribute to Flaubert" (x). In that early novel, Dreyer is a composite of Charles, Homais, and Lheureux. Although nearly drowned by the lovers, he survives to prosper at the end. His nephew Franz is a vapid reflection of Léon. The Emma-figure, Martha, treats her dog cruelly as Emma mistreats her daughter Berthe. To conceal her adultery, she pretends to be taking exercise classes with a Madame l'Empereur, a name nearly identical to that of Emma's imaginary piano teacher. But she is a philistine tramp without any of Emma's relatively superior refinement and intelligence compared to others in her milieu. Other cruder, more sexually provocative versions of the Emma Bovary figure appear in Margot in *Laughter in the Dark* and in the teenage Lolita. The latter begins piano lessons with a Miss Emperor and then starts skipping them to meet her lover Quilty, until her teacher calls Humbert Humbert. The long drive around the United States in *Lolita* echoes Léon and Emma's ride in an enclosed cab in Rouen.[25]

OTHER RECENT AMERICAN AND FRENCH WRITERS

Mary McCarthy wrote a rich, sensitive, original essay "On *Madame Bovary*," and she too wrote realistic satiric fictions.[26] She admired Flaubert's portrayal of Emma: "I think that in general men write better about women than women write about men. . . . I can't imagine that a woman novelist could become as intimate with a male hero as Tolstoy is with Anna Karenina or Flaubert with Emma Bovary."[27] But she reacted strongly against his impersonality, because she felt that it stifled authorial self-expression. In a 1962 interview with Elizabeth Niebuhr, she was asked, "Other than the arrangement of time, are there other specific technical difficulties about the novel you find yourself particularly concerned with?" She replied, "Well, the whole question of the point of view, which tortures everybody. It's the problem that everybody's been up against since Joyce, if not before. Of course James really began it, and Flaubert even. You find it as early as *Madame Bovary* . . . *style indirect libre*—the author's voice, by a kind of ventriloquism, disappearing in and completely limited by the voices of his characters. What it has meant is the complete banishment of the author. I would like to restore the author! … I think this technical development has been absolutely killing to the novel" (Gelderman, 25–26).

The greatest novelist qua novelist to undergo Flaubert's influence on his creative work in the second half of the twentieth century no doubt is Michel Tournier, whose two critical essays in *Le Vol du vampire* (1981) praise *Madame Bovary* as the most celebrated novel in French literature. As William Cloonan has explained, Tournier imitates features of Flaubert's style in several of his works. Like Flaubert, he weaves together allusions to various myths, as Robert Griffin and Anne Mullen Hohl among others have demonstrated. In an interview, Tournier said that his masterpiece, *Le Roi des aulnes*, borrows extensively from various texts of Flaubert.

Finally, for the contemporary French novelist Nathalie Sarraute (1902–99), language is a powerful instrument of social control. In many of her works, she undermines linguistic authority by distorting and fragmenting the discourses of her text. Her interest in how our language always and necessarily belongs to someone else and her sense of the difficulty of achieving originality or narrative authority owe much to Flaubert. Both Flaubert and Sarraute reject the commonplace as unable to express the individual. They both find stupidity an integral part of language, one that overwhelms its textual setting through excessive description. Like Flaubert's, Sarraute's readers are obliged to do the work of interpretation, to discover the meanings behind words.[28] She considers *Madame Bovary* a masterpiece for its depiction of inauthentic, rationalized, self-justifying feelings and believes that such inauthenticity has become the very substance of Flaubert's final novel, *Bouvard et Pécuchet*. Sarraute's own innovative prose sketches, *Tropismes* (Paris: Denoël, 1939), analyze the unconscious and preconscious propensities that influence our behavior regardless of our intent and volition.

PLAYFUL REWORKINGS OF FLAUBERT

In at least three delightful recent fictions, playful authors have turned Flaubert's irony against his critics. Woody Allen's spoof "The Kugelmass Episode" tells of a New York intellectual who lusts after Emma Bovary and finds a mad scientist with a machine that can transport him into the pages of her novel. But he cannot do so discreetly; hundreds of startled readers in their college classrooms exclaim: "Who's that bald Jew kissing Madame Bovary?" When he takes her for a luxurious holiday at the Plaza Hotel in New York, readers wonder why she has disappeared from Normandy. Emma loves the shopping and sophistication of the city and quickly aspires to get an agent and become a film star. After predictable imbroglios, Kugelmass frees himself from her and swears off fiction traveling, but after a few weeks, he cannot resist the chance to enter another sexy novel. The machine explodes, killing its inventor, and trapping Kugelmass forever in the arid landscape of an elementary Spanish textbook.[29] Julian Barnes satirizes Flaubert trivia buffs and source hunting in his *Flaubert's Parrot* (1985). And Philippe Sollers brings Emma Bovary back from the dead in his essay "Emma B." All the characters from the novel, Sollers imagines, have survived into the present, unchanged except that Rodolphe has married and that Emma has a second daughter, Marie. They all have moved to Paris, and they socialize in the full knowledge of Emma's infidelities, while she maintains affairs with both Léon and Rodolphe. Despite Emma's attempt to blackmail Rodolphe by feigning suicide, he still will not divorce in order to devote himself entirely to her. All the characters pass indulgent, detached judgments on their former creator. Emma's only consolation is in raising her daughters "in the spirit of a total revenge"—presumably against men.[30]

Georges Perec's supersegmental pastiches, lists of sentences admittedly extracted from *Madame Bovary* and other texts by Flaubert for reuse in Perec's own work, are actually not pastiches but collages, foreign objects pasted into an autonomous, overarching scheme. Or perhaps they are parts of a jigsaw puzzle like the one that provides a guiding structure in *La Vie Mode d'emploi*, or like the finer-grained puzzles *La Disparition* and *Les Revenentes*, where the pieces are letters (the missing or ubiquitous letter *e*). Postmodern entropy steadily erodes the dominance of the master-text, as the borrowed building blocks for new literary productions shrink from topics to sentences to letters of the alphabet.

LITERARY CRITICS' REACTIONS TO *MADAME BOVARY*

Aside from other authors' admiring reactions, Flaubert criticism so far has evolved through four main overlapping stages: moralistic, thematic, textualist, and socially committed. Moralistic, or normative, criticism attacks the author for having failed to meet the critic's standards—moral, aesthetic, or both. Thematic criticism seeks the messages of some higher wisdom in an author's works. Textualist criticism analyzes the words in literary works as self-sufficient systems. And socially committed criticism—whether favorable or not toward an author—seeks to address and redress social wrongs, such as the oppression of women, or workers, or ethnic minorities, by examining fictive reflections on a warped society to raise readers' consciousness about real wrongs.

Normative criticism sides with social order against the artist. It believes itself entitled to legislate how literature should benefit society. It found Flaubert's realism wanting because he did not affirm lofty ideals. Normative responses to Flaubert predominated from the appearance of *Madame Bovary* in late 1856 (in *La Revue de Paris*) and 1857 (in volume form) until the centenary of Flaubert's birth, in 1921. L'abbé Batteux summed up the underlying presupposition of normative criticism early in the eighteenth century, in what became an axiom of neoclassical aesthetics in general: literature should devote itself to "l'imitation de la belle nature." Actually, this expression means "the imitation of [the] beautiful [in] nature," but Batteux was not literally recommending a literature of landscape descriptions. By *nature* he meant "human nature," and by *beautiful*, "what is beautiful in human nature"—in particular, the moral sublime, the willingness to risk or sacrifice one's personal interests or even one's life for a transcendent value. In other words, literature, like a sermon, should select from human behavior what is most noble and inspiring, so as to set a good example for its readers. The major corollary to this view was that the reader needed guidance: an author should therefore explicitly intervene to praise virtue and condemn vice, as George Eliot or Dickens do, tugging the reader by the sleeve and telling him or her what to feel.

Flaubert roundly condemned such moralizing literature. But most critics of Flaubert's time advocated it, being too moralistic to appreciate realistic literature as fully as we can today. After reading *Madame Bovary* in 1857, they granted that Flaubert observed keenly and described with power, but they condemned him—as they were to do even more fervently to Zola—for having selected only what was base and trivial in human nature and neglecting whatever might have been uplifting. Worse yet, they complained, Flaubert did not denounce his characters' baseness. Instead, he reported it calmly, impersonally, without telling us how we should react. His dispassionateness seemed by default to condone the immorality he depicted. And he failed to defend the good: when his impersonal narrator observes that in *this* adultery Emma "rediscovered all the platitudes of marriage," he implies that *some* adulteries might be superior to marriage. The word *this* was eliminated by the editors, but the phrase that remained still gave offense by putting adultery and marriage on a par. Critics of Flaubert's time found his detachment cynical and depressing, if not depraved.

So, typically for his contemporaries, Charles Augustin Sainte-Beuve, the leading literary critic of the nineteenth century, saw only "meanness, misery, pretentiousness, stupidity" in Flaubert's characters. "Why not provide the good in one figure at least," he lamented, "in one charming or venerable face.... That provides relief and consolation, and the view of humanity is only the more complete."[31] (See also the judgments of Edmond Duranty and Barbey D'Aurevilly, quoted previously.) During the remainder of Flaubert's career, critics gradually came round to a grudging, backhanded appreciation of *Madame Bovary*, contrasting it favorably with his later novel and claiming that he had outlived his genius. In the same vein, but with even more peremptory language, Henry James exempts *Madame Bovary* from the general condemnation he pronounces on Flaubert's novels only because of its moral utility: "It is an elaborate picture of vice, but it represents it as so indefeasibly commingled with misery that in a really enlightened system of education it would form exactly the volume to put into the hands of young persons in whom vicious tendencies had been distinctly perceived." Otherwise, he lamented, "Many American readers probably have followed [Flaubert's] career, and will readily recall it as an extraordinary exam-

ple of a writer outliving his genius. ... And yet we would not for the world have
had M. Flaubert's novels unwritten. Lying there before us so unmistakably still-
born, they are a capital refutation of the very dogma [realism] in defence of
which they appeared. The fatal charmlessness of each and all of them is an eloquent plea for the ideal."[32]

Normative criticism continued to dominate the Victorian Age and the French
belle époque (1880–1914). It reappeared in new guises after World War I. Re-
vulsion at the horrors of the war, added to a groundswell of reaction against late
nineteenth-century positivism and scientism, produced strong religious revivals
in France and England. As a result, critics such as J. Middleton Murry appeared,
condemning Flaubert for not being a Christian. During the first half of the twentieth century, critical reaction divided into two major streams. One can characterize them clearly by using four main examples. By the 1950s, the major French
writers of that period were considered to be Claudel, Valéry, Proust, and Gide.
Claudel, along with other writers associated with the Catholic Renaissance of
the first half of the century, used Flaubert as a whipping boy for the sins of god-
less materialism. As Claudel wrote to Gide, "our generation has a great task to
accomplish, and we must undo the horrible consequences, which we see everywhere, of our predecessors' crimes [he means the disestablishment of the Catholic Church]. The Flauberts, the Taines, the Renans, the Goncourts, the Zolas and
that whole bunch are filled only with wickedness, emptiness, skepticism, despair,
pessimism, and mockery of everything wholesome and good."[33] The anti-
Semite Léon Daudet, monarchist editor of *L'Action Française*, allegedly bel-
lowed, "I'd give away everything Flaubert ever wrote for two cents."[34] Fellow-
traveling Far Right agnostics such as Maurice Barrès and Henry de Montherlant expressed similarly dismissive views. Motivated by envy, Barrès declaimed:
"Listen to a tableful of writers. The majority of them are mediocre, so they pre-
fer mediocrity. That explains the success of a writer like Flaubert, a mediocre
writer."[35] The clumsy style of this denunciation hoists Barrès ludicrously on his
own petard. Montherlant seems moved here as elsewhere by homosexual panic,
which apparently prevented him from becoming familiar with Flaubert's life
and works: "Flaubert was certainly a queer; that he never married, and had only
one woman in his life, proves it."[36]

Unlike Claudel and his ilk, Valéry and Proust disapproved of Flaubert on
aesthetic rather than moral grounds. Valéry's fastidiousness produced a my-
opic view of Flaubert. Depending on the immediate context of his reading,
Valéry at times taxes Flaubert for being too much a realist (in *La Tentation de
saint Antoine*) and, at other times, for being too much an idealist. In *Variété
V*, he grumbles about Flaubert's cult of art: "Flaubert was convinced that each
idea can assume only one adequate form, which the writer must discover or
construct, and labor without ceasing until having done so. Unfortunately, that
fine doctrine makes no sense."[37] Proust felt ambivalent toward Flaubert. The
awkward way that mentions of Flaubert surface in and then disappear from
Proust's writings as they develop neatly reveals the anxiety of influence. Ac-

cording to that psychic principle, a revered but crushingly dominant precursor must be misinterpreted and disparaged so that an emerging author may feel justified in expressing his or her own originality. Two pastiches of Flaubert by Proust, in *Les Plaisirs et les jours* of 1896 and in the journal *Le Figaro* for March 14, 1908, both reprinted in *Contre Sainte-Beuve*, betray Proust's strong feelings of rivalry. These pastiches almost seem to claim that Proust could imitate Flaubert's style as a diversion, without being influenced by him in his own novels. For example, the novelist Bergotte in *A la recherche du temps perdu* would not be Flaubert, but Anatole France. In 1920, Proust contributed to the then-current debate surrounding the correctness of Flaubert's French by criticizing his supposedly inept use of metaphor and simile. But at the same time, Proust praised Flaubert's habitual use of the imperfect tense to create a new style of narration that makes event blend with memory and with repetition, as he himself had done.

André Gide's relationship to his precursor was more complex. He frequently returned to Flaubert in his *Journal:* he obviously admired him, but he used him as a private *repoussoir* (an example of what to avoid). Gide found the artistic problems that Flaubert set himself unvarying and the solutions unimaginative. He rewrites this remark almost verbatim, years after having first written it.[38] Flaubert's obsession with assailing stupidity, Gide felt, seemed to constrain him: "Flaubert fought all his life, and wore himself out doing so, to oppose that negative thing: human stupidity! ... Toward the end of his life he hunted no other game. He used to become indignant at, or mock, expressions such as 'the depths of the sky.' What could one do about them?" Gide respects Flaubert's underlying kindness but resists his depression: "Implicit or shouted forth, blasphemy against life, that permanent blasphemy, in the mouth of one I love, pains me greatly. I feel the *duty* to be happy" (311, 715).

Normative criticism tries to locate the ultimate meaning of a literary work outside the work, in a parallel but more extensive frame of reference. It is *extrinsic*. In contrast, thematic criticism is *intrinsic;* it seeks the work's meaning within itself or within the corpus of the author's works. The main assumption is that an author does not explain everything and that the task of criticism is to bring out what the author has implied or hidden. Thematic criticism serves not society, but the artist, working to disclose his or her richness, complexity, and enduring interest. Thematic criticism sees the work of art either as existing in harmony with its tradition or as inaugurating a new and equally valid one. This approach dominated Flaubert criticism from around 1920 to 1970. It called Flaubert an idealist—one frequently frustrated by the shortcomings of society and the material order. Thematic critics such as Harry Levin depicted Flaubert as a saint of art, a martyr to style, sequestering himself in an eremitic retreat to devote himself to his writing. After Flaubert's correspondence became widely known in the 1930s, critics could find abundant evidence of his idealism. More than once, inspired by the philosophical eclecticism of Victor Cousin, he invoked and praised platonic ideas.[39]

Georges Poulet encapsulated the attitudes of thematic criticism by insisting on the organic unity of the work of art. "The main purpose [of *Madame Bovary*] is to maintain relation and order."[40] "What man attains in the Flaubertian experience is ... the intuition of life in its cosmic expansion," Poulet affirms elsewhere. His phenomenological criticism assumes that only our subjective representations of the world—of time and space, self and other, thought and object—are knowable, while that world in and of itself is not. Indeed, Poulet continues, "Flaubert arrived at an integral phenomenalism. The mind being what it represents, and the object existing only in its representation in the mind, what remains is simply a unique being that can be called indifferently mind or matter" (407).[41] Poulet tries to show how Flaubert enters this awareness and then reemerges from it to compose a novel. The weakness of Poulet's method is to consider as a single, uniform whole everything that Flaubert ever wrote and to assume that Flaubert's thought was always already fully formed. Eighty-five percent of Poulet's citations in "Flaubert" refer to the letters or to the juvenilia.

The decisive shift from a thematic to a textualist emphasis in Flaubert criticism occurred in 1962, when the most frequently reprinted essay in Flaubert criticism, Jean Rousset's "*Madame Bovary:* Flaubert's Anti-novel," stressed Flaubert's declared aim to make *Madame Bovary* "a book about nothing, a book without reference outside itself." Rousset claimed that this enterprise made Flaubert "the first in date of the non-figurative novelists" such as Joyce or Woolf (59). If true, this means that Flaubert anticipated these modernist authors' role as forebears of postmodernism by seventy years.[42] Such criticism treats Flaubert as an indeterminist, skeptical concerning the ability of the intellect to arrive at any truths other than the ultimate reality of human folly and self-deception. However, Flaubert's *L'Education sentimentale* surely deserves more attention than it has yet received, as a "book about nothing" more radical than *Madame Bovary*. That Frédéric Moreau's story grazes *la grande histoire* without truly being touched by it and that the convulsions of that history will not produce any noteworthy social change emphasize by contrast the moral and intellectual void at the core of the novel, a void Flaubert emphasizes by touching many points along its periphery. Unlike Emma Bovary or Mathilde de La Mole or Julien Sorel, Frédéric lacks passion and ambition fueled by a sense of emulation. Less lucid even than Emma in many ways, Frédéric does not realize when he is engaging in vapid repetitions.

Most recently, literary criticism in general often tries to rescue victims: postcolonialist criticism condemns authors' complacent acceptance of the benefits they derive from their first-world society's unjust power; feminist criticism connects female characters to historical women enslaved by patriarchal repression. A refreshingly divergent recent tendency is genetic criticism, which tries to rescue literary works from the fetishism that accrues to the completed, manufactured object of cultural consumption by tracing the author's creative process from *avant-textes* (larval versions of the finished work) and *paratexts* (popularizations through which great predecessors' thought often reaches new au-

thors) to *macrotexts* (the body of a single author's work within which one particular text resonates and completes its meaning). Yvan Leclerc, who has taken
over the editorship of the fifth and final volume of Jean Bruneau's great edition
of Flaubert's correspondence, recently published a noteworthy diplomatic edition of Flaubert's scenarios and sketches for *Madame Bovary*, preserved in the
municipal library of Rouen.[43]

MARXIST CRITICISM: JEAN-PAUL SARTRE

More complex and influential was the position of Marxist criticism, which preserved a strong normative strain in Flaubert criticism until at least the early
1970s, owing to the guilty class-consciousness of privileged French academics.
From this viewpoint, the French Revolution had been led by and worked primarily for the benefit of the middle class: the formerly dominant aristocracy
was replaced by capitalists (as Flaubert himself shows in the figure of Monsieur
Dambreuse of *L'Education sentimentale*—a man who had changed his name
from d'Ambreuse to conceal his aristocratic origins and to curry favor with the
Left Wing—and as Stendhal before him had shown in *Le Rouge et le Noir*). By
developing more efficient means of production, middle-class capitalists accu-
mulated wealth at the expense of the growing urban proletariat. The latter were
exploited without mercy. Around the middle of the nineteenth century, writers,
also middle-class, reluctantly recognized themselves as members of a social
group that had become morally bankrupt. Seeing no positive values to uphold,
they reacted with disillusionment, despair, and nihilism, becoming—in Sartre's
phrase—"knights of nothingness."[44]

The most influential representatives of Marxist criticism of *Madame Bovary*
were Roland Barthes in his middle period and Jean-Paul Sartre. In *Writing Degree Zero*, Barthes argues that *Madame Bovary* exemplifies a crisis of the loss
of values in the novel around 1850: Flaubert tries to revalidate the novel in capitalist terms, on the basis of how much work has gone into producing it. More
pointedly and more self-righteously, the third volume of Sartre's monumental
study of Flaubert, *The Family Idiot* (1972), criticizes Flaubert for sharing the
"bad faith" of the middle class, the self-deception that masks a deliberate initial
choice to claim special privileges for oneself at the expense of justice and logic.
Sartre claims that Flaubert tried to escape from his social class into pseudono-
bility during the last nine years of the Second Empire (1861–70). In 1866,
Flaubert accepted the cross of the Legion of Honor, nine years after having
ridiculed his character Homais for prostituting himself in order to gain that same
cross, and he became a regular guest of Princess Mathilde, who admired his work
and to whom he referred as "*Our* Princess." After the disaster of the Franco-
Prussian War in 1870, Sartre continues, Flaubert was forced to recognize the
sham of the bourgeois values by which he lived, but he could only reaffirm them
without conviction. He refrained from writing a satiric novel about the Second Em-

pire, although he had thought about one, because the loss of his special status as an honored guest of the Imperial Family depressed him.[45]

Surely the most intense, prolonged, and tragic encounter of a creative writer with Flaubert in the twentieth century was Jean-Paul Sartre's in the 3,000-page *L'Idiot de la famille* (1971–72). This work was the third and last of a series of writerly successes that failed to define an existentialist morality. First, from 1945 to 1949, Sartre published three volumes of the wartime novel *Les Chemins de la liberté,* where the fluid representation of consciousness through *style indirect libre* may have owed something to Flaubert as well as to Dos Passos. The fourth volume, intended to define the existentialist praxis of a secular morality, never was finished. By accident, the late George Bauer found the hundred fifty pages of notes for that fourth volume at a bookseller's, where an unscrupulous former secretary of Sartre's had sold them. Bauer edited them for the Pléiade volume of Sartre's novels. A decade later, in 1960, Sartre published his *Critique de la raison dialectique,* a Thomistic attempt to reconcile Marxism with existentialism. "Questions de méthode," the hundred-page essay that opens volume 1, uses Sartre's psychological insights into Flaubert to criticize the Marxists for overlooking the formative influence of childhood on the individual and the mediating role of the family in inserting an individual into his or her class. Again, the planned second volume of suggestions for practical ethical applications of his theoretical insights never went beyond notes and sketches. In 1966, Sartre's two-part article in *Les Temps modernes,* "Flaubert: Du poète jusqu'à l'artiste," examined Flaubert's youthful writings of the 1830s to define the dualism of the real and the ideal in the nineteenth-century author—his hope of escaping his condition as a bourgeois by assuming the aristocratic essence of a writer and his "misunderstood child's" disgust at those who think too basely (meaning, with exclusively utilitarian values) to appreciate him. All these preliminary studies culminated in Sartre's massive attempt to determine Flaubert's character and career retrospectively through existentialist psychoanalysis in *L'Idiot.* Sartre claims that Flaubert's nihilism results from a projection of his contempt for his own social class onto all humanity. But he unwittingly and self-defeatingly implies that "motivated is determined," although no amount of second-guessing could predict or explain Flaubert's greatest achievements. A final short fourth part of *L'Idiot,* intended to explicate *Madame Bovary,* never materialized. Sartre vainly tries to control Flaubert's creativity *après la lettre* because he no longer can control his own. *L'Idiot de la famille* stands as the tragic ruin of a misguided intellect that earlier stood next to Proust's as the greatest in twentieth-century French letters.

More recent literary developments suggest that Flaubert has become more a cultural icon than a master—an instantly recognizable celebrity whose best-known work can be freely transformed by being unfaithful to the faithless heroine's story and even cut and pasted into postmodernist constructions such as the paintings of Andy Warhol or Larry Rivers—or Marcel Duchamp, decades before them. The British author Posy Simmonds's novel *Gemma Bovery* (2000) resets the story in current times. The village baker (echoing Boulanger, the name of Emma's first lover) is the local intellectual, who envies Gemma's lovers and spies on her with a voyeuristic curiosity. He has already read *Madame Bovary*, recognizes an uncanny recurrence, and tries to control events. Gemma dies anyway. He steals her diary from her bedroom and uses it to reconstruct her story. Lionel Acher, in *Cette diablesse de Madame Bovary* (2001), imagines that the devil brings her back to life to exact revenge on the men who have wronged her.

In the teacher-novelist Daniel Pennac's *Comme un roman*, *Madame Bovary* becomes the chief token of cultural assimilation for young people who are learning to read and then to interpret literature. Flaubert's novel first appears as a daunting, formidable homework assignment and then as a numbing question on the oral part of the *agrégation*, the highly competitive state examination that admits a few chosen French people to prestigious careers in higher education. As Pennac's benevolent tutelage gradually frees us and his students from indifference, fear, and resentment toward literature, the ever-reappearing Flaubert comes to be associated with increasing degrees of personal liberty: the right to tell one's own stories about the classics; the right to *Bovarysme* in the sense of reading for the instant gratification of one's emotions alone (we are always convinced, Pennac observes with wry humor, that Madame Bovary is everybody else but ourselves; "Emma would surely have shared this conviction" [249]); and the right to read out loud, as Flaubert did in his famous *gueuloir*—dramatizing and shouting his text to test its sensory qualities.[46]

THE ENDURING INFLUENCE OF *MADAME BOVARY*

Since 1980, *Bouvard et Pécuchet* and *L'Education sentimentale* have been neglected, whereas the popularity of *Madame Bovary* has remained constant, and *La Tentation de saint Antoine* has passed nearly unnoticed since the beginning of the First World War. If you consider the dates during which Flaubert's influence on other writers seemed most pronounced, you will note an inward turn of the French tradition: until 1943, three-quarters of the writers listed on Table 6.1 are foreigners. From 1951 onward, about half are French. One wonders whether the sphere of Flaubert's influence—or of the cultural presence of France in the world—has shrunk, and whether, outside France, Flaubert has not been superseded by Faulkner, whom a surprising number of third-world writers regard as the richest model for their attempts at prose fiction, despite the racist world that he depicts. One may explain the apparently self-perpetuating prestige of *Madame Bovary* inside France simply. Because inspiration is the product of familiarity and time, French writers' contact with Emma's story early in their schooldays makes that work readily available to them when they start to write. For practicing novelists in France, Flaubert's masterpiece remains something that one has to outgrow.

Table 6.1 *A Chart of Flaubert's Influence on Creative Writers*

Influence Dates and Author	Sources in Flaubert's Work	Results and Trends
1842–69 Bouilhet, Louis	Joint theatrical projects	Close collaboration
1847–54 Colet, Louise	Critique and copyediting	Two *romans à clé*
1857–58 Feydeau, Ernest	MB	Imitates for financial gain
1859–81 les Goncourt	Friendship, misogyny	Many portraits in *Journal*
1870–1902 Zola, Emile	MB, ES	Narrative art, s.i.l.
1874–77 Tolstoy, Leo	MB as *repoussoir*	*Anna Karenina*
1874–1902 James, Henry	MB	Satire, s.i.l., craft
1878 Queirós, Eça de	MB	*O primo Basilio*, adultery
1880–88 Maupassant, Guy de	MB, ES, TC, BP	Style, cult of art, discipleship
1881–1911 Pardo Bazán, E.	TSA, ES, MB	Pessimism, mysticism
1881–1932 Martin du Gard, R.	MB, TSA, TC	Bourgeois critique
1882 Verga, Giovanni	MB	*Il marito di Elena*, adultery
1884–91 Clarín (L. Alas)	All	Echoes of childhood, s.i.l.
1888 Darío, Rubén	TSA	*Azul*, cult of exotic words
1890–1914 France, Anatole	SAL, TSA, TC	Satire, exotic religions
1895–97 Conrad, Joseph	BP, ES, MB, SAL	Realism, character portrayal
1896–1921 Proust, Marcel	BP, CORR	Male bonding, pastiches
1898–1935 Unamuno, Miguel	MB as model	Flawed perception, *Niebla*
1899 Chopin, Kate	MB	Female bildungsroman
1902–44 Maugham, Somerset	TSA	Sexual frustration, reworking
1903–39 Yeats, Wm. Butler	ES, SAL	Rich detail
1906–25 Ford, Ford Madox	UCS, CORR, ES, TC	History, detached observer
1909–46 Stein, Gertrude	MP, BP	*Three Lives*, cult of art
1913–24 Kafka, Franz	MB	Altered consciousness, the absurd
1913–26 Cather, Willa	BP, TSA	Models of passion, adultery
1914–39 Joyce, James	*Le Candidat*	Anatomy, interior monologue
1915 Sternheim, Carl	BP, ES	Translated and staged
1917 Eliot, T. S.	BP, ES	Irony

1923 Romains, Jules	MB, "le Garçon," Homais	Medical farce, *Knock*
1925–57 Faulkner, William	MB	s.i.l., interior monologue
1928–67 Nabokov, Vladimir	Often reworks MB	Lyrical style
1931–39 Mann, Heinrich	ES, MB	"Pippo Spano," *Die kleine Stadt*, the cult of art
1933–43 Mann, Thomas	SAL as counter-example	*Joseph and His Brothers*
1939 Lewis, Sinclair	MB (denies influence)	*Main Street*, satire
1941 Auden, W.H.		Figure of the artist-hero
1943 Azorín (pseud.)	BP	Realism shifting to idealism
1951–59 Salinger, J.D.	ES as bildungsroman	Irony, cult of *le mot juste*
1957 Borges, Jorge Luis	Essays on BP	Metaliterature
1959 Gallant, Mavis	Plots of MB and ES	"Green Water, Green Sky"
1960–72 Sartre, Jean-Paul	Over 3,000 pages on Flaubert	Nihilism, bourgeois critique
1962–70 McCarthy, Mary	Essay on MB	Opposes impersonalism
1962–99 Vargas Llosa, M.	Book on MB	Art of characterization
1963–84 Robbe-Grillet, A.	MB, SAL	Flaubert as pioneer New Novelist
1965 Sarraute, Nathalie	BP, MB, SAL; dislikes ES	"Tropisms," inauthenticity
1965–80 Perec, Georges	BP, MB, ES, TSA	Pastiches, the cult of art
1968–73 Barthes, Roland	UCS, MB	Reality effect, *texte du plaisir*
1970–81 Tournier, Michel	MB, TC, SAL (redoes)	Exoticism; myth; *Gaspard, Melchior, et Balthazar*
1970–84 Butor, Michel	TSA	The text as subversion
1977–82 Allen, Woody	MB (parodies)	"The Kugelmass Episode"
1983–2000 Sollers, Philippe	MB (parodies)	*Les Femmes*
1985 Barnes, Julian	UCS (parodies)	*Flaubert's Parrot*, satire
1989 Jelinek, Elfriede	MB?	Lust, adultery, abjection
1992 Pennac, Daniel	MB	Flaubert as our acculturation
1993 Bessa-Luís, Agustina	MB as model	*Vale Abraão* and film
2000 Simmonds, Posy	Parody of MB	*Gemma Bovery*
2001 Acher, Lionel	Parody of MB	*Cette diablesse de Madame Bovary* [on-line]

KEY: BP = *Bouvard et Pécuchet*; UCS = "Un cœur simple"; CORR = *Correspondance*; ES = *L'Éducation sentimentale*; MB = *Madame Bovary*; SAL = *Salammbô*; TSA = *La Tentation de saint Antoine*; TC = *Trois Contes*; s.i.l. = *style indirect libre*

The chronological list in Table 6.1 is arranged according to the periods during which individual authors seemed most influenced by *Madame Bovary* when composing their own creative works.[47] The dates when Flaubert's impact on each literary figure was at its height were gleaned from authors' publications; they therefore represent an artificially belated appearance of influence. Publication dates overlook the long gestation periods during which Flaubert's example inspired creative work that was not yet detectable beyond the writer's worktable. The list also says nothing about the varying rhythms of social, political, and intellectual history that accelerated or delayed Flaubert's effect on a country's writers. When his impact seems strongly concentrated on a particular work by another author, that work, rather than a more general tendency, is listed under Results and Trends at the far right.

Table 6.1 suggests that *Madame Bovary*'s general influences on creative writers have not unfolded in a clear pattern. Characterization, bourgeois critique, and emphasis on the writer's craft seem to have alternated fairly regularly, without any one of these emphases gaining a clear ascendancy. Professor Stéphane Michaud of the Sorbonne Nouvelle (Paris III) informs us that an article in the October 2001 issue of *Le Magazine littéraire* discusses Flaubert's influence on the prolific, well-known contemporary French novelists Florence Delay (1941–) and Jean Echenoz (1947–).

MADAME BOVARY INTO FILM

The deliberate drabness of the novel's setting and characters for a time discouraged directors from adapting it for the screen, particularly during the era of black-and-white film. Another major impediment, in the era of silent film, when subtitles needed to be almost entirely devoted to the characters' words and thoughts or to introductory remarks intended to set the stage, was the difficulty in rendering Flaubert's irony. Only when voice-overs could provide a flexible ironic counterpoint to the characters' words was a relatively faithful rendering of Flaubert's narrative viewpoint possible. So "event theater" tempted earlier film producers more than did subtle psychological dramas, as Eisenstein's celebrated treatment of the sailors' revolt on the battleship *Potemkin* illustrates. Hugo's sprawling account of crime, revolution, and redemption, *Les Misérables*, became the first full-length feature film in the United States, in 1905.

The first of Flaubert's works to be filmed was *La Tentation de saint Antoine*, by Georges Méliès in 1898. Adaptations of *Madame Bovary* other than the three discussed previously include *Unholy Love*, a Hollywood production (1932); a German *Madame Bovary* with Pola Negri in 1935; an Argentine version in 1947; a German-Italian version variously entitled *I Peccati di Madame Bovary*, *Die nackte Bovary*, or *Les Folles Nuits de la Bovary*. Translated into English as *Play the Game or Leave the Bed* (1969), the film was revised to provide a happy ending. An Indian film directed by Ketan Metha appeared in 1991. A television version directed by Georges Neveux in 1972 was re-released on videotape in 1986 by (the overly expensive) Films for the Humanities. A TV miniseries version directed by Rodney Bennett appeared on BBC2 in 1975, and another on that network in 2000. And in 1994, Aleksandr Sokhurov directed a Soviet version, *Spasi i sohrani* (translated as *Sauve et protégé*). For other lists of versions, see Mary Donaldson-Evans, "Film Adaptations of Flaubert's Works" in Porter, ed., *A Gustave Flaubert Encyclopedia*, 129–30; John Tibbetts and James M. Welsh, eds., *The Encyclopedia of Novels into Film* (New York: Facts on File, 1998); and Jean Tulard, *Guide des films*, new ed. 2 vols. (Paris: Laffont, 1997).

So far, the best-known film versions of *Madame Bovary*, each by a famous director, have been Jean Renoir's classic in black and white (1934), Vincente Minnelli's version (1949), and Claude Chabrol's (1991). Today, Renoir's free adaptation "stands as a period piece, offering modern viewers a revealing glimpse of American attitudes in the late 1940s."[48] Minelli's even freer treatment frames the story of Emma's adulteries not with scenes from her husband's childhood and short life as a widower, but with scenes from the historical Flaubert's trial. Played by James Mason, Flaubert takes the stand to defend Emma and himself. After the main story begins, he remains as a phantom presence in persistent voice-overs that establish and recall his point of view. The ball at La Vaubyessard in Minelli's version is one of the great tableaux in the history of film. The figure of the charming viscount there is implausibly fused with that of Rodolphe later. Charles becomes much more intelligent, lucid, and likeable than in the novel. Although Emma threatens to not love him any more unless he performs the clubfoot operation, he wisely, morally recognizes his limitations as a doctor and, after an intense inner struggle, spares the stable boy Hippolyte. Nevertheless, Emma's death scene, greatly idealized as if to conform with her romantic self-image, partially redeems her in a way the novel does not (Donaldson-Evans, 118–19).

Chabrol's recent version is ploddingly faithful to Flaubert's text, although his insistence on casting the icily beautiful, self-possessed Isabelle Huppert as the hysterical Emma seems inappropriate, especially because the actress added far more prefeminist nuances to her interpretation than one can find in the novel. Chabrol treats the ironic juxtaposition of political and sexual seduction speeches at the agricultural fair quite crudely, while reducing the comic roles of Homais and Bournisien and attenuating the confusion between religious ecstasy and sensuality in Emma's mind. Chabrol, like Minnelli, suppresses scenes from Charles' life before and after Emma. He indulges in arch quotations from the novel, displaced from their original location, as if to suggest that the clichés Flaubert denounced had acquired a parasitical, independent life. Whether Minnelli's or Chabrol's film would be the better introduction or supplement to the novel remains an open question.[49]

Since 1995, the rapidly developing World Wide Web has sparked an explosion of scholarly interest in Flaubert, as the final section of our bibliography, devoted to Internet resources, demonstrates. Brief comments are included there. Teams of researchers in Paris and in Rouen are providing excellent digitized (*numérisé*) versions of Flaubert's most reliable texts and some of his manuscripts, iconography, and current bibliography, all available and downloadable, mainly free, online. They are ably seconded by the new society for nineteenth-century French studies in the United Kingdom, where, as in the United States, more researchers study Flaubert than any other French author of his century. At the Université de Rouen, Yvan Leclerc's team is publishing a hypertext edition of the manuscripts of *Madame Bovary* in 2003. The 4,392 pages of manuscripts are thoroughly hot-linked to the definitive printed version. Leclerc also offers free materials for secondary school teachers of Flaubert.

NOTES

1. See Benjamin F. Bart, *Flaubert* (Syracuse, NY: Syracuse University Press, 1967), 354–66, and Dominick La Capra, Madame Bovary *on Trial* (Ithaca, NY: Cornell University Press, 1982).

2. Edmond Duranty, [Review of *Madame Bovary*], *Réalisme* 5 (March 15, 1857): 79–80, reprinted in Laurence M. Porter, ed., *Critical Essays on Gustave Flaubert* (Boston: Hall, 1986), 49. For a broader view of the literary-historical context of Flaubert's times, see George Becker, comp. and trans., *Documents of Modern Literary Realism* (Princeton, NJ: Princeton University Press, 1963).

3. Barbey D'Aurevilly, "M. Gustave Flaubert," in Porter, ed., *Critical Essays on Gustave Flaubert*: 50–57 (50). First published in D'Aurévilly, *Des Œuvres et des Hommes* (1865) 4:61–76.

4. Bertolt Brecht, "Alienation Effects in Chinese Acting" (1936), in John Willett, ed. and trans., *Brecht on Theatre: The Development of an Esthetic* (New York: Hill and Wang, 1996), 91–99. In the same volume, see also Brecht's "Short Description of a New Technique of Acting which Produces an Alienation Effect" (1940), intended "to make the spectator adopt an attitude of inquiry and criticism," 136–47; and "A Short Organum for the Theatre" (1949), 179–205, esp. 191–95.

5. In *Le Moniteur* for June 14, 1858. See also Pierre Martino, *Le Roman réaliste sous le Second Empire* (Paris: Hachette, 1913), 180–204.

6. See Eugene F. Gray, "Guy de Maupassant," in Laurence M. Porter, ed., *A Gustave Flaubert Encyclopedia* (Westport, CT: Greenwood, 2001), 215–16.

7. Guy de Maupassant, *Pierre et Jean* (New York: Scribner's, 1936), xlvi–xlviii.

8. See Brunetière on Flaubert's style; Bascelli, Bismut, and Goetz on the Goncourts' style; and Sachs on Daudet's style.

9. See Priscilla Meyer's "Anna Karenina: Tolstoy's Polemic with *Madame Bovary*," *The Russian Review* 54.2 (1995): 243–59. I would suggest investigating Goethe's *Elective Affinities* (1809) as a possible common source.

10. See Gilbert Chaitin, "Listening Power: Flaubert, Zola, and the Politics of *style indirect libre*, " *The French Review* 72.6 (1999): 1023–37.

11. Sheila Teahan, "Henry James," in Laurence M. Porter, ed., *A Gustave Flaubert Encyclopedia* (Westport, CT: Greenwood, 2001), 184–85 (184).

12. Henry James, *The Portrait of a Lady*, Nicola Bradbury, ed. (Oxford, UK: Oxford University Press, 1995), 187. Thanks to Sheila Teahan for this information.

13. Anatole France, *La Vie littéraire*, 4 vols. (Paris: Calmann-Lévy, 1889–92), 2.19.

14. Roger Martin du Gard, *Correspondance générale* (Paris: Gallimard, 1980–) 1:17–18.

15. Roger Martin du Gard, letter to his wife, October 13, 1918, in *Correspondance générale*, 2:981.

16. Jules de Gaultier, *Le Bovarysme* (Paris: Mercure de France, 1902), 13.

17. A disagreement between the publisher and the director prevented the project from being accomplished, but Martin du Gard's preliminary plans have survived. See Claude Sicard, "Roger Martin du Gard and Gustave Flaubert," in Jean-Louis Cabanes, ed., *Voix de l'écrivain: mélanges offerts à Guy Sagnes* (Toulouse: Presses Universitaires du Mirail, 1996: 277–87), 284–85.

18. See Arthur F. Kinney, "Faulkner and Flaubert," *Journal of Modern Literature* 6 (1977): 222–47 (222).

19. Cited in Frederick L. Gwynn and Joseph L. Blotner, eds., *Faulkner in the University* (Charlottesville, VA: University of Virginia Press, 1959), 55–56.

20. Dawn Trouard, "X Marks the Spot: Faulkner's Garden," in Donald M. Kartiganer and Ann J. Abadie, eds., *Faulkner in Cultural Context: Faulkner and Yoknapatawpha* (Jackson, MS: University Press of Mississippi, 1997), 99–124.

21. Nathalie Sarraute, "Flaubert le précurseur," in *Paul Valéry et l'enfant d'éléphant* (Paris: Gallimard, 1986), 61–89.

22. "Robbe-Grillet, ho ucciso Balzac," interview with Antonio Debenedetti in the *Corriere della Sera*, August 17, 1998 (25).

23. All these quotations and references are taken from Vanessa Kamkhagi, "Alain Robbe-Grillet: 'Flaubert, c'est moi,'" in Liana Nissim, ed., *Le Letture/La Lettura di Flaubert* (Milan: Cisalpino, 2000), 371–86. This volume is highly recommended.

24. See the studies by Banuls and by Weisstein.

25. Much of this information concerning parallels between Nabokov and Flaubert has been drawn from Maurice Couturier, "Nabokov and Flaubert," 405–12 in Vladimir E. Alexandrov, ed., *The Garland Companion to Vladimir Nabokov* (New York: Garland, 1995). The works by Nabokov mentioned include *Speak, Memory: An Autobiography Revisited* (1967; New York: Vintage, 1989); *Nikolai Gogol* (New York: New Directions, 1944, rev. 1961); *Bend Sinister* (1947; New York: Vintage, 1990); *King, Queen, Knave* (1928; New York: Vintage, 1989); *Laughter in the Dark* (1938; New York: Vintage, 1989); *Lolita* (1955; New York: Vintage, 1989); and *Lectures on Literature*, Fredson Bowers, ed. (New York: Harcourt Brace Jovanovich, 1980).

26. McCarthy, "On *Madame Bovary*" (1964), in McCarthy, *The Writing on the Wall, and Other Literary Essays* (New York: Harcourt, Brace & World, 1970), 72–94.

27. [Interview with Peter Duval Smith, 1963], in Carol Gelderman, ed., *Conversations with Mary McCarthy* (Jackson, MS: University Press of Mississippi, 1991), 58.

28. With minimal rephrasing, up to this point the discussion of Sarraute is borrowed from E. Nicole Meyer in our joint entry on "Sarraute, Nathalie (1902–1999)" in Porter, ed., *A Gustave Flaubert Encyclopedia*: 294–95.

29. Woody Allen, "The Kugelmass Episode," in *Side Effects* (New York: Ballantine, 1982), 59–78. For an amusing commentary, see Douglas Robinson, "Kugelmass, Translator (Some Thoughts on Translation and Its Teaching)," in Peter Bust and Kirsten Malmkjaer, *Rimbaud's Rainbow: Literary Translation in Higher Education* (Amsterdam: Benjamins, 1998), 47–61. In *Manhattan*, a film directed by and starring Allen, his character, Isaac, at the end, lists Flaubert's *L'Education sentimentale* as one of the few things that make life worth living.

30. Philippe Sollers, "Emma B.," in *Eloge de l'infini* (Paris: Gallimard, 2001), 307–13 (first published in his *Femmes*, 1983).

31. Charles-Augustin Sainte-Beuve, "*Madame Bovary* par M. Gustave Flaubert," in *Causeries de lundi*, 16 vols. (Paris: Garnier, 1850–60), 13:346–63, reprinted in George Becker, ed., *Documents of Modern Literary Realism* (Princeton, N.J.: Princeton University Press, 1963), 99–104 (103).

32. Henry James, "Flaubert's *Temptation of St. Anthony*," in Porter, *Critical Essays*, 141–45 (142, 141, 142), reprinted from James, *Literary Reviews and Essays* (New Haven, CT: New College and University Press, 1957), 145–50 (originally published in 1874).

33. Paul Claudel/André Gide, *Correspondance 1899–1926*, R. Mallet, ed. (Paris: Gallimard, 1949), 96.

34. Léon Daudet, cited in Jules Renard, *Journal*, L. Guichard and G. Sigaux, eds. (Paris: Gallimard, 1960), 150.

35. Maurice Barrès, *Mes Cahiers*, 14 vols. (Paris: Plon, 1929–57), 3:284.

36. Henry de Montherlant, *Pitié pour les femmes* in Montherlant, *Romans* (Paris: Gallimard, 1962), 1186.

37. Paul Valéry, *Variété V* (Paris: Gallimard, 1944), 95, 199, 205.

38. André Gide, *Journal*, vol. 1 (Paris: Gallimard, 1960), 209, 720.

39. "The major difficulty, for me, always remains the style, the form, the indefinable Beauty *resulting from the concept itself* and which is the resplendence of the Truth, as Plato said" (letter to Mademoiselle Leroyer de Chantepie, March 18, 1857, in Bruneau, ed., *Correspondance*, [5] vols. Paris: Gallimard, 1973–[98], 2:691). See also the letter to Louise Colet on March 27, 1853 [2.285], and later letters on January 16, 1866, March 23, 1868, and April 3, 1876. For critical commentary, see Benjamin F. Bart, *Flaubert* (Syracuse, NY: Syracuse UP, 1967), 48–49, 117; and Jacques Derrida, "Une idée de Flaubert: la lettre de Platon," *Revue d'Histoire Littéraire de la France* 81 (1981): 658–76, translated in *MLN* 99 (1984): 748–68.

40. "The Circle and the Center: Reality and *Madame Bovary*" (1955), in *Madame Bovary: Backgrounds and Sources; Essays in Criticism*, Paul de Man, ed. (New York: Norton, 1965), 392–407.

41. Poulet, "Flaubert," in Poulet, *Studies in Human Time* (Baltimore: Johns Hopkins University Press, 1956), 248–61.

42. Denis Diderot's experimental novel *Jacques le Fataliste* (1771–83) would be an equally good candidate for those who did not wish to exaggerate the importance of Flaubert in literary history—and before Diderot, Lawrence Sterne's *Tristram Shandy* (1759) or François Rabelais's *Tiers Livre* (1546), both of which refuse to resolve themselves into a plot.

43. Yvan Leclerc, *Plans et scénarios de* Madame Bovary (Paris: CNRS/Zulma, 1995). A "diplomatic edition" reproduces the exact sizes, positions, and forms of the letters on an author's manuscript pages, as closely as typography can approximate handwriting.

44. See Jean-Paul Sartre, *L'Idiot de la famille: Gustave Flaubert de 1821–1857*, 3 vols. (Paris: Gallimard, 1971–72), 3:160–206, esp. 193–202.

45. See Hazel E. Barnes, *Sartre & Flaubert* (Chicago: University of Chicago Press, 1981), 278–309.

46. Daniel Pennac, *Reads Like a Novel*, David Gunn, trans. (London: Quartet, 1994; *Comme un roman* [Paris: Gallimard, 1992]), 57–59, 65–66, 70, 93–97, 127–28, 165–67, 175 (167).

47. Modernist writers themselves, such as Proust or Joyce, seem to have favored *Bouvard et Pécuchet* over *Madame Bovary* and to have read Flaubert as part of a postmodernist, ludic holiday.

48. Geoffrey Wagner, *The Novel and the Cinema* (Rutherford, NJ: Fairleigh Dickinson University Press, 1975), 253, cited by Mary Donaldson-Evans, "Teaching *Madame Bovary* through Film," in Laurence M. Porter and Eugene F. Gray, *Approaches to Teaching Flaubert's* Madame Bovary (New York: MLA, 1995): 114–21 (114).

49. Donaldson-Evans, 120–21; François Boddaert and Pierre-Marc de Biasi, et al., *Autour d'Emma* (Paris: Hatier, 1991). See also Stephen Harvey, *Directed by Vincente Minnelli* (New York: Harper, 1989), and Desmond Ryan, "Claude Chabrol Adapts Flaubert's Masterpiece for the Screen," *The Philadelphia Inquirer*, December 25, 1991: 6D.

Chapter 7

Bibliographical Essay

FRANCE AND NORMANDY IN THE TIME OF EMMA BOVARY AND FLAUBERT

Other than traveling to Normandy, the best way to acquire a sense of the landscapes where Flaubert's story is set may be to read Jean Canu's old article "La couleur normande de *Madame Bovary*," a detailed study of the background of the novel, that is, the geography, geology, architecture, customs, costumes, and vocabulary of the "pays de Caux," the region of chalky plains and escarpments that runs west from Rouen to the Atlantic Coast between Le Havre and Dieppe. To learn about everyday life there one hundred fifty years ago, read André Guérin's *La Vie quotidienne en Normandie au temps de Madame Bovary* (1975; Paris: Hachette, 1991). See also the two Web sites in Normandy that provide attractive images of Flaubert's haunts, and Jean Bruneau's *Album Flaubert*.

Pierre Larousse's *Grand Dictionnaire universel du dix-neuvième siècle* offers a mine of information about the period: see, for example, the article "Officier de santé," which explains that public health officers such as Charles Bovary could practice only in the district where they had been licensed, could not be licensed to practice in Paris, and were not allowed to do major surgery. The profession was officially abolished at the end of the nineteenth century. Thus we understand why Charles feels so flattered when Homais calls him "doctor" and why he and Emma could not live in a more exciting place even if he wanted to. Emma could not divorce Charles because divorce was illegal between 1814 and 1886. She is trapped.

The best source for historical background is Gordon Wright's frequently revised *France in Modern Times,* covering from the late eighteenth century to the present. Each section concludes with a bibliographical essay entitled "The Varieties of History," which presents scholars' divergent interpretations of the events of each period. George Joseph Becker and Bernard Weinberg (140–14, 159–76) provide helpful overviews of the realist movement in French literature (Flaubert himself, however, refused the label "realist"). Cesar Grana's *Bohemian versus Bourgeois* contrasts liberal and conservative lifestyles in the middle class, illuminating the ludicrousness of the very bourgeois Homais's and Léon's superficial flirtations with bohemianism. The first two chapters of Dominick La Capra's *Flaubert on Trial* analyze the institution of official censorship from which Flaubert and his publishers suffered under the Second Empire (1851–70). In a recent book on the government prosecuting attorney, Ernest Pinard (2001), the lawyer Alexandre Najjar applied his expertise to analyzing the case of the State against Flaubert, in chapters 5 and 6. Najjar makes him out to be quite repellent but cannot find conclusive proof that he wrote pornographic verse, as Flaubert claimed. The social histories by Eugen Weber *(Peasants into Frenchmen)* and Theodore Zeldin *(France, 1848–1945),* although they respectively treat the periods just before and just after Emma's fictive life, are still quite useful. F. W. J. Hemmings's three studies *The Age of Realism; Culture and Society in France, 1789–1848;* and *Culture and Society in France, 1848–1898: Dissidents and Philistines* also provide much information on Flaubert's times. Asa Briggs's collection of essays *The Nineteenth Century: The Contradictions of Progress* provides an attractively illustrated, wide-ranging overview of Western Europe. *Approaches to Teaching Flaubert's* Madame Bovary, edited by Laurence M. Porter and Eugene F. Gray, contains a bibliographic essay drawn from a national survey of college and university teachers of Flaubert, who suggest a rich variety of background materials. Two essays in the volume, Lilian R. Furst's "Emma Bovary: The Angel Gone Astray" (21–27) and Edward J. Ahearn's "A Marxist Approach to *Madame Bovary"* (28–33) are particularly valuable on the condition of women and on economic conditions under the constitutional monarchy of Louis-Philippe (1830–48), when Emma supposedly lived.

BIOGRAPHIES AND THE CORRESPONDENCE OF FLAUBERT

Despite the publication of later biographies by Herbert Lottman (1990), Jean-Paul Sartre (1971–72), and Enid Starkie (1967–71), the best remains Benjamin F. Bart's monumental but highly readable *Flaubert* (1967). It adopts a searching but restrained psychological approach and contains noteworthy interpretations of all the major works *except* for *Madame Bovary.* Enid Starkie's two-volume study, which coincidentally appeared at the same time, is less wide-ranging and insightful. Starkie seems fixated on Flaubert's possible homo- or bisexuality. Her overall conclusion, however, is a masterful synthesis (2:336–56). Herbert Lottman's biography, although far more recent (1990), adds information only on several minor issues. Noteworthy contributions concerning Flaubert's love relationships appear in books by Jacques-Louis Douchin (who dispels the myth of Flaubert's lifelong devotion to Elisa Schlésinger and somewhat rehabilitates Louise Colet and Maxime Du Camp) and Oliver Hermia. The most accessible, entertaining treatment of Flaubert's life is Francis Steegmuller's *Flaubert and Madame Bovary: A Double Portrait*. Among memoirs by Flaubert's contemporaries, Maxime Du Camp's two-volume *Souvenirs littéraires* (1882–83; 1: chaps. 7, 9–14; 2: chaps. 21, 25, 28–30) and the Goncourt brothers' bitchy *Journal*, respectively, reveal much concerning the first and the latter part of Flaubert's career. His niece Caroline Commanville, who was raised by Flaubert and his mother, offers a first-hand view. All three sources must be approached with caution.

Flaubert wrote marvelous, impassioned, revealing letters, of which at least some 3,600 survive, although most of his letters to and from his close friends Louis Bouilhet, Maxime Du Camp, and Guy de Maupassant have been destroyed, as well as those from his lovers Louise Colet and Juliet Herbert, "the English governess." Many private owners of Flaubert's letters have refused to release them, in hopes of increasing their value. The definitive edition of Flaubert's *Correspondance* edited by Jean Bruneau is close to completion (only volume 5, covering 1876–80 and a general index, remain unfinished), and he gives the names of these dogs in the manger there. Owing to Bruneau's ill health, Yvan Leclerc has assumed responsibility for completing this final volume. Occasional letters and excerpts from letters by others to Flaubert are included in volumes 1–4, along with painstakingly detailed notes. Bernard Masson published a French-language anthology of Flaubert's best letters in 1998. Francis Steegmuller had earlier done so in English. Flaubert's opinions remained remarkably consistent over time. Geneviève Bollème, Jean Bruneau, Wendy Deutelbaum, Hélène Frejlich, Maurice Schöne, and Mieczyslava Sekreka all offer useful comments on what Flaubert's letters reveal about him and on his epistolary art.

Some English translations can be found in Francis Steegmuller's edition of *The Letters of Gustave Flaubert*. Steegmuller and Bray also edited and translated the letters between Flaubert and George Sand. Barbara Beaumont edited and translated Flaubert's correspondence with the Russian writer Turgenev, a devoted friend in Flaubert's later years, who also greatly helped advance the career of Flaubert's beloved protégé, Guy de Maupassant. Raymonde Debray-Genette and Jacques Neefs have collected a volume of essays analyzing Flaubert's letters.

A compendium of many of the clichés that Flaubert satirized in *Madame Bovary* and elsewhere can be found in Lea Caminiti's edition of Flaubert's *Dictionnaire des idées reçues*. Jacques Barzun wrote a penetrating introduction for an English translation of the foregoing text, entitled *The Dictionary of Accepted Ideas: A Gustave Flaubert Encyclopedia* (2001), edited by Laurence M. Porter, containing much recent information on all aspects of Flaubert's times, background, life, friends and acquaintances, ideas and opinions, and works, although the present volume, a year later, synthesizes even more knowledge concerning Flaubert's impact on creative writers in the twentieth century.

EDITIONS AND TRANSLATIONS: *MADAME BOVARY* AND OTHER WORKS

Now unfortunately out of print, Claudine Gothot-Mersch's Garnier edition of *Madame Bovary* (1971) is an excellent choice for scholarly work. Her incisive introduction traces the origins of the novel and discusses Flaubert's use of description and irony. It corrects thirty-seven misprints and obvious errors in its base text, the edition of 1873, called "definitive" because of a widely accepted scholarly criterion: it was the last one reviewed by the author during his lifetime. Gothot-Mersch does not correct numerous copyists' errors that remained in subsequent editions, but a careful list of manuscript variants allows the reader to reconstitute the stage of the autograph manuscript. Given Flaubert's desultory attitude toward the task of correcting his proofs, the autograph manuscript remains the best starting point for verifying the accuracy of the printed text.

Three scholarly editions of the *Œuvres complètes* are recommended most often by researchers: Bernard Masson's (2 vols., Seuil), convenient because compact; Maurice Nadeau's (18 vols., Editions Rencontre), whose small format contains all the essentials; and Maurice Bardèche's (16 vols., Club de l'Honnête Homme). The editorial team of this elegant edition, named one of the *cinquante beaux livres* for 1971, achieved the most comprehensive publication to date of Flaubert's works. They assembled the standard previously published works with their associated scenarios, outlines, notebooks, notes, and other documentation. So the scholar can expect to find in this one collection nearly everything needed for the serious study of Flaubert's texts. The transcriptions of his letters are significantly more correct than those in the Conard edition. Yet some omissions, misreadings, and faulty texts reproduced unchanged from previous editions still appear. This monument to scholarship must be used with caution as well as gratitude.

The best inexpensive edition of *Madame Bovary* in French remains Bernard Ajac's Garnier-Flammarion volume. The 1986 version, like Gothot-Mersch's 1971 Garnier text, reproduces the 1873 Charpentier edition. Ajac's introduction is competent, and he includes the lawyers' and the judges' speeches at Flaubert's trial for subverting public morals. The Classiques Garnier and the Folio editions offer valid alternatives. Thierry Laget's 2001 edition, a new Folio Classique, may also be considered.

In English, the most widely used edition is Paul de Man's, published in the Norton Critical Editions series (1965). He retouched the nineteenth-century translation by Karl Marx's daughter Eleanor Marx Aveling—and took full credit for it. De Man includes some of Flaubert's preliminary scenarios and sketches of scenes for the novel, plus sixteen critical essays and three of the author's letters. There are some errors in the translation. Norton is preparing an updated edition. Other respected translations have been made by Lowell Bair (Bantam Classics); Gerard Manley Hopkins (Oxford University Press, edited by Terence

Cave); Alan Russell (Viking Penguin); and Francis Steegmuller (The Modern College Library, Random House). Some say Bair's version is more accurate than Steegmuller's and less stilted than Aveling's.

Steegmuller has written an engaging article about the challenges that a translator faces in understanding the culture of rural and small-town France two centuries ago, as described by Flaubert, and in finding appropriate English equivalents to the French-language descriptions of that culture. Ronald Bush's chapter in *The Future of Modernism* (1997) tells the painful story of Karl Marx's idealistic daughter Eleanor. By translating *Madame Bovary*, she hoped to continue her father's struggles for justice by extending them to women. She also fervently supported Ibsen's theater in England, where she lived, believing that *A Doll's House* was a feminist manifesto rather than—as Ibsen saw it—a poignant recognition of two absolutely incompatible, gender-bound value systems. She had sought a common-law marriage with the scoundrel Edward Aveling, to foster the principle of a pact between members of a couple that was based on mutual trust and honor rather than legal compulsion. When she learned that Aveling had betrayed her by contracting a legal marriage with an actress, she proposed a suicide pact to him. He accepted, purchased the poison, and then reneged at the last moment, to inherit Eleanor Marx's substantial fortune, including the ample revenues from the translation of *Madame Bovary*.

GENERAL CRITICAL STUDIES OF FLAUBERT

Useful recent selections of major essays have been compiled by Raymonde Debray-Genette, Laurence M. Porter, and the late Naomi Schor and Henry Majewski. The last is a truly outstanding collection. Victor Brombert's opening chapters in *Flaubert par lui-même* richly characterize Flaubert's imagination, and many critics admire Brombert's lucid overview of *The Novels of Flaubert*, which emphasizes the thematic continuity of Flaubert's imagination. Eric Gans, Rosemary Lloyd, Maurice Nadeau, Charles-Augustin Sainte-Beuve, Jean-Paul Sartre, Albert Thibaudet, and Anthony Thorlby have also written well-regarded general studies of Flaubert or *Madame Bovary*. The projected fourth volume of Sartre's *L'Idiot de la famille*—a close reading of *Madame Bovary*—never appeared during his lifetime, but his notes for that study are reproduced in volume 3 of the revised edition (663–812). Sartre's 3,000-page, three-volume study was reissued in five volumes in the English translation published by the University of Chicago Press. The first volume of the latter contains numerous errors in translation.

Several major writers have devoted sensitive, insightful essays to Flaubert's craftsmanship, which are well worth reading. These include Charles Baudelaire, Emile Zola, Henry James, Marcel Proust, Mary McCarthy, Vladimir Nabokov, Michel Tournier, and Mario Vargas Llosa, discussed in the previous chapter.

INFLUENCE STUDIES

It would be impossible to survey this field in less than a full chapter: I shall simply list my favorite books and articles concerning Flaubert's influence on other authors, to be supplemented by chapter 6 of this volume and by *A Gustave Flaubert Encyclopedia* (Greenwood, 2001) for references to studies of influences on him. Stephen Heath reveals how Kate Chopin's *The Awakening* "rewrites and transforms *Madame Bovary*" in his "Chopin's Parrot" (*Textual Practice* 8.1 [Spring 1994]: 11–32). Maurice Couturier presents a substantial, scholarly statement on "Nabokov and Flaubert" in *The Garland Companion to Vladimir Nabokov* (1995: 405–12). Claude Burgelin discusses Flaubert's strong influence on postmodernism in "Perec lecteur de Flaubert" (*Revue des lettres modernes* 703–6 [1984]: 135–71). Henk Hillenaar sensitively surveys the surprising close friendship between "George Sand and Gustave Flaubert" in *(En) jeux de la communication romanesque: hommage à Françoise van Rossum-Guyon* (Amsterdam: Rodopi, 1994: 135–49). Hazel Barnes's masterful *Sartre and Flaubert* cannot be recommended too highly. Priscilla Meyers offers suggestive speculations on Tolstoy's response to Flaubert in "*Anna Karenina:* Tolstoy's Polemic with *Madame Bovary*" in the April 1995 *Russian Review* (54.2: 243–59). Gilbert Chaitin discusses the democratizing potential of represented discourse in "Listening Power: Flaubert, Zola, and the Politics of *style indirect libre*" (*French Review* 72,6 [1999]: 1023–37).

More generally, studies of and recommendations concerning the formal art of the novel by New Critics (of the 1920s and 1930s), rhetorical critics, and structuralist critics frequently choose Flaubert as a leading example. See the indexes to classics such as Wayne C. Booth's *The Rhetoric of Fiction*, Robert Scholes and Robert Kellogg's *The Nature of Narrative*, or, most notably, Percy Lubbock's *The Craft of Fiction* (New York: Viking, 1957), 60–92. Indeed, one might say that the disappearance of Flaubert's name from books of critical theory and the profusion of playful reworkings of his texts by authors such as Audureau, Woody Allen, Georges Perec, and Philippe Sollers mark the transition from normative modernism to ludic postmodernism. On Flaubert's aesthetics, see Benjamin F. Bart's two articles in *PMLA* (1954, 1965) and René Wellek, "Gustave Flaubert," 4:6–12 in Wellek, *A History of Modern Criticism*.

CRITICAL STUDIES OF *MADAME BOVARY*

General Studies of the Novel

Albert Thibaudet's overview, first published in 1914 and substantially revised in 1935 (with an added section of Flaubert's style), for decades was the lion in the path for Flaubert critics. The best sections treat *Madame Bovary* and style. Today this landmark work is dated. Erich Auerbach reads one scene closely to derive a famous characterization of Flaubert's particular brand of realism. George Poulet took issue with Auerbach in a classic phenomenological essay: "The mind, the body, nature, and life, all participate in the same moment of the same becoming," which contracts and expands in the consciousness of the author and of his heroine ("Flaubert," 18). Albert Béguin wrote a beautiful lament for Flaubert's self-mutilating sacrifices of his rich psychological insights, an act that produces a great poem of ennui.

Also highly regarded by North American teachers and scholars are the books or chapters by Jonathan Culler (the most influential of all), Tony Tanner, and Mario Vargas Llosa. Nearly as influential have been essays by Charles Baudelaire, Roland Barthes, Leo Bersani, Stirling Haig, Georges Poulet, Jean-Pierre Richard, Michael Riffaterre, and Richard Terdiman.[1]

Characters Other Than Emma Bovary

David A. Williams has written a fine study of Binet as a parody of artistic self-consciousness as he endlessly turns out useless napkin rings on his lathe. Peter M. Wetherill, skeptical concerning the heavy symbolic meanings attached by critics to the Blind Man, claims that he "merely reinforces that impression of meaningless experience [that] typifies the majority of Flaubert's works" (42). René Jasinski perspicaciously examines the important role of the contrasting couple of the priest Bournisien and the pharmacist Homais. Lilian Furst (1993–94) situates the portrait of Charles as a medical professional in the context of fictions of the time. Graham Falconer's essay on Charles is outstanding. In a radical revision of accepted opinion, Norioki Sugaya speculates that he died happily of love. Mary Orr calls attention to the ambiguous sexuality of the richly characterized but neglected Lheureux (who reminds one a bit of Dickens's Uriah Heep in *David Copperfield*). Patricia Reynaud-Pactat probes Rodolphe's character in the scene where he writes a letter breaking with Emma.

Deconstructionist Studies

The deconstructionist movement passed its peak twenty-five years ago, but not without producing lasting changes—as did Freud—in the way we see a text: as a dynamic field of shifting meanings, not as a static and monumental residue. Jonathan Culler's excellent book, still probably the most influential single critical work on Flaubert, unequivocally opposes the long critical tradition concerned with "making sense" of Flaubert's texts, in particular, of those passages deemed "puzzling" owing to their descriptions, episodic characters, shifting viewpoints, and irony. The rapidly changing perspectives prevent the reader from determining who speaks; without a privileged narrative point of view, the text becomes an aesthetic object rather than a communicative act. Culler examines the paramount role of irony in creating a discrepancy between novelistic sign and novelistic function, resulting in that distancing effect that makes the text—and all language—appear "stupid," the characteristic of all great art according to Flaubert. Culler sees irony used ultimately to disclose the sacred, defined as "the necessary correlate of our desire to order experience in ways that escape delusion and destructive irony" (126).

Jean Rousset and Leo Bersani, discussed elsewhere, reveal deconstructivist tendencies in their work. Nathaniel Wing offers a stimulating study of the opposing narrative families of Emma's desire for love and for money. Wing treats the opera scene particularly well. Dorothy Kelly teaches us much about deconstructive criticism by showing us how to teach the method to students. The Master, Jacques Derrida, applied his paradoxical questioning to Flaubert's aesthetic theories themselves, not to their product. Victor Brombert, the most eloquent member of the old guard, and Porter, Prendergast, and Williams have written in opposition to various instances of deconstructive criticism, considering them either as betrayals of the true intent of the movement (Porter) or as horrible examples of a fundamentally flawed enterprise.

Feminist and Gender Studies

Charles Baudelaire pioneered in noticing and discussing the androgynous nature of Flaubert's narrative persona and of Emma Bovary's virile, and therefore transgressive, qualities. S. Murphy presents a forceful feminist view of how Flaubert condemns his society in depicting the education and rearing of women. Carla Peterson discusses Emma as reader: perusing novels forms a natural outlet for intelligent women denied autonomy and a serious education; Emma's suicide is an act of self-assertion that the men around her cannot prevent. Naomi Schor takes the other tack, discussing Emma as victim, exemplified in her intermittent but critical failures to find the right words, as opposed to Homais's facility in writing. Her love letters create an ideal lover, but by that token, an inaccessible one. Three varied, informative feminist essays, by Lilian Furst, Susan Wolf, and Lauren Pinzka—the first in cultural studies and the latter two psychoanalytic—appear in Laurence M. Porter and Eugene F. Gray's *Approaches to Teaching* Madame Bovary.

Genetic Studies (How Flaubert Conceived, Developed, and Perfected His Novel)

The indispensable studies in the area of genetic studies are Claudine Gothot-Mersch's *La Genèse de* Madame Bovary and Yvan Leclerc's edition of the outlines, scenarios, and sketches of scenes. These, and nine volumes of drafts and notes for the novel, were bequeathed to the Rouen town library; a few other notes are found in the Bodmer collection in Geneva. Giovanni Bonaccorso wrote in Italian "Sul testo di Madame Bovary," explaining the errors persisting in the 1873 Charpentier edition and the superiority of the Lemerre edition in adhering to Flaubert's intentions. Graham Falconer studies the manuscript variants to show how Flaubert progressively made Charles Bovary less intelligent and likable as he developed Homais's and Emma's personalities. Eric Le Calvez, the leading genetic scholar of *L'Education sentimentale*, has an important article on the use of genetic criticism—applied, in this instance, to *Madame Bovary*—in teaching the novel. To these treasures, Yvan Leclerc has just recently added a scholarly study of the books in Flaubert's library.

Psychological Studies

The two outstandingly original psychological studies to illuminate *Madame Bovary* have been René Girard's and Jean-Paul Sartre's. Girard's *Deceit, Desire, and the Novel*, which advances the compelling theory of "mediated desire" (based on but extending Freud's theory of the Oedipus complex [which Oedipus himself, of course, did not have]). We learn what to want from what others prize. Debased forms of romanticism mediate and motivate Emma's desires. Sartre's *The Family Idiot* deploys existentialist psychoanalysis, which tries to modify Marxist insights into class dynamics with considerations of one's family and milieu (social setting). He emphasizes ways in which our lives become "inauthentic" through convenient, self-justifying self-deceptions operating in our preconscious on awareness that we have successfully suppressed (as opposed to Freudian repression, which never allows unconscious material to emerge to awareness). Hazel Barnes's brilliant, respectful analysis clarifies Sartre greatly and exposes the weaknesses of his approach: he neglects Emma's milieu, projects his own suppressed self-hatred (liberal guilt) onto Flaubert, and fails to situate that author convincingly in literary history.

Less original, but still noteworthy, are the achievements of Charles Bernheimer, Leo Bersani, Simon O. Lesser, Bernard J. Paris, and Avita Ronell. Ronell innovates in finding the key to Emma's psyche in her thrill-seeking, addictive personality, which thrives on powerful sensations of every kind. Paris has pioneered in applying the theories of Karen Horney to the analysis of characters in realistic novels. Horney concentrates on interactive strategies that parallel animal behavior (although she omits altruism), neurosis being the excessive and often inappropriate use of only one of them: fight, flight, or compliance. In "The Role of Unconscious Understanding in Flaubert and Dostoevsky" (*Daedalus* 92 [1963]: 363–82), Lesser analyzes how Flaubert "splits the ambivalence" toward his father—glorifying him in the portrait of Dr. Larivière and satirizing him in Charles (and, one could add, in Canivet). Bernheimer tried to update psychoanalytic object-relations theory so that it could subsume deconstruction. Bersani assails the concept of "that unity of personality assumed by all humanistic psychologies." For him, the essence of personhood is desire, projected outward onto constantly shifting objects. Skeptical of the systematic application of psychoanalytic theory to fiction, Laurence M. Porter uses a strict constructionist approach via contemporary psychoanalytical practice, as reflected in the DSM (the official handbook of diagnoses that justify insurance payments), to show how the aesthetic demands of a novel necessitate incoherence whenever we attempt to read Emma as if she were a real person.

Louise Kaplan's chapter on Emma in her seductively titled book *Female Perversions* invokes the notion of sexual bondage inspired by Richard von Krafft-Ebing's *Psychopathia Sexualis* (trans. Franklin S. Klaf. New York: Bell, 1965) and by Annie Reich's *Psychoanalytic Contributions* (New York: International Universities Press, 1973) to explain Emma's morbid attachment to Rodolphe and Léon's to her. But her skimming treatment of the text tells us no more than we already have learned from the novel. She does not illumine the rest of the novel or of Flaubert's characterizations. And she overreaches herself by claiming that Charles was seeking a sexual dominatrix.

Several ingenious but dangerously misleading critics such as Ion Collas (1985), Kristina Curry (1996–97), and Roberto Speziale-Bagliacca (first in 1974), influenced mainly by Melanie Klein's recasting of Freud's notion of melancholia (loss elicits rage, which then turns masochistically against the self), distort many details in the text in order to invent elaborate parallel stories that present Emma as if she were an actual client in therapy but that serve only as vehicles for their own psychic projections. References to these meretricious, unsound works will not be provided here.

Stylistic Studies

Flaubert's style has inspired much research. Eugene F. Gray offers a succinct overview in *A Gustave Flaubert Encyclopedia*, s.v. "Stylistic studies," 311–17. Ferdinand Brunetière's pioneering essay (1880) called attention to several characteristic traits of Flaubert's writing in *Madame Bovary:* impressionist style, flashbacks, and tableaux. Philippe Hamon wrote a still-influential survey of the art of description in prose fiction, which should be supplemented with Jean Ricardou's chapter and Roland Barthes's brief comments on "the reality effect" Flaubert achieves by depicting a brute, alien world of objects (Sartre's *en-soi*) gratuitous in relation to the plot. Claude Duchet describes characteristic situations—commonplace in Balzac or the fantastic, unexpected in a purportedly objective novel—in which these objects seem to acquire an independent life. Gray (1978) points out the epistemological consequences of Flaubert's descriptions, which often imply flawed perception and limited awareness on the part of the characters that inhabit them.

Mieke Bal and Gerald Prince are noteworthy among those whose general elaborations of narratological theory have particular relevance for Flaubert's sophisticated but in many ways classical story telling. Vaheed Ramazani published three well-regarded studies of Flaubert's irony, an almost universal feature of his writing. He points out that because in the nineteenth century books are mass manufactured and distributed for commercial gain (as contrasted, for instance, with the circulation of the Encyclopedists' handwritten manuscripts throughout European intellectual circles in the eighteenth century), the literary work of art loses much justification for its claims of transcendence. These claims are further undermined by Flaubert's painful awareness that what language can communicate is mainly what the writer has in common with the public; much of the superiority that writers believe themselves to possess is unknowable by others.

Charles Bruneau and Albert Thibaudet offer important general studies of Flaubert's style, whereas Brunetière, John Porter Houston, Gustave Lanson, and Alf Lombard situate that style among nineteenth-century conventions. Charles Bally and Stephen Ullmann each offer helpful clarifications of the difficult concept of the *style indirect libre* (represented discourse, *erlebte Rede*) that is Flaubert's hallmark; Benjamin Bart (1954), Claudine Gothot-Mersch (1971), R. J. Sherrington, and more recently Stirling Haig and Michal Peled Ginsburg treat Flaubert's use of it in detail. Haig points out how often Emma Bovary's prosaic but pretentious style in the drafts was later replaced by *style indirect libre*. Gérard Strauch provides a historical overview of that device, which dates back at least to *La Cantilène de sainte Eulalie*, one of the earliest-known literary texts in French.

Thematic Studies

Thematic studies include two of the most influential essays on Flaubert. In his *Studies in Human Time* (1956; in French 1949), which includes "Flaubert," Georges Poulet adopts a phenomenological approach to study how the younger Flaubert uses memory to shorten the distance between consciousness and outside events, producing ecstasy. In his maturity, through the rational construction of some kind of order, Flaubert tries to overcome his sense that an abyss separates his consciousness from outside events. Jean-Pierre Richard's widely cited, highly impressionistic "La creation de la forme chez Flaubert," published in his *Littérature et sensation* (1954), concentrates on food and eating: it reviews images of digestion, absorption, assimilation, and liquefaction in Flaubert's works, to argue that the endomorphic Flaubert seeks to establish his identity vis-à-vis the all-engulfing universe but is doomed to failure.

In less sweeping studies, Tony Tanner's stimulating, uneven study includes 130 pages on adultery in *Madame Bovary*. Bersani (1976), Kaplan, and LaCapra also treat this motif competently, and Riffaterre devotes a brilliant, controversial study to how the cultural cliché of condemning marital infidelity generates the entire novel. Issacharoff treats the comic. Engstrom offers a richly detailed analysis of the motif of fate and fatality. Lapp discusses hallucinations—the epileptic Flaubert's experience of second states of consciousness enriched his portrait of the hypersensitive Emma. Nelles provides a close reading of horse symbolism (virility, bridled and unbridled passion) in Western tradition and in Flaubert. Rothfield has contributed a highly recommended study of medical discourse. Hasumi discusses space. Chambers offers an original view of suicide; and Starobinski has a fine, original essay on Emma's sensitivity to ambient temperature. See also, in *A Gustave Flaubert Encyclopedia*, the entries on adultery (2–3), androgyny (7–8), art (15–16), *bêtise* (stupidity or philistinism, or both; 26–27), the book (31), colors (66–67), copies and copying (72–74), death (93–95), decadence (97–98), fetishism (126–27; see also Tanner, 284–96), food (136; see also Richard), history (169–70), homosexuality (172–73), medievalism (218–19), mirror symbolism (224), neurosis (238–39), nihilism (239), romanticism (275–76), and suicide (317–18).

CONCORDANCES

The concordance to *Madame Bovary*, compiled by Charles Carlut, Pierre Dubé, and Raymond Duggan, was prepared in the standard keyword-in-context format: the indexed word appears in the middle of a line of text. Common grammatical words—articles and the most frequent prepositions, pronouns, and conjunctions—are omitted. The frequencies of all words are noted, however. Claudine Gothot-Mersch's edition is used as a base. This reference work, particularly when used in conjunction with the ARTFL (American and French Research on the Treasury of the French Language) electronic database (to be discussed), greatly facilitates semantic and thematic studies of Flaubert's masterpiece (for example, the term *fatalité* occurs a dozen times).

OTHER MEDIA: ART, FILM, MUSIC, PAINTING, AND PHOTOGRAPHY

Kenneth Clark's video program "The Fallacies of Hope," part 12 of his *Civilisation*, was distributed by the BBC in 1970. The three best-known film versions of *Madame Bovary* are available on videotape: those by Jean Renoir (1934), Vincente Minnelli (1949), and Claude Chabrol (1991). Mary Donaldson-Evans compares them perceptively.

Jean Bruneau and Jean-A. Ducourneau have compiled an impressive collection of documents, sketches, and photographs related to Flaubert in their *Album Flaubert* (Pléiade, 1972). René Dumesnil's *Flaubert et* L'Education sentimentale (1943) contains images of Flaubert, his family, acquaintances, haunts, and key pages from his notes and manuscripts. More recently, Peter Wetherill's compilation L'Education sentimentale: *Notes et documents* (1985) presents interesting contemporary portraits and images that may roughly correspond to what Flaubert saw or imagined.

ELECTRONIC RESOURCES

Chief among electronic resources for the study of Flaubert is the ARTFL, an indispensable and constantly expanding on-line database for textual research in French literature. It is free, accessible, and downloadable via Netscape. Located at the University of Chicago, this corpus allows one to search hundreds of French fictional texts, including several by Flaubert, for a given word or phrase. The format is keyword-in-context, and the editions used are specified. (Unfortunately, older texts such as the incomplete, inaccurate Conard edition of his correspondence are often used.) As time permits, the context is being extended to paragraph length, with links to the previous and following paragraphs and to the entire page on which the example in question appears. Writers' journals and memoirs are a prominent feature.

The most serious scholarly site for information on contemporary research on Flaubert and on *Madame Bovary* in particular is Yvan Leclerc's *www .univ-rouen.fr*. F. J. Venezia's Flaubert info.com site, the *http://perso .wanadoo.fr/jb guinot/pages/accueil.html,* and *www.hull.ac.uk/item.ens.fr* all offer many valuable and varied links and features. A selective general site that combines eighty search engines is *www.copernic.com.* If instead you use a search engine such as Google, you will be overwhelmed with literally millions of sites, choked with advertisements and listed without discrimination. The ClicNet site provides links to nine Flaubert texts with advanced search features. The best source for on-line, downloadable texts is *http://gallica.bnf.fr,* with forty-nine digitized titles and a sound choice of editions. Even more texts (132) from the same source, the Bibliothèque Nationale, are found at *http://catalog num.bnf.fr/html/i—frames.htm.* Timothy Unwin, himself a Flaubert specialist and a founder of the new Société des dix-neuvièmistes (started in 2001) in the UK, provides addresses of a number of Web sites of interest to specialists, in his chapter "A Report on Flaubert and the New Technologies." More recently, Andrew Oliver (2001) has surveyed Internet resources for nineteenth-century French scholars.

NOTE

1. These results were derived from a national survey devised, circulated, and tabulated by Laurence M. Porter and Eugene F. Gray as they prepared *Approaches to Teaching Flaubert's* Madame Bovary (1995) for the Modern Language Association of America.

Bibliography

WORKS BY FLAUBERT IN FRENCH

Flaubert, Gustave. *Classement et analyse des brouillons de* Madame Bovary *de Gustave Flaubert.* Ed. Marie Durel. Thèse: L'Université de Rouen, 2000.

———.*Les Comices agricoles de* Madame Bovary *de Flaubert. Transcription intégrale et genèse.* Ed. Jeanne Goldin. 2 vols. Geneva: Droz, 1984.

———. *Correspondance.* Ed. Jean Bruneau and Yvan Leclerc. [5] vols. Paris: Gallimard, 1971–[98; vol. 5 is near completion].

———. *Correspondance* [selection]. Ed. Bernard Masson. Paris: Gallimard, Folio Classique, 1998.

———. *Dictionnaire des idées reçues.* Ed. Lea Caminiti. Diplomatic edition of the Rouen mss. Paris: Nizet, 1966.

———. *Gustave Flaubert, Plans et scénarios de* Madame Bovary. Ed. Yvan Leclerc. Paris: CNRS/Zulma, 1995.

———. *Madame Bovary.* Ed. Bernard Ajac. Paris: Garnier-Flammarion, 1986.

———. *Madame Bovary.* Ed. Claudine Gothot-Mersch. Paris: Garnier, 1971.

———. *Madame Bovary.* Ed. Thierry Laget. Paris: Gallimard, Folio Classique, 2001.

———. *Madame Bovary: Ébauches et fragments inédits, recueillis d'après les manuscrits.* Ed. Gabrielle Leleu. 2 vols. Paris: Conard, 1936.

———. *Madame Bovary. Nouvelle Version précédée de scénarios inédits: Textes établis sur les manuscrits de Rouen avec une introduction et des notes.* Ed. Jean Pommier and Gabrielle Leleu. Paris: Corti, 1949.

———. *Œuvres.* Ed. Maurice Nadeau. 18 vols. Lausanne: Rencontre, 1964–65.

———. *Œuvres complètes.* Ed. Maurice Bardèche et al. 16 vols. Paris: Club de l'Honnête Homme, 1971–76.

———. *Œuvres complètes.* Ed. Bernard Masson. 2 vols. Paris: Seuil, 1964.

———. *Pour Bouilhet.* Ed. Alan Raitt. Exeter, UK: University of Exeter Press, 1994.

ENGLISH TRANSLATIONS OF WORKS BY FLAUBERT

Flaubert, Gustave. *Bouvard and Pécuchet*. Trans. T. W. Earp and G. W. Stonier. With an introduction by Lionel Trilling. New York: New Directions, 1964.

————. *The Dictionary of Accepted Ideas*. Trans. and with an introduction by Jacques Barzun. Norfolk: New Directions, 1954.

————. *Early Writings. Gustave Flaubert*. Ed. and trans. Robert Griffin. Lincoln, NE: University of Nebraska Press, 1991.

————. *The Letters of Gustave Flaubert*. Ed. and trans. Francis Steegmuller. Cambridge, MA: Harvard UP, 1980.

————. *Madame Bovary*. Trans. Lowell Bair. New York: Bantam, 1987.

————. *Madame Bovary*. Trans. Alan Russell. New York: Viking Penguin, 1951.

————. *Madame Bovary*. Trans. Francis Steegmuller. New York: Random, 1981.

————. Madame Bovary: *Backgrounds and Sources: Essays in Criticism*. Ed. Paul de Man. Trans. Eleanor Marx Aveling. New York: Norton, 1965.

————. Madame Bovary: *Life in a Country Town*. Ed. Terence Cave. Trans. Gerard Manley Hopkins. World's Classics. New York: Oxford University Press, 1989.

Flaubert–Sand: The Correspondence. Ed. and trans. Francis Steegmuller and Barbara Bray. London: Harvill, 1993.

Flaubert and Turgenev, a Friendship in Letters: The Complete Correspondence. Ed. and trans. Barbara Beaumont. London: Athlone, 1985.

UNESCO. *http://databases.unesco.org/xtrans/xtra-form.html*. 585 listings under "AUTHOR = Flaubert" (as of October 2001).

BIBLIOGRAPHIES

French Dissertations on Flaubert: *http://www.sudoc.abes.fr/* lists 134 defended since 1909, including 14 on *Madame Bovary*.

Gray, Eugene F., and Laurence M. Porter. "Gustave Flaubert." 2:801–66 in David Baguley, ed. *A Critical Bibliography of French Literature*. Vol. 5, *The Nineteenth Century*. 2 vols. Syracuse, NY: Syracuse University Press, 1994 [coverage through 1989].

Guidis, Odile de. Paris, Equipe Flaubert, ITEM–CNRS [annual bibliography at] *http://www.item.ens.fr/contenus/equiprojet/EQPaccueil.htm*.

MLA 1963–90; 1991–[present]. Modern Language Association of America. On-line bibliographies with advanced search functions, available through libraries that subscribe; also on CD-ROM. Includes dissertations completed.

www.univ-rouen.fr/Flaubert/index.htm. Regular updates supervised by Yvan Leclerc.

The Year's Work in Modern Language Studies. London: The Modern Humanities Research Association, UK. Critical and selective.

WORKS ABOUT FLAUBERT, HIS TIMES, AND HIS INFLUENCE

Acher, Lionel. *Cette diablesse de Madame Bovary*. A parodistic novel (2001), available on-line at *http:/www.planet4u.com/*.

————. "Réécritures et suites de *Madame Bovary*." *Bulletin Flaubert-Maupassant* 6 (1998): 79–91. From late fall 2001 on, updated on-line: *http://www. univ-rouen.fr/Flaubert/index.htm/*.

Ahearn, Edward J. "A Marxist Approach to *Madame Bovary*." 28–33 in Laurence M. Porter and Eugene F. Gray, eds. *Approaches to Teaching Flaubert's* Madame Bovary. New York: Modern Language Association of America, 1995.

Allen, Woody. "The Kugelmass Episode." 59–78 in Allen, *Side Effects*. New York: Ballantine, 1982.

Aprile, Max. "L'aveugle et sa signification dans *Madame Bovary*." *Revue d'Histoire Littéraire de la France* 76 (1976): 385–92.

Auerbach, Erich. *Mimesis: The Representation of Reality in Western Literature*. Trans. Willard R. Trask. Princeton, NJ: Princeton University Press, 1953.

Bailbé, Joseph-Marc. "*Salammbô* de Reyer: Du roman à l'opéra." *Romantisme* 38 (1982): 93–103.

Bal, Mieke. "Descriptions: Pour une théorie de la description narrative: À propos de *Madame Bovary* de Flaubert," 87–111 in *Narratologie; les instances du récit: Essais sur la signification narrative dans quatre romans modernes*. Paris: Klincksieck, 1977.

Ballanger, Claude, et al. *Histoire générale de la presse française*. 3 vols. Paris: Presses Universitaires de France, 1969.

Bally, Charles. "Le style indirect libre en français moderne." *Germanisch-Romanische Monatsschrift* 4 (1912): 549–56, 597–606.

Balzac, Honoré de. *Mercadet*. Paris: Librairie Théâtrale, 1851 [date first performed].

————. *La Comédie humaine*. 12 vols. Paris: Gallimard, 1976–80.

Banuls, André. "L'Education sentimentale" [on "Pippo Spano" by Heinrich Mann]. 161–84 in *Heinrich Mann: Le poète et la politique*. Paris: Klincksieck, 1966.

Banville, Théodore de. *Odes funambulesques*. Paris: Calmann-Lévy, 1859.

Barbey d'Aurevilly, Jules Amédée. "Gustave Flaubert" in "Les Romanciers." 61–76 in Volume 4 of *Le XIXe Siècle: Des Œuvres et des hommes*. 15 vols. Paris: Amyot et al., 1860–95.

————. "M. Gustave Flaubert." 50–57 in Laurence M. Porter, ed. *Critical Essays on Gustave Flaubert*. Boston: Hall, 1986. First published in Barbey d'Aurevilly, *Des Œuvres et des hommes* 4:61–76.

Barnes, Hazel E. *Sartre & Flaubert*. Chicago: University of Chicago Press, 1981.

Barrès, Maurice. *Mes Cahiers*. 14 vols. Paris: Plon, 1929–57.

Bart, Benjamin F. "Aesthetic Distance in *Madame Bovary*." *PMLA* 69 (1954): 1113–26.

————. *Flaubert*. Syracuse, NY: Syracuse University Press, 1967.

————. "Flaubert's Concept of the Novel." *PMLA* 80 (1965): 84–89.

————. *Flaubert's Landscape Descriptions*. Ann Arbor, MI: University of Michigan Press, 1956.

————. "Louis Bouilhet: Flaubert's accoucheur." *Symposium* 17 (1963): 183–201.

————. "Psyche into Myth: Humanity and Animality in Flaubert's *Saint Julien*." *Kentucky Romance Quarterly* 20 (1973): 317–42.

Barthes, Roland. "L'artisanat du style." 89–94 in *Le Degré zero de la littérature*. Paris: Seuil, 1953. 62–66 in *Writing Degree Zero*. Trans. Annette Lavers and Colin Smith. New York: Hill and Wang, 1968.

————. "L'Effet de réel." *Communications* 11 (1968): 84–89.

Bascelli, Anthony L. "Flaubert as Seen through the Eyes of the Brothers Goncourt: A Neglected and Somewhat Flawed Artistical Judgment." *Nineteenth-Century French Studies* 5 (1977): 277–95.

Baudelaire, Charles. "*Madame Bovary,* par Gustave Flaubert." *L'Artiste.* October 18, 1857. Translation in Paul de Man, ed., *Madame Bovary:* 336–43.

Becker, George Joseph, comp. and trans. *Documents of Modern Literary Realism.* Princeton, NJ: Princeton University Press, 1963.

Béguin, Albert. "Relire *Madame Bovary.*" *La Table Ronde* 1950: 160–64. Translation in Paul de Man, ed., *Madame Bovary:* 292–97.

Beizer, Janet, Raymonde Debray-Genette, and Jacques Neefs, eds. *Œuvre de l'œuvre: Études sur la correspondance de Flaubert.* Paris: Presses Universitaires de Vincennes, 1993.

Bellanger, Claude, et al. *Histoire générale de la presse française.* 3 vols. Paris: Presses Universitaires de France, 1969.

Bellet, Roger, ed. *Femmes de lettres au XIXe siècle, autour de Louise Colet.* Lyon: Presses Universitaires de Lyon, 1982.

Bernheimer, Charles. *Flaubert and Kafka: Studies in Psychopoetic Structure.* New Haven, CT: Yale University Press, 1982.

Bersani, Leo. "Flaubert and the Threats of Imagination." 140–91 in *Balzac to Beckett: Center and Circumference in French Fiction.* New York: Oxford University Press, 1970.

————. "*Madame Bovary* and the Sense of Sex." 89–105 in *A Future for Astyanax: Character and Desire in Literature.* Boston: Little, Brown, 1976.

Billy, André. *La Présidente et ses amis.* Paris: Flammarion, 1945.

Bismut, Roger. "Henri Monnier, modèle de Flaubert." *Les Amis de Flaubert* 27 (December 1965): 15–17.

————. "Le narrateur dans *Germinie Lacerteux.*" *Cahiers de l'Association Internationale des Etudes Françaises* 36 (1984): 21–33.

————. "Sur une chronologie de *Madame Bovary.*" *Les Amis de Flaubert* 42 (May 1973): 4–9.

Bloy, Léon. *Journal* 2 (1907): 288. Paris: Mercure de France, 1956–63.

Bollème, Geneviève. *Extraits de la correspondance, ou préface à la vie d'écrivain.* Paris: Seuil, 1963.

————. *Le Second Volume de* Bouvard et Pécuchet. Paris: Denoël, 1966.

Bonaccorso, Giovanni. "Sul testo di Madame Bovary." *Rivista di letterature moderne e comparate* 31 (1978): 129–50.

Bonwit, Marianne. "Gustave Flaubert et le principe d'impassibilité." *University of California Publications in Modern Philology* 33 (1950): 263–420.

Brecht, Bertolt. "Alienation Effects in Chinese Acting." 1936. 91–99 in John Willett, ed. and trans. *Brecht on Theatre: The Development of an Esthetic.* New York: Hill and Wang, 1996.

————. "Short Description of a New Technique of Acting which Produces an Alienation Effect." 1940. 136–47 in John Willett, ed. and trans. *Brecht on Theatre: The Development of an Esthetic.* New York: Hill and Wang, 1996.

————. "A Short Organum for the Theatre." 1949. 179–205 in John Willett, ed. and trans. *Brecht on Theatre: The Development of an Esthetic.* New York: Hill and Wang, 1996.

Briggs, Asa, ed. *The Nineteenth Century: The Contradictions of Progress.* New York: McGraw-Hill, 1970.

Brombert, Victor. "Flaubert and the Status of the Subject." 100–115 in Naomi Schor and Henry F. Majewski, eds. *Flaubert and Postmodernism.* Lincoln, NE: University of Nebraska Press, 1984.

———. *Flaubert par lui-même.* Paris: Seuil, 1971.

———. *The Novels of Flaubert: A Study of Themes and Techniques.* Princeton, NJ: Princeton University Press, 1966.

Bruneau, Charles. "Le style littéraire." 7–46 in Ferdinand Brunot, ed. *L'Epoque réaliste.* Part 2, vol. 13 of *Histoire de la langue française, des origines à 1900.* Paris: Colin, 1972.

Bruneau, Jean. *Les Débuts littéraires de Gustave Flaubert.* Paris: Colin, 1962.

Brunetière, Ferdinand. "Le naturalisme français: Etude sur Gustave Flaubert." 1883. 149–203 in *Le roman naturaliste.* Paris: Calmann-Lévy, 1896.

Brush, Stephen G. "Thermodynamics and History." *The Graduate Journal* 7 (1967): 477–566.

Bush, Ronald. "James Joyce, Eleanor Marx, and the Future of Modernism." 49–77 in Hugh Witemeyer, ed. *The Future of Modernism.* Ann Arbor, MI: University of Michigan Press, 1997.

Camus, Albert. *L'Homme révolté.* Paris: Gallimard, 1951.

Canu, Jean. "La 'Couleur normande' de *Madame Bovary.*" *PMLA* 48 (1933): 167–208.

———. *Flaubert auteur dramatique.* Paris: Ecrits de France, 1946.

Carlut, Charles, Pierre Dubé, and J. Raymond Duggan, comps. *A Concordance to Flaubert's* Madame Bovary. 2 vols. New York: Garland, 1978.

Carpenter, Scott D. "*L'Education sentimentale* (1845)." 108–12 in Laurence M. Porter, ed. *A Gustave Flaubert Encyclopedia.* Westport, CT: Greenwood Press, 2001.

Cassagne, Albert. *La Théorie de l'art pour l'art en France.* Paris: Dorbon, 1959.

Chaitin, Gilbert. "Listening Power: Flaubert, Zola, and the Politics of *style indirect libre.*" *French Review* 72.6 (May 1999): 1023–37.

Champfleury [pseud. of Jules Husson]. *Henry Monnier: Sa vie, son œuvre.* Paris: Dentu, 1889.

———. Histoire *de la caricature moderne.* Paris: Dentu, n.d.

Chateaubriand, François-René de. *Itinéraire de Paris à Jérusalem.* 1811. Ed. Jean Mourot. Paris: Garnier-Flammarion, 1968. Seventy editions of this work appeared during the nineteenth century.

Claudel, Paul. *Paul Claudel/André Gide, Correspondance 1899–1926.* Ed. R. Mallet. Paris: Gallimard, 1949.

Clayman, Charles B., ed. *Encyclopedia of Medicine.* New York: Random House, 1989.

Cloonan, William. "Michel Tournier." 333–34 in Laurence M. Porter, ed. *A Gustave Flaubert Encyclopedia.* Westport, CT: Greenwood, 2001.

———. *Michel Tournier.* Boston: Twayne, 1985.

Commanville, Caroline. *Souvenirs sur Gustave Flaubert.* Paris: Ferroud, 1895. Republished as "Souvenirs intimes" under her new married name, Franklin-Grout, as the preface to Gustave Flaubert, *Œuvres complètes.* Vol. 1. 22 vols. Paris: Conard, 1910–33.

Cousin, Victor. *Cours de philosophie sur le fondement des idées absolues du vrai, du beau et du bien.* Ed. Adolphe Garnier. Paris: Hachette, 1836.

Couturier, Maurice. "Nabokov and Flaubert." 405–12 in Vladimir E. Alexandrov, ed. *The Garland Companion to Vladimir Nabokov*. New York: Garland, 1995.

Culler, Jonathan. *Flaubert: The Uses of Uncertainty*. Ithaca, NY: Cornell University Press, 1974, rev. 1985.

DSM-IV (The Diagnostic and Statistical Manual of Mental Disorders, Fourth Edition). Washington, DC: American Psychiatric Association, 1994, s.v. "Narcissistic Personality Disorder," 658–61.

Daudet, Léon. Cited in Jules Renard. *Journal*. Ed. L. Guichard and G. Sigaux. P. 150. Paris: Gallimard, 1960.

Daumier, Honoré. *Les cent Robert Macaire*. Paris: Les Arts et le livre, 1926.

Daunais, Isabelle. *Flaubert et la scénographie romanesque*. Paris: Nizet, 1993.

Debray-Genette, Raymonde, ed. *Flaubert*. Paris: Didot, 1970.

Delavigne, Casimir. *Œuvres complètes de Casimir Delavigne*. Paris: Didier, 1855.

Derrida, Jacques. "Une idée de Flaubert: La lettre de Platon." *Revue d'Histoire Littéraire de la France* 81 (1981): 658–76. Translated in *MLN* 99 (1984): 748–68.

Descharmes, René. *Flaubert, sa vie, son caractère et ses idées avant 1857*. Paris: Ferroud, 1909.

Descharmes, René, and René Dumesnil. *Autour de Flaubert*. 2 vols. Paris: Mercure de France, 1912.

Deutelbaum, Wendy. "Desolation and Consolation: The Correspondence of Flaubert and George Sand." *Genre* 15 (1982): 281–302.

Donato, Eugenio. "The Museum's Furnace: Notes toward a Contextual Reading of *Bouvard et Pécuchet*." 207–22 in Laurence M. Porter, ed. *Critical Essays on Gustave Flaubert*. Boston: Hall, 1986.

Douchin, Jacques-Louis. "La Satire 'Prud'hommesque' dans la correspondance de Flaubert." *Les Amis de Flaubert* 25 (December 1964): 13–23.

———. *La Vie érotique de Flaubert*. Paris: Pauvert, 1984.

Du Bos, Charles. *Journal*. 4 vols. Paris: Correa, 1946–50.

Dubuc, André. "Une amitié littéraire: Gustave Flaubert et Emile Zola." *Les Cahiers Naturalistes* 10 (1964): 129–36.

Du Camp, Maxime. *Lettres inédites à Gustave Flaubert*. Ed. Giovanni Bonaccorso and Maria di Stefano. Messina: EDAS, 1978.

———. *Souvenirs et paysages d'Orient, Smyrne, Ephèse, Magnésie, Constantinople, Scio*. Paris: Bertrand, 1848.

———. *Souvenirs littéraires*. 1906. Paris: Aubier, 1994.

Duchet, Claude. "Discours social et texte italique dans *Madame Bovary*." 143–63 in Michael Issacharoff, ed. *Langages de Flaubert*. Paris: Lettres Modernes, 1976.

———. "Roman et objets: L'exemple de *Madame Bovary*." *Europe* 485–87 (1969): 171–201.

Duranty, Edmond. Review of *Madame Bovary*. *Réalisme* 5 (March 15, 1857): 79–80. Reprinted in Laurence M. Porter, ed. *Critical Essays on Gustave Flaubert*, 49. Boston: Hall, 1986.

Durry, Marie-Jeanne. *Flaubert et ses projets inédits*. Paris: Nizet, 1950.

Engstrom, Alfred. "Flaubert's Correspondence and the Ironic and Symbolic Structure of *Madame Bovary*." *Studies in Philology* 46 (1949): 470–95.

Falconer, Graham. "Flaubert assassin de Charles." 115–41 in Michael Issacharoff, ed. *Langages de Flaubert*. Paris: Lettres Modernes, 1976.

Feldman, Irving. "A Sentimental Education Circa 1956." 32–36 in Sanford Pinsker, ed. *Critical Essays on Philip Roth.* Boston: Hall, 1982.

Felman, Shoshana. "Modernity of the Commonplace." 29–48 in Laurence M. Porter, ed. *Critical Essays on Gustave Flaubert.* Boston: Hall, 1986.

France, Anatole. *La Vie littéraire.* 4 vols. Paris: Calmann-Lévy, 1889–92.

France, Peter, ed. *The New Oxford Companion to Literature in French.* Oxford, UK: Clarendon, 1995.

Frejlich, Hélène. *Flaubert d'après sa correspondance.* Paris: Société française d'éditions littéraires et techniques, 1933.

Fromentin, Eugène. *Between Sea and Sahara: An Algerian Journal.* Columbus, OH: Ohio State University Press, 1999.

Furst, Lilian R. "The Power of the Powerless: A Trio of Nineteenth-Century Disorderly Eaters." 153–66 in Lilian R. Furst and Peter W. Graham, eds. *Disorderly Eaters: Texts in Self-Empowerment.* University Park, PA: Pennsylvania State University Press, 1992.

———. "Realism and Hypertrophy: A Study of Three Medico-Historical 'Cases.'" *Nineteenth-Century French Studies* 22.1–2 (Fall–Winter 1993–94): 29–47.

———, ed. *Realism.* New York: Longman, 1992.

Gans, Eric. Madame Bovary: *The End of Romance.* Boston: Twayne, 1989.

Gauguin, Paul. *Lettres de Gauguin à sa femme et à ses amis.* Paris: Grasset, 1949.

Gaultier, Jules de. *Le Bovarysme.* Paris: Mercure de France, 1902.

Gautier, Théophile. *Constantinople: Et autres textes sur la Turquie.* 1852. Paris: La Boîte aux documents, 1990.

Gavarni [pseud. of Sulpice-Guillaume Chevalier]. *Œuvres choisies.* 2 vols. Paris: Hetzel, 1847.

Gay, Peter. *The Bourgeois Experience: Victoria to Freud.* New York: Oxford University Press, 1984.

Gengembre, Gérard. *Gustave Flaubert:* Madame Bovary. Paris: Presses Universitaires de France, 1990.

Gérard-Gailly, Emile. *Le Grand Amour de Flaubert.* Paris: Aubier, 1944.

Gide, André. *Journal 1889–1939.* In *Journal.* Vol. 1. 2 vols. Paris: Gallimard, 1960.

Ginsburg, Michal Peled. *Flaubert Writing: A Study in Narrative Strategies.* Stanford, CA: Stanford University Press, 1986.

Girard, René. *Deceit, Desire, and the Novel: Self and Other in Literary Structure.* Trans. Yvonne Freccero. Baltimore: Johns Hopkins University Press, 1965. Published in French as *Mensonge romantique et vérité romanesque.* Paris: Grasset, 1961.

Goetz, Thomas H. "Edmond Louis Antoine and John Alfred Huet de Goncourt." 7:1395–1419 in George Stade, ed. *European Writers: The Romantic Century.* New York: Scribners, 1980.

Goncourt, Edmond and Jules de. *Journal.* 4 vols. Paris: Flammarion, 1959.

Gothot-Mersch, Claudine. "Aspects de la temporalité dans les romans de Flaubert." 6–55 in P. M. Wetherill, ed. *Flaubert: La dimension du texte.* Manchester, UK: Manchester University Press, 1982.

———. *La Genèse de* Madame Bovary. Paris: Corti, 1966.

Gothot-Mersch, Claudine, and Raphaël Célis, eds. *Narration et interprétation.* Brussels: Facultés Universitaires Saint-Louis, 1984.

Gourmont, Rémy de. "Flaubert et la bêtise humaine." In *Promenades littéraires.* 2 vols. Paris: Mercure de France, 1963.

Grana, Cesar. *Bohemian versus Bourgeois: French Society and the French Man of Letters in the Nineteenth Century.* New York: Basic Books, 1964.

Gray, Eugene F. "Emma by Twilight: Flawed Perception in *Madame Bovary*." *Nineteenth-Century French Studies* 6.3–4 (Spring–Summer 1978): 231–40.

———. "Guy de Maupassant." 215–16 in Laurence M. Porter, ed. *A Gustave Flaubert Encyclopedia.* Westport, CT: Greenwood, 2001.

———. "Stylistic Studies," 311–17 in Laurence M. Porter, ed. *A Gustave Flaubert Encyclopedia.* Westport, CT: Greenwood, 2001.

Gray, Eugene F., and Laurence M. Porter. *Flaubert.* 2:801–66 in David Baguley, ed. *A Critical Bibliography of French Literature.* Vol. 5, *The Nineteenth Century.* 2 vols. Syracuse, NY: Syracuse University Press, 1994.

Green, Julien. *Journal.* 5 vols. Paris: Plon, 1938–51.

Gwynn, Frederick L., and Joseph L. Blotner, eds. *Faulkner in the University.* Charlottesville, VA: University of Virginia Press, 1959.

Haig, Stirling. *Flaubert and the Gift of Speech: Dialogue and Discourse in Four Modern Novels.* Cambridge, UK: Cambridge University Press, 1986.

———. "The Madame Bovary Blues." 79–93 in *The Madame Bovary Blues: The Pursuit of Illusion in Nineteenth-Century French Fiction.* Baton Rouge, LA: Louisiana State University Press, 1987.

Hamon, Philippe. *Introduction à l'analyse du descriptif.* Paris: Hachette, 1981.

———. "What Is a Description?" 147–78 in Tzvetan Todorov, ed. *French Literary Theory Today.* Cambridge, UK: Cambridge University Press, 1982.

Hasumi, Shiguéhiko. "Ambivalence flaubertienne de l'ouvert et du clos: La mort de deux personnages principaux de *Madame Bovary*." *Cahiers de l'Association internationale des études françaises* 23 (1971): 261–75.

Hemmings, F. W. J. *Culture and Society in France, 1789–1848.* Leicester: Leicester University Press, 1987.

———. *Culture and Society in France, 1848–98.* London, UK: Batsford, 1971.

Herval, René. *Les véritables origines de* Madame Bovary. Paris: Nizet, 1957.

Holmes, Oliver Wendell. "Some of My Early Teachers." *Medical Essays 1842–1882.* 9:420–40 in *The Writings.* 13 vols. Boston & New York: Houghton Mifflin, 1892–93.

Houston, John Porter. "Flaubert." 204–31 in *The Traditions of French Prose Style: A Rhetorical Study.* Baton Rouge, LA: Louisiana State University Press, 1981.

Hugo, Victor. *Les Misérables.* Ed. René Journet. 3 vols. Paris: Garnier-Flammarion, 1967.

Huysmans, Joris-Karl. *Là-bas.* Vol. 12 in *Œuvres complètes.* Ed. Lucien Descaves and Charles Grolleau. 23 vols. in 18. Paris: Crès, 1939.

James, Henry. "Flaubert's *Temptation of St. Anthony*." 141–45 in Laurence M. Porter, ed. *Critical Essays on Gustave Flaubert.* Boston: Hall, 1986.

———. *Literary Criticism: French Writers, Other European Writers.* New York: The Library of America, 1984.

———. *The Portrait of a Lady.* Ed. Nicola Bradbury. Oxford, UK: Oxford University Press, 1995.

Jasinski, René. "Le Couple Bournisien-Homais." 249–68 in *A travers le XIXe siècle.* Paris: Minard, 1975.

Kamkhagi, Vanessa. "Alain Robbe-Grillet: 'Flaubert, c'est moi.'" 371–86 in Liana Nissim, ed. *Le Letture/La Lettura di Flaubert.* Milan: Cisalpino, 2000.

Kaplan, Louise. "The Temptations of Emma Bovary." 201–36 in *Female Perversions: The Temptations of Emma Bovary*. New York: Doubleday, 1991.

Kaufmann, Vincent. *L'Equivoque épistolaire*. Paris: Minuit, 1990.

Kelly, Dorothy. *Fictional Genders: Role and Representation in Nineteenth-Century French Narrative*. Lincoln, NE: University of Nebraska Press, 1989.

———. "Teaching *Madame Bovary* through the Lens of Post-structuralism." 90–97 in Laurence M. Porter and Eugene F. Gray, eds. *Approaches to Teaching Flaubert's* Madame Bovary. New York: Modern Language Association of America, 1995.

Kempf, Roger. "Flaubert: Le double pupitre." 69–95 in Kempf, *Mœurs: Ethnologie et fiction*. Paris: Seuil, 1976.

Kinney, Arthur F. "Faulkner and Flaubert." *Journal of Modern Literature* 6 (1977): 222–47.

La Capra, Dominick. Madame Bovary *on Trial*. Ithaca, NY: Cornell University Press, 1982.

Lamartine, Alphonse de. *Souvenirs, impressions, pensées et paysages pendant un voyage en Orient*. Paris: Gosselin, 1835. Approximately one-third has been excerpted in Lotfy Fam, ed. *Voyage en Orient*. Paris: Nizet, 1959.

Langer, Suzanne. *Feeling and Form*. New York: Scribners, 1953.

Lanson, Gustave. *L'Art de la prose*. Fayard, 1908. Paris: Nizet, 1968.

Lapp, John. "Art and Hallucination in Flaubert." *French Studies* 10 (1956): 322–34.

Larousse, Pierre. *Grand dictionnaire universel du dix-neuvième siècle*. 17 vols. Paris: Administration du Grand Dictionnaire Universel, 1866–90.

Le Bidois, Georges, and Robert Le Bidois. *Syntaxe du français moderne*. 2 vols. Paris: Picard, 1935–38.

Le Calvez, Eric. "*Le Père Goriot* and *La Comédie humaine:* From Text to Macrotext." 23–31 in Michal Peled Ginsburg, ed. *Approaches to Teaching Balzac's* Old Goriot. New York: Modern Language Association of America, 2000.

Ledré, Charles. *Histoire de la presse*. Paris: Fayard, 1958.

Leleu, Gabrielle. "Du nouveau sur *Madame Bovary*, II: Une source inconnue de *Madame Bovary*, Le Document Pradier." *Revue d'Histoire Littéraire de la France* 47 (1947): 227–44.

———. Madame Bovary: *Ebauches et fragments inédits*. 2 vols. Paris: Conard, 1936.

Letellier, Léon. *Louis Bouilhet (1821–1869): Sa vie et ses œuvres d'après des documents inédits*. Paris: Hachette, 1919.

Lloyd, Rosemary. *Madame Bovary*. London: Unwin Hyman, 1990.

Lombard, Alf. *Les constructions nominales dans le français moderne*. Uppsala: Almqvist, 1930.

Lottman, Herbert R. *Flaubert: A Biography*. New York: Fromm, 1990.

Louis, Pierre-Charles-Alexandre. *Recherches sur les effets de la saignée dans quelques maladies inflammatoires*. Paris: Baillière, 1835.

Lubbock, Percy. *The Craft of Fiction*. 1921. Pp. 60–92. New York: Viking, 1957.

Magazine Littéraire 401 (September 2001). Special issue on *Flaubert, l'invention du roman moderne*.

Martin du Gard, Roger. *Correspondance générale*. Ed. Maurice Rieuneau, Jean-Claude Airal, et al. [7] vols. [through 1944]. Paris: Gallimard, 1980–[97].

Martino, Pierre. *Le Roman réaliste sous le Second Empire*. Paris: Hachette, 1913.

Maupassant, Guy de. *Lettres d'Afrique: Algérie, Tunisie*. Ed. Michèle Salinas. Paris: La Boîte aux Documents, 1990.

———. "Le Roman." In *Romans*, 703–15 (715). Paris: Gallimard, 1987.

Maynial, Edouard. *La Jeunesse de Flaubert*. Paris: Mercure de France, 1913.

McCarthy, Mary. [Interview with Peter Duval Smith, 1963]. In Carol Gelderman, ed. *Conversations with Mary McCarthy*. Jackson, MS: University Press of Mississippi, 1991.

————. "On *Madame Bovary*." 72–94 in *The Writing on the Wall, and Other Literary Essays*. New York: Harcourt, Brace & World, 1970.

McKenna, Andrew. "Desire, Difference, and Deconstruction in *Madame Bovary*." 106–13 in Laurence M. Porter and Eugene F. Gray, eds. *Approaches to Teaching Flaubert's Madame Bovary*. New York: Modern Language Association of America, 1995.

Meyer, E. Nicole. "Sarraute, Nathalie (1902–1999)." 294–95 in Laurence M. Porter, ed. *A Gustave Flaubert Encyclopedia*. Westport, CT: Greenwood, 2001.

Meyer, Priscilla. "Anna Karenina: Tolstoy's Polemic with *Madame Bovary*." *The Russian Review* 54.2 (1995): 243–59.

Milbauer, Asher Z., and Donald G. Watson, eds. *Reading Philip Roth*. London: Macmillan, 1988.

Monnier, Henry. *Scènes populaires*. Paris: Flammarion, 1973.

Montaigne, Michel de. "De l'art de conférer"; "Du repentir"; "Apologie de Raymond Sebond" in Montaigne, *Œuvres complètes*. Ed. Maurice Rat. Paris: Gallimard, 1962.

Montherlant, Henry de. *Pitié pour les femmes*. In *Romans*. Paris: Gallimard, 1962.

Mouchard, Claude, and Jacques Neefs. *Flaubert*. Paris: Balland, 1986.

Nabokov, Vladimir. *Bend Sinister*. 1947. New York: Vintage, 1990.

————. *King, Queen, Knave*. 1928. New York: Vintage, 1989.

————. *Laughter in the Dark*. 1938. New York: Vintage, 1989.

————. *Lectures on Literature*. Ed. Fredson Bowers. New York: Harcourt Brace Jovanovich, 1980.

————. *Lolita*. 1955. New York: Vintage, 1989.

————. *Nikolai Gogol*. New York: New Directions, 1944, rev. 1961.

————. *Speak, Memory: An Autobiography Revisited*. 1967. New York: Vintage, 1989.

Nadeau, Maurice. *Gustave Flaubert écrivain*. Paris: Lettres nouvelles, 1969. Published in English as *The Greatness of Flaubert*. New York: Library, 1972.

Najjar, Alexandre. *Le Procureur de l'Empire, Ernest Pinard (1822–1909)*. Chapters 5–6. Paris: Balland, 2001.

Neefs, Jacques. "La Figuration réaliste: L'exemple de *Madame Bovary*." *Poétique* 4.16 (November 1973): 466–76.

Nelles, William. "Myth and Symbol in *Madame Bovary*." 55–60 in Laurence M. Porter and Eugene F. Gray, eds. *Approaches to Teaching Flaubert's Madame Bovary*. New York: Modern Language Association of America, 1995.

Nerval, Gérard de. *Le Voyage en Orient*. Ed. Michel Jeanneret. 2 vols. Paris: Garnier-Flammarion, 1980.

Nettement, Alfred. *Etudes critiques sur le feuilleton-roman*. Paris: Lagny Frères, 1845–46.

Norioki, Sugaya. "La Mort de Charles." In Shiguéhiko Hasumi and Yoko Kudo, eds. *Flaubert, Tentation d'une écriture*. University of Tokyo, 2001 (pagination not yet available).

Olds, Marshall. *Au pays des perroquets: Féerie théâtrale et narration chez Flaubert*. Amsterdam: Rodopi, 2001.

Oliver, Hermia. *Flaubert and an English Governess: The Quest for Juliet Herbert*. Oxford, UK: Clarendon, 1980.

Orr, Mary. *Flaubert: Writing the Masculine*. Oxford, UK: Oxford University Press, 2000.

Paliyenko, Adrianna. *Misreading the Creative Impulse: The Poetic Subject in Rimbaud and Claudel, Restaged.* Carbondale: Southern Illinois University Press, 1997.

Paris, Bernard J. *Imagined Human Beings: A Psychological Approach to Character and Conflict.* New York: New York University Press, 1997.

———. "The Search for Glory in *Madame Bovary:* A Horneyan Analysis." *American Journal of Psychoanalysis* 57.1 (1997): 5–24.

Pasco, Allan H. *Sick Heroes: French Society and Literature in the Romantic Age, 1750–1850.* Exeter, UK: University of Exeter Press, 1997.

Pennac, Daniel. *Reads Like a Novel.* Trans. David Gunn. London: Quartet, 1994. Published in French as *Comme un roman.* Paris: Gallimard, 1992.

Perec, Georges. *Les Choses: Une histoire des années soixante.* 1965. Ed. Jacques Leenhardt. Paris: 10/18, 1999.

———. "Emprunts à Flaubert." *L'Arc* 79 (1980): 49–50. This list is incomplete.

———. *La Vie, mode d'emploi.* Paris: Hachette, 1978.

Peterson, Carla L. "The Heroine as Reader in the Nineteenth Century Novel: Emma Bovary and Maggie Tulliver." *Comparative Literature Studies* 17 (1980): 168–83.

Pichois, Claude. *Le romantisme.* 2 vols. Paris: Arthaud, 1979.

Pierrot, Jean. *L'Imaginaire décadent (1880–1900).* Paris: Presses Universitaires, 1977.

Pinsker, Sanford, ed. *Critical Essays on Philip Roth.* Boston: Hall, 1982.

Pinzka, Lauren. "A Psychoanalytic Approach to *Madame Bovary.*" 42–48 in Laurence M. Porter and Eugene F. Gray, eds. *Approaches to Teaching Flaubert's* Madame Bovary. New York: Modern Language Association of America, 1995.

Pommier, Jean. "Flaubert et la naissance de l'acteur." *Journal de Psychologie Normale et Pathologique* (April–June 1947): 187–88.

Pommier, Jean, and Gabrielle Leleu. "Du Nouveau sur *Madame Bovary.*" *Revue d'histoire littéraire de la France* 47 (1947): 216–26.

Porter, Laurence M. "Decadence and the *Fin-de-Siècle* Novel." 93–110 in Timothy Unwin, ed. *The French Novel from 1880 to the Present.* Cambridge, UK: Cambridge University Press, 1997.

———. "Emma Bovary's Narcissism Revisited." 85–97 in Graham Falconer and Mary Donaldson-Evans, eds. *Kaleidoscope: Essays on Nineteenth-Century French Literature in Honor of Thomas H. Goetz.* Toronto: Centre d'Etudes Romantiques Joseph Sablé, Saint Michael's College, The University of Toronto, 1996.

———. "Le faux fantastique de *La Peau de chagrin.*" 29–38 in Didier Maleuvre and Catherine Nesci, eds. *L'œuvre d'identité: Essais sur le romantisme de Nodier à Baudelaire. Paragraphes:* Département d'Etudes françaises, l'Université de Montréal, 1996.

———. "Flaubert's Characters." Forthcoming in Timothy Unwin, ed,. *The Cambridge Companion to Flaubert.* Cambridge, UK: Cambridge University Press, 2004.

———. "L'Inconscient religieux dans *Connaissance de l'Est* de Paul Claudel." 261–71 in Jerry C. Nash and Gérard Defaux, eds. *A French Forum: Mélanges de littérature française offerts à Raymond et Virginie La Charité.* Paris: Klincksieck, 2000.

———. "Modernist Maldoror: The De-euphemization of Metaphor." *L'Esprit Créateur* 18.3 (Fall 1978): 25–34.

———. "Nuance in the Novel: Teaching *Old Goriot* in the Context of a Course on French or World Literature." 160–67 in Michal Peled Ginsburg, ed. *Approaches to Teach-*

ing Balzac's Old Goriot. New York: Modern Language Association of America, 2001.

————. "The Rhetoric of Deconstruction: Donato and Flaubert." *Nineteenth-Century French Studies* 20.1–2 (Fall–Winter 1991–92): 128–36.

————, ed. *Critical Essays on Gustave Flaubert.* Boston: Hall, 1986.

————. *A Gustave Flaubert Encyclopedia.* Westport, CT: Greenwood, 2001.

————. "Introduction." *Approaches to Teaching Baudelaire's* Flowers of Evil. New York: Modern Language Association of America, 2000.

Porter, Laurence M., and Eugene F. Gray, eds. *Approaches to Teaching Flaubert's* Madame Bovary. New York: Modern Language Association of America, 1995.

Poulet, Georges. "The Circle and the Center: Reality and *Madame Bovary.*" 392–407 in *Madame Bovary: Backgrounds and Sources: Essays in Criticism.* Ed. Paul de Man. Trans. Eleanor Marx Aveling. New York: Norton, 1965.

————. "Flaubert." 248–61 in *Studies in Human Time.* Baltimore: Johns Hopkins University Press, 1956. Reprinted in Laurence M. Porter, ed. *Critical Essays on Gustave Flaubert,* 15–27. Boston: Hall, 1986.

Pradier, James. *Correspondance.* Ed. Douglas Siler. 3 vols. Geneva: Droz, 1984–88.

Pradier, Louise. "Mémoires de Madame Ludovica." Ms g 226⁴, fol. 233ff, Bibliothèque de Rouen.

Prendergast, Christopher. *The Order of Mimesis: Balzac, Stendhal, Nerval, Flaubert.* Cambridge, UK: Cambridge University Press, 1986.

Prince, Gerald. *Narrative as Theme: Studies in French Fiction.* Lincoln, NE: University of Nebraska Press, 1992.

————. "On Attributive Discourse in *Madame Bovary.*" 269–75 in Robert L. Mitchell, ed. *Pre-text, Text, Context.* Columbus, OH: Ohio State University Press, 1980.

Proust, Marcel. "A propos du 'style' de Flaubert." *Nouvelle Revue Française,* January 1, 1920. Reprinted in Proust, *Contre Sainte-Beuve.*

————. *Contre Sainte-Beuve; précédé de* Pastiches et Mélanges; *et suivi de* Essais et articles. Ed. Pierre Clarac. Paris: Gallimard, 1971.

Ramazani, Vaheed. *The Free Indirect Mode.* Charlottesville, VA: The University of Virginia Press, 1988.

————. "Historical Cliché: Irony and the Sublime in *L'Education sentimentale.*" *PMLA* 108.1 (September 1993): 121–35.

————. "Lacan/Flaubert: Towards a Psychopoetics of Irony." *Romanic Review* 80 (1989): 548–59.

Reichenbach, Hans. *Elements of Symbolic Logic.* New York: Free Press, 1947.

Renard, Jules. *Journal.* Ed. Léon Guichard and Georges Sigaux. Paris: Gallimard, 1960.

Reybaud, Louis. *Jérôme Paturot à la recherche d'une position sociale.* Paris: Paulin, 1846.

Reynaud-Pactat, Patricia. "La lettre de rupture de Rodolphe à Emma Bovary: L'énonciation parle l'économie." *Nineteenth-Century French Studies* 19.1 (Fall 1990): 83–94.

Ricardou, Jean. *Nouveaux problèmes du roman.* Paris: Seuil, 1978.

Rice, James L. *Dostoevsky and the Healing Art: An Essay in Literary and Medical History.* Ann Arbor, MI: Ardis, 1985.

Richard, Jean-Pierre. "La création de la forme chez Flaubert." 119–219 in Richard, *Littérature et sensation.* Paris: Seuil, 1954.

Rifelj, Carol. "Ces tableaux du monde: Keepsakes in *Madame Bovary*." *Nineteenth-Century French Studies* 25:3–4 (Spring–Summer 1997): 360–85.

Riffaterre, Michael. "Flaubert's Presuppositions." 76–86 in Laurence M. Porter, ed. *Critical Essays on Gustave Flaubert*. Boston: Hall, 1986.

Robbe-Grillet, Alain. [Interview with Antonio Debenedetti]. "Robbe-Grillet, ho ucciso Balzac." *Corriere della Sera*. August 17, 1998: 25.

———. [Interview with Jean-Pierre Salgas]. "Robbe-Grillet: 'Je n'ai jamais parlé d'autre chose que de moi.'" *La Quinzaine littéraire* 432 (1985): 7.

———. *Le Miroir qui revient*. Paris: Minuit, 1984.

———. *Pour un nouveau roman*. Paris: Minuit, 1963.

Robinson, Douglas. "Kugelmass, Translator (Some Thoughts on Translation and Its Teaching)." 47–61 in Peter Bust and Kirsten Malmkjaer, eds. *Rimbaud's Rainbow: Literary Translation in Higher Education*. Amsterdam: Benjamins, 1998.

Ronell, Avital. *Crack Wars: Literature Addiction Mania*. Lincoln, NE: University of Nebraska Press, 1992.

Roth, Phillip. [Interview with Alvin P. Sanoff]. *U.S. News and World Report*. February 2, 1987: 61–62.

———. "Reading Myself." *Partisan Review* 40 (1973) 404–17.

Rothfield, Lawrence. "From Semiotic to Discursive Intertextuality: The Case of *Madame Bovary*." *Novel* 19 (1985): 57–81.

Rousset, Jean. "*Madame Bovary* ou le livre sur rien." 109–33 in *Forme et signification: Essais sur les structures littéraires de Corneille à Claudel*. Paris: Corti, 1962.

Sachs, Murray. *The Career of Alphonse Daudet*. Cambridge, MA: Harvard University Press, 1965.

———. "The Role of the Blind Beggar in *Madame Bovary*." *Symposium* 22 (1968): 72–80.

Said, Edward. *Orientalism*. New York: Vintage, 1979.

Sainte-Beuve, Charles-Augustin. "De la littérature industrielle." *Revue des Deux Mondes* ser. 4, vol. 19 (September 1, 1839): 675–91.

———. "*Madame Bovary* par M. Gustave Flaubert." 13:346–63 in Sainte-Beuve, *Causeries de Lundi*. 16 vols. Paris: Garnier, 1850–60. Reprinted in Becker, ed., 99–104.

———. [Review of Ernest Feydeau's *Fanny*.] *Le Moniteur*. June 14, 1858.

Sarraute, Nathalie. "Flaubert le précurseur." 61–89 in *Paul Valéry et l'enfant d'éléphant*. Paris: Gallimard, 1986.

Sartre, Jean-Paul. "La Conscience de classe chez Flaubert." *Les Temps Modernes* 21 (1966): 1921–51, 2114–53.

———. "Flaubert: Du poète à l'artiste." *Les Temps Modernes* 22 (1966): 197–253, 423–81, 598–674.

———. *L'Idiot de la famille: Gustave Flaubert de 1821–1857*. 3 vols. Paris: Gallimard, 1971–72.

———. *Les Mots*. Paris: Gallimard, 1964.

———. "Question de méthode." 15–111 in *Critique de la raison dialectique*. Vol. 1, *Théorie des ensembles poétiques*. 2 vols. Paris: Gallimard, 1960.

Schöne, Maurice. "Langue écrite et langue parlée: A propos de la correspondance de Flaubert." *Le Français moderne* 11 (1943): 87–108, 175–91, 263–76; 12 (1944): 25–42.

Schor, Naomi. "For a Restricted Thematics: Writing, Speech, and Difference in *Madame Bovary.*" 3–28 in *Breaking the Chain: Women, Theory, and French Realist Fiction.* New York: Columbia University Press, 1985.

Schor, Naomi, and Henry F. Majewski, eds. *Flaubert and Postmodernism.* Lincoln, NE: University of Nebraska Press, 1985.

Searles, George J., ed. *Conversations with Philip Roth.* Jackson, MS: The University Press of Mississippi, 1992.

Sekreka, Mieczyslava. "Flaubert d'après sa nouvelle correspondance" [the 4-vol. supplement to the Conard]. *Roczniki humanistyczne* 6 (1957): 51–94.

Serres, Michel. *Hermes III.* Paris: Minuit, 1974.

Sherrington, R. J. *Three Novels by Flaubert: A Study of Techniques.* Oxford, UK: Clarendon, 1970.

Sicard, Claude. "Roger Martin du Gard et Gustave Flaubert." 277–87 in Jean-Louis Cabanes, ed. *Voix de l'écrivain: Mélanges offerts à Guy Sagnes.* Toulouse: Presses Universitaires du Mirail, 1996.

Siler, Douglas. "Du nouveau sur la genèse de *Madame Bovary.*" *Revue d'Histoire Littéraire de la France* 79 (1979): 26–49.

———. "Du nouveau sur les Mémoires de Madame Ludovica." *Revue d'Histoire Littéraire de la France* 78 (1978): 36–46.

———. *Flaubert et Louise Pradier: Le texte intégral des Mémoires de Madame Ludovica.* Paris: Minard, 1973. *Archives des Lettres Modernes,* 145.

Simmonds, Posy. *Gemma Bovery.* London: Cape, 2000.

Smith, Bonnie G. *Ladies of the Leisure Class: The Bourgeoises of Northern France in the Nineteenth Century.* Princeton, NJ: Princeton University Press, 1981.

Sollers, Philippe. "Emma B." 307–13 in *Eloge de l'infini.* Paris: Gallimard, 2001. First published in his *Femmes,* 1983.

Staël-Holstein, Germaine, baronne de. *De la littérature.* 2 vols. Ed. Paul van Tieghem. Geneva: Droz, 1959.

Starkie, Enid. *Flaubert: The Making of the Master.* New York: Atheneum, 1967.

———. *Flaubert, the Master.* New York: Atheneum, 1971.

Starobinski, Jean. "L'échelle des températures." 45–78 in Gérard Genette and Tzvetan Todorov, eds. *Travail de Flaubert.* Paris: Seuil, 1983.

Steegmuller, Francis. *Flaubert and* Madame Bovary: A Double Portrait. 1939. Rev. ed. Chicago, IL: University of Chicago Press, 1977.

———. "Translating *Madame Bovary.*" 227–32 in *Stories and True Stories.* Boston: Little, Brown, 1973.

Stivale, Charles J. *The Art of Rupture: Narrative Desire and Duplicity in the Tales of Guy de Maupassant.* Ann Arbor, MI: University of Michigan Press, 1994.

Strauch, Gérard. "De quelques interprétations récentes du style indirect libre." *Recherches anglaises et américaines* 7 (1974): 40–73.

Tanner, Tony. *Adultery in the Novel: Contract and Transgression.* Baltimore: Johns Hopkins University Press, 1979.

Teahan, Sheila. "James, Henry (1843–1916)." 184–85 in Laurence M. Porter, ed. *A Gustave Flaubert Encyclopedia.* Westport, CT: Greenwood, 2001.

Terdiman, Richard. *Discourse/Counter-discourse: The Theory and Practice of Symbolic Resistance in Nineteenth-Century France.* Ithaca, NY: Cornell University Press, 1985.

Thibaudet, Albert. *Gustave Flaubert.* 1922, 1935. Rev. ed. Paris: Gallimard, 1963.

Thorlby, Anthony. *Gustave Flaubert and the Art of Realism.* New Haven, CT: Yale University Press, 1957.

Tournier, Michel. "Une mystique étouffée: Madame Bovary." 150–60 in *Le Vol du vampire: Notes de lecture.* Paris: Mercure de France, 1981.

Trouard, Dawn. "X Marks the Spot: Faulkner's Garden." 99–124 in Donald M. Kartiganer and Ann J. Abadie, eds. *Faulkner in Cultural Context: Faulkner and Yoknapatawpha.* Jackson, MS: University Press of Mississippi, 1997.

Tucker, Martin. "The Shape of Exile in Philip Roth, or the Part is Always Apart." 33–49 in Asher Z. Milbauer and Donald G. Watson, eds. *Reading Philip Roth.* London: Macmillan, 1988.

Twyman, Michael. *Lithography, 1800–1850.* London: Oxford University Press, 1970.

Ullmann, Stephen. "Reported Speech and Internal Monologue in Flaubert." 94–120 in *Style in the French Novel.* 1957. New York: Barnes & Noble, 1964.

Unwin, Timothy. *Art et infini: L'Œuvre de jeunesse de Gustave Flaubert.* Amsterdam: Rodopi, 1991.

———. "A Report on Flaubert and the New Technologies." 235–43 in Tony Williams and Mary Orr, eds. *New Approaches in Flaubert Studies.* Lewiston, NY: Mellen, 1999.

Valéry, Paul. *Variété V.* Paris: Gallimard, 1944.

Vallès, Jules. *L'Enfant.* Paris: Garnier-Flammarion, 1968.

Vargas Llosa, Mario. *The Perpetual Orgy: Flaubert and* Madame Bovary. 1978. Trans. Helen Lane. New York: Farrar, 1986.

Villeneuve-Bargemont, Alban de. *Economie politique chrétienne ou Recherche sur la nature et les causes du paupérisme en France et en Europe et sur les moyens de le soulager et de le prévenir.* 1834.

Villermé, Louis-René. *Tableau de l'état physique et moral des ouvriers employés dans les manufactures de coton, de laine et de soie.* Paris: Renouard, 1840; Paris: Etudes et documentation internationale, 1989.

Waller, Margaret. *The Male Malady: Fictions of Impotence in the French Romantic Novel.* New Brunswick, NJ: Rutgers University Press, 1993.

Weber, Eugen. *Peasants into Frenchmen.* Stanford, CA: Stanford University Press, 1976.

Weinberg, Bernard. *French Realism: The Critical Reaction, 1830–1870.* London: Oxford University Press, 1937.

Weisstein, Ulrich. "Heinrich Mann und Flaubert" [on *Die kleine Stadt*]. *Euphorion* 57 (1963): 132–55.

Wellek, René. *A History of Modern Criticism: 1750–1950.* Vol. 4, *The Later Nineteenth Century.* New Haven, CT: Yale University Press, 1965: 6–12.

Wetherill, Peter M. "*Madame Bovary*'s Blind Man: Symbolism in Flaubert." *Romanic Review* 61.1 (February 1970): 35–42.

Williams, David A. "Le Rôle de Binet dans *Madame Bovary*." 90–120 in Peter M. Wetherill, ed. *Flaubert: La dimension du texte.* Manchester, UK: Manchester University Press, 1982. Translated in the *Romanic Review* 71 (1980): 149–66.

Winegarten, Renée. *The Double Life of George Sand, Woman and Writer.* New York: Basic Books, 1978.

Wing, Nathaniel. "Emma's Stories: Narrative, Repetition and Desire in *Madame Bovary*." 41–77 in *The Limits of Narrative: Essays on Baudelaire, Flaubert, Rimbaud, and Mallarmé.* Cambridge, UK: Cambridge University Press, 1986.

Wolf, Susan L. "The Same or (M)Other: A Feminist Reading of *Madame Bovary*." 34–41 in Laurence M. Porter and Eugene F. Gray, eds. *Approaches to Teaching Flaubert's* Madame Bovary. New York: Modern Language Association of America, 1995.

Wright, Gordon. *France in Modern Times, from the Enlightenment to the Present*, 5th ed. New York: Norton, 1995.

Zeldin, Theodore. *France, 1848–1945*. 2 vols. Oxford, UK: Clarendon, 1973–77. Vol. 2 rev., Oxford University Press, 1980.

Zola, Emile. "De la description." In Henri Mitterand, ed. Zola, *Œuvres Complètes*. 15 vols. Vol. 10, *Les romanciers naturalistes*. Paris: Cercle du Livre Précieux, 1966–69.

AUDIOVISUAL AND ELECTRONIC RESOURCES

Bart, Benjamin F. "Flaubert and the Graphic Arts: A Model for His Sources, His Texts, and His Illustrators." *Symposium* 40 (1987): 259–95.

Boddaert, François, and Pierre-Marc de Biasi, et al. *Autour d'Emma*. Paris: Hatier, 1991.

Bonnefis, Philippe, and Pierre Reboul. *Des mots et des couleurs. Etudes sur le rapport de la littérature et de la peinture (19e–20e siècles)*. Lille: Presses Universitaires de Lille, 1970.

Bruneau, Jean, and Jean-A. Ducourneau. *Album Flaubert* [iconography]. Paris: Gallimard, 1972.

CD-ROMS in Print. Westport, CT: Meckler, annual.

Chabrol, Claude, dir. *Madame Bovary*. With Isabelle Huppert, Jean-François Balmer, Christophe Malavoy, Jean Yanne, and Lucas Belvaux. MK2 Productions, 1991.

Chatman, Seymour. "What Novels Can Do That Films Can't and Vice Versa." *Critical Inquiry* 7 (1980): 121–40.

Clark, Kenneth. "The Fallacies of Hope." In *Civilisation*, part 12 (on romanticism). BBC, 1970. Distr. Time-Life Films, 1000 Eisenhower Drive, Paramus, NJ 07652.

Cœuroy, André. *Musique et littérature*. Paris: Bloud & Gay, 1923.

Donaldson-Evans, Mary. "Film Adaptations of Flaubert's Works." 129–30 in Laurence M. Porter, ed. *A Gustave Flaubert Encyclopedia*. Westport, CT: Greenwood, 2001.

———. "Teaching *Madame Bovary* through Film." 114–21 in Porter and Gray, eds. *Approaches to Teaching Flaubert's* Madame Bovary. New York: Modern Language Association of America, 1995.

Dumesnil, René. *Flaubert et* L'Education sentimentale. Paris: Les Belles Lettres, 1943.

Finke, Ulrich, ed. *French 19th-Century Painting and Literature*. Manchester, UK: Manchester University Press, 1972.

Flaubert, Gustave. *Madame Bovary*. Collection "L'Autre Plume." Paris: Ubi Soft, 1997. Text, background, sound, and graphics on CD-ROM.

———. *L'Œuvre Romanesque, texte intégral*. Collection "Catalogue des Lettres." Paris: Egide, 1997. CD-ROM, designed for advanced search functions.

Guichard, Léon. *La musique et les lettres au temps du romantisme*. Paris: Presses Universitaires de France, 1955.

Harvey, Stephen. *Directed by Vincente Minnelli*. New York: Harper, 1989.

Hautecœur, Louis. *Littérature et peinture en France. Du XVIIe au XXe siècle*. Paris: Colin, 1942.

Internet Movie Database. http://us.imdb.com/

Jullian, René. *Le mouvement des arts du romantisme au symbolisme. Arts visuels, musique, littérature.* Paris: Albin Michel, 1979.

Minnelli, Vincente, dir. *Madame Bovary.* With James Mason, Louis Jourdan, Jennifer Jones, Van Heflin, and Christopher Kent. MGM, 1949.

The Multimedia and CD-ROM Directory. Stockton, CA, annual.

Oliveira, Manoel de, dir. *Vale Abraão.* A film version of Agostina Bessa Luis's free twentieth-century version of Emma Bovary's story. 1993–94.

Le Pavillon Flaubert. www.napoleon.fr/scripts/napoleon-biin/gide-detail.idc?num = 106.

Renoir, Jean, dir. *Madame Bovary.* With Pierre Renoir, Robert LeVigan, Max Dearly, and Valentine Tessier. Paris: Editions Gallimard, 1934.

Ryan, Desmond. "Claude Chabrol Adapts Flaubert's Masterpiece for the Screen." The *Philadelphia Inquirer,* December 25, 1991: 6D.

Serres, Michel. *Hermès: Littérature, science, philosophie.* Ed. Josué V. Harari and David F. Bell. Baltimore, MD: Johns Hopkins University Press, 1982.

Sherrard, Jean, dir. *Madame Bovary.* Adapt. Jean Sherrard and John Siscoe. Based on the Francis Steegmuller translation. National Public Radio Playhouse. Globe Radio Repertory Theatre. Seattle, WA, 1986.

Tibbetts, John, and James M. Welsh, eds. *The Encyclopedia of Novels into Film.* New York: Facts on File, 1998.

Tulard, Jean. *Guide des films,* rev. ed. 2 vols. Paris: Laffont, 1997.

Unwin, Timothy. "A Report on Flaubert and the New Technologies." 235–43 in Tony Williams and Mary Orr, eds. *New Approaches in Flaubert Studies.* Lewiston, NY: Mellen, 1999.

Wagner, Geoffrey. *The Novel and the Cinema.* Rutherford, NJ: Fairleigh Dickinson University Press, 1975.

Wetherill, Peter, ed. L'Education sentimentale. *Images et documents.* Paris: Garnier, 1985. The iconography proper, 99–220, contains contemporary portraits and images that may roughly correspond to what Flaubert saw or imagined.

www.users.imaginet.fr/~dloss/adc/n3va.html (L'Art du cinéma, 3: a 5,000-word review of Manoel de Oliveira's film *Val Abraham* and a close comparison with Flaubert's novel).

AUDIOCASSETTES

Half a dozen different editions of *Madame Bovary* are available from Amazon.com.

VIDEOCASSETTES

For price and supplier, see the *Video Source Book,* 15th ed. Julia C. Furtaw, ed. Detroit: Gale, 1994.

Madame Bovary. 1949. Dir. Vincente Minnelli. MGM/UA Home Video.
Madame Bovary. 1991. Dir. Claude Chabrol. Columbia Pictures Home Video.
Paris in the Time of Balzac. Films for the Humanities and Sciences, 1989.
Paris in the Time of Zola. Films for the Humanities and Sciences, 1989.

THE WEB (SELECTED SITES NOT LISTED PREVIOUSLY)

ARTFL (*American and French Research on the Treasury of the French Language*). The University of Chicago.

http://catalog num.bnf.fr/html/i—frames.html/. Offers 132 digitized texts of works by Flaubert.

http://gallica.bnf.fr/. 49 digitized texts of works by Flaubert. Excellent choice of editions. Like the previous site, this one draws on the resources of the Bibliothèque Nationale.

Gustave Flaubert (1821–1880). www://scopus.ch/users/torent_j/Flaubert.html/.

http://persoo.wanadoo.fr/jb guinot/pages/accueil.html.

http://www.Bristol.ac.uk/dix-neuf/. (*Dix-Neuf. Ressources sur le dix-neuvième siècle*). The site of the new UK Society for research in nineteenth-century French studies, founded 2001. Open to other nationals. Has an extensive network of hyperlinks.

http://www.copernic.com/. Combines eighty search engines. Ideal for weeding out ephemeral and trivial sites on Flaubert.

http://www.flaubert—nl.com/.

http://www.franclink.com/radio stations/Sorbonne/rey.html/. Ten lectures on *Madame Bovary* by the Sorbonne Professor Pierre-Louis Rey. Free; continuously available.

http://hull.ac.uk.item.ens.fr.

http://www.msu.edu/~graye/caricature/. Contemporary images with captions, illustrating many of Flaubert's satiric targets.

http://univ-rouen.fr/Flaubert/index.html/. The best site, offering a wealth of resources. Directed by Yvan Leclerc.

Normandy: attractive images of Flaubert's homes and haunts and from the Musée Flaubert are found at *http://auteurs.normands.free.fr/la maison de Flaubert.html/* and at *http://www.chu-rouen.fr/musee/index.html/*.

Oliver, Andrew. "Le XIXᵉ siècle et les recherches sur Internet." The excellent article on Flaubert sites, which appeared in *Dix-neuvième siècle* 33 (June 2001), is available on-line at *http://www.chass.utoronto.ca/French/xix/chronique4/*.

At present (July 1, 2002) Google lists 6,530 Web sites devoted to Emma Bovary or *Madame Bovary*; Amazon.com lists 125 books or tapes, and 389 "products" by and about Flaubert, both in and out of print. These include French items and a few titles in other languages. FNAC, the largest French book dealer, has 268 such titles. Beware of so-called tenure presses and vanity presses. A product that pays to be listed on-line is not necessarily the best of its kind.

Index

176   Index

Barthes, Roland, 79; the reality effect, 108; *Writing Degree Zero,* 108, 131
Barzun, Jacques, 145
Batteux, Charles, l'abbé, as exemplar of neoclassical aesthetics, 126–27
Baudelaire, Charles, 150; on Emma Bovary as an hysteric, 119
Baudry, Frédéric, 73
Bauer, George, 132
Beaumont, Barbara, 145
Beauty, as artist's supreme goal, 71
Becker, George Joseph, 144
Béguin, Albert, 144
Bernheimer, Charles, 151
Bersani, Leo, 151–52
Binet (character in *Madame Bovary*), 20; as automaton, 82–83; as self-parodying artist figure, 71; symbols of meaningless repetition, 96
Bismut, Roger, 49
Blanc, Louis, 48
The Blind Man (character in *Madame Bovary*), 17, 21, 22, 80, 90–91, 102
Bonaccorso, Giovanni, 151
Bouilhet, Louis, 23, 64, 145; *Mademoiselle Aïssé* (play), xxxiv; *Le Sexe faible* (play), xxxiv
Bourgeois critique, 58; Le Garçon as vehicle for, 60–61
Bournisien, l'abbé (character in *Madame Bovary*), 21, 23, 37
Bovary, Berthe (character in *Madame Bovary*), 23, 102; surrogate for Emma Bovary, 101
Bovary, Charles (character in *Madame Bovary*), 2–5, 16, 21–23, 51, 101, 110, 143, 152; awkwardness, 2, 4; break with mother, 23; characterization, 32, 39, 137; corrupted by Emma after her death, 22; parents, 2–3; physical descriptions, 34–35; relationship to first wife, 114–15
Bovary, Emma (character in *Madame Bovary*), 3, 101, 110, 124, 143; acting out by, 110; allure, 96; boredom, 19; burial, 22; characterization, 32, 35–36, 39; Chateaubriand's *René* as a model, 53–54; clichés, ambivalence toward,

xxx; codependency, 13–14, 18, 32, 110; commodity fetishism, 6; conflict with mother-in-law, 10; daydreams, 13, 15; death, 21; demoralization, 32, 99; depression, 7; dishonesty, 16, 17; disillusionment, 18; distancing by narrator, 32; divorce, impossibility of, 7; ecstatic experiences, 79; entitlement, sense of, xxx; envy of male privilege, 37; as *femme sensible* and *femme galante*, financial problems, 18–20, 96–97, 102; frustration in marriage, xi; and gender roles, 8, 16, 17, 18; glory, desire for, 12; hallucination, 20; humiliation, 14, 19, 113, 137; hypocrisy, 9; illness, 14; Léon, encounters, 37; moods, symbolic representations of, 98–99; narcissism, 6, 7, 96; pride, 9, 12–13, 14; profligacy, 8; psychosomatic illnesses, 7; religious experiences, ix, 14; scandalous behavior, 38–39; seduction by, 15–16; seduction of, 10–11; self-destructiveness, 99; self-indulgence, 17; sentimentality, 13, 17; sexuality, 18
Bovary, Madame (character in *Madame Bovary*; Charles's mother), 22, 38
Brecht, Bertolt, 118
Briggs, Asa, 144
Brombert, Victor, 147, 150
Broussais, François, 52
Bruneau, Jean, 143, 145, 154
Brunetière, Ferdinand, 152
Burgelin, Claude, 148
Bush, Ronald, 147
Byron, George Gordon, Lord: *Childe Harold's Pilgrimage,* xxi; orientalism as influence on Flaubert, 70

Caminiti, Léa, 145
Camus, Albert, on Homais, 90
Canu, Jean, 143
Caricature, vogue of, 57–59
Carlut, Charles, 154
Carnot, Nicolas Léonard Sadi, 49
Carvalho (pseud. of Léon Carvaille), xxxiv
Catholic Church, influence of, 46

About the Authors

LAURENCE M. PORTER is Professor of French and Comparative Literature at Michigan State University. His previous books include *A Gustave Flaubert Encyclopedia* (2001).

EUGENE F. GRAY is Professor of French at Michigan State University. His essays have appeared in such journals as *Nineteenth-Century French Studies* and *The French Review.*